English Literary Stylistics

1·2010

PERSPECTIVES ON THE ENGLISH LANGUAGE

Series Editor: Lesley Jeffries

Published

Siobhan Chapman   Thinking About Language: Theories of English
Urszula Clark   Studying Language: English in Action
Christiana Gregoriou   English Literary Stylistics
Lesley Jeffries   Discovering Language: The Structure of Modern English

Forthcoming

Stephen Bax   Discourse and Genre
Jonathan Culpeper   The Pragmatics of the English Language
Simon Horobin   History of the English Language
Lesley Jeffries   Critical Stylistics
Rob Penhallurick   Studying Dialect

Perspectives on the English Language Series
Series Standing Order
ISBN 0-333-96146-3 hardback
ISBN 0-333-96147-1 paperback
(outside North America only)

You can receive future titles in this series as they are published by placing a standing order. Please contact your bookseller or, in the case of difficulty, write to us at the address below with your name and address, the title of the series and one of the ISBNs quoted above.

Customer Services Department, Macmillan Distribution Ltd, Houndmills, Basingstoke, Hampshire RG21 6XS, England

English Literary Stylistics

Christiana Gregoriou

palgrave
macmillan

First published 2009 by
PALGRAVE MACMILLAN
Houndmills, Basingstoke, Hampshire RG21 6XS and
175 Fifth Avenue, New York, N.Y. 10010
Companies and representatives throughout the world

PALGRAVE MACMILLAN is the global academic imprint of the Palgrave Macmillan division of St. Martin's Press, LLC and of Palgrave Macmillan Ltd. Macmillan® is a registered trademark in the United States, United Kingdom and other countries. Palgrave is a registered trademark in the European Union and other countries.

ISBN-13: 978–0–230–52543–6   hardback
ISBN-10: 0–230–52543–1   hardback
ISBN-13: 978–0–230–52541–2   paperback
ISBN-10: 0–230–52541–5   paperback

This book is printed on paper suitable for recycling and made from fully managed and sustained forest sources.

A catalogue record for this book is available from the British Library.

A catalog record for this book is available from the Library of Congress.

10 9 8 7 6 5 4 3 2 1
18 17 16 15 14 13 12 11 10 09

Printed and bound in China

For Phylactis

Contents

Series editors' preface   ix
Acknowledgements   x

Introduction: An overview of literary stylistics   1
    What is 'style'?   1
    Why should we do stylistics?   3

1   Naming poetic parts   8
    1.1   Analysing poetry   8
    1.2   Rhythm and metre   8
    1.3   Poetic sound effects   17
    1.4   Relating poetic form to poetic meaning   19
    1.5   Chapter review   23

2   Poetic figures, foregrounding and metaphor   24
    2.1   Figure and ground   24
    2.2   Linguistic foregrounding   26
        2.2.1   Deviation   28
        2.2.2   Parallelism   36
    2.3   Metaphor   38
    2.4   Chapter review   42

3   Stylistics of poetry practice   43

4   Narrators, viewpoint, speech and thought   63
    4.1   Narratives: some introductory terminology   63
    4.2   Types of narration   64

	4.3	Point of view	67
	4.4	Mind style	72
	4.5	Speech and thought presentation	73
	4.6	Chapter review	78
5		**Narrative worlds, schemata and frames**	**79**
	5.1	Possible worlds and text world theory	79
	5.2	Schema theory	86
	5.3	Telling stories	89
		5.3.1 Labov's oral narratives model	89
		5.3.2 Propp's morphology of the folktale	91
	5.4	Emmott's frame theory	94
	5.5	Chapter review	97
6		**Stylistics of prose practice**	**98**
7		**Structure and characterisation in drama**	**129**
	7.1	Analysing drama's discourse levels	129
	7.2	The form of dramatic conversation	130
	7.3	Text, production and performance	137
	7.4	Characterisation	139
	7.5	Chapter review	141
8		**The pragmatics of drama**	**143**
	8.1	What is pragmatics?	143
	8.2	Speech acts	143
	8.3	Grice's maxims	146
	8.4	Politeness theory	153
	8.5	Chapter review	161
9		**Stylistics of drama practice**	**163**
		Concluding remarks	**183**
		Afterthought	183
		Ideas for further stylistic practice	184
		Notes	*187*
		Bibliography	*191*
		Index	*198*

Series editors' preface

The first three books to be published in the Perspectives on the English Language series (Jeffries, *Discovering Language*, Chapman, *Thinking About Language* and Clark, *Studying Language*) together formed the first wave of what will ultimately be a comprehensive collection of research-based textbooks covering the wide variety of topics in English Language studies. These initial three books provide the basics of English Language description, theory and methodology that students need, whether they are specialists in English Language or taking only one or two modules in the subject. The idea was that these books would be used differently by such different students, and indeed they have already proved useful to postgraduate students as well as undergraduates.

Now we are beginning the process of adding to the series the envisaged set of higher-level textbooks which will build on the core books by bringing together the latest thinking in a range of topics in English Language. This 'second wave' comprises books written by current researchers in the field, and far from simply providing an overview or summary of work so far, these books are distinctive in making the latest research available to a student audience. They are not 'dumbed down', but are written accessibly, with exercises and questions for the reader to consider where relevant. And for the HE teacher, these books provide a resource that s/he can use to bring out the best in students of all abilities.

The book you are holding will ultimately be part of a large series of topic-based books in English Language, and we are confident that you will find them useful and interesting. Although this series was begun with only one series editor, the rate of production of the second wave calls for more help in editing and proofreading. We look forward to surfing this second wave together!

Lesley Jeffries and Dan McIntyre
June 2008

Acknowledgements

I take this opportunity to thank Lesley Jeffries, the series editor, for giving me the opportunity to write this book, and Peter Stockwell, for his professional advice and suggestions on an earlier proposal and preliminary chapter drafts for this book. I would also like to thank Kate Haines, the 'in-house' editor, whose help and faith in this project was invaluable. I am also indebted to all stylisticians I've encountered and learnt from over so many years, throughout my career as a student, teacher, and researcher on the subject of stylistics: particularly all PALAns at Lancaster, Nottingham, Huddersfield and Leeds University. Of course, just as important were my stylistics students, particularly Ann Thompson, whose helpful ideas benefited my work greatly.

Last but by no means least, I would like to thank my friends and family for their support and encouragement when working on this project. I am grateful to all, particularly my grandfather Phylactis, whose love of the English language has influenced and stayed with me for life. This book is dedicated to him.

For the purpose of my book, I am using various short extracts from contemporary films, poems and prose. I analyse the language of the relevant extracts using a range of stylistic theories, to enable my readers to investigate the effects of these genres through the structure of their language.

The author and publisher would like to thank the following for permission to reproduce copyright material:

Carcanet Press, for the extracts from William Carlos Williams, 'To a Poor Old Woman' and 'Landscape With The Fall of Icarus' in *The Collected Poems of William Carlos Williams, 1939–1962* (vol. 2, edited by C. MacGowan: Carcanet, 1988);

Michael Connelly, for the extract from *The Poet* (Orion Books, 1996), by permission of The Orion Publishing Group and David Higham Associates;

Columbia Pictures, for the extract from 'As Good as it Gets' © 1997 Tristar Pictures, Inc. All Rights Reserved; and for the extract from 'Erin Brockovich' © 2000 Universal City Studios, Inc. and Palisade Investors, LLC. All Rights Reserved. Courtesy of Columbia Pictures.

Andre Dubus, for extracts from *House of Sand and Fog* (William Heinemann Ltd, 2001). Reprinted by permission of The Random House Group Ltd and WW Norton and Company, Inc;

Faber and Faber Ltd, for 'Funeral blues' from *The Ascent of F6: A Tragedy in Two Acts* by W.H. Auden, and C. Isherwood (Faber, 1936) and the extract from 'Metaphors' from *The Collected Poems of Sylvia Plath* (Faber, edited by T. Hughes, 1981) by Sylvia Plath;

Ricky Gervais, for the extract from *The Office*, by permission of United Agents, as agents for the author

Mark Haddon, for the extract from *The Curious Incident of the Dog in the Night-Time* (Jonathan Cape/David Fickling, 2003). Reprinted by permission of The Random House Group Ltd and Aitken Alexander Associates Ltd;

Tony Harrison, for the extract from 'Them & [uz]' in *Collected Poems* (Penguin 2007), by permission of Gordon Dickenson, on behalf of the author;

Russell Hoban, for the extract from *Riddley Walker* (Bloomsbury, 1980), by permission of David Higham Associates;

Jackie Kay, for extracts from 'The adoption papers' in *Darling: New & Selected Poems* (Bloodaxe Books, 2007), by permission of Bloodaxe Books;

The Random House Group Ltd, for the use of Robert Frost, 'The road not taken' from *The Poetry of Robert Frost* (edited by Edward Connery Lathem), published by Jonathan Cape;

Lionel Shriver, for the extract from *We Need to Talk About Kevin* (Serpent's Tail, 2005) by permission of Profile Books;

Jim Thompson, for the extract from *The Killer Inside Me* (Orion Books, 1952, 2002) by permission of The Orion Publishing Group;

Twentieth Century Fox, for the extracts from *There's Something About Mary* © 1998 Courtesy of Twentieth Century Fox. Story by Ed Decter and John J.

Strauss. Screenplay by Ed Decter and John J. Strauss and Peter Farrelly and Bobby Farrelly. All rights reserved;

Universal Studios, for the extracts from *Notting Hill*, courtesy of Universal Studios Licensing LLLP © 1999 Universal City Studios, Inc;

Benjamin Zephaniah, for extracts from 'White comedy' and 'De wrong song' in *Propa Propaganda* (Bloodaxe Books, 1996), by permission of Bloodaxe Books.

The film transcripts reproduced in this book were accessed from a variety of online resources.

Every effort has been made to trace all copyright-holders, but if any have been inadvertently overlooked, the publishers will be pleased to make the necessary arrangement at the first opportunity.

Christiana Gregoriou

Introduction: An Overview of Literary Stylistics

What is 'style'?

What do you understand by 'style'? In the word's everyday sense, it can be used to talk about such things as fashion, music and architecture, in addition to writers and their language, and seems to be a word with positive connotations. To say that a woman has style or that a house is decorated with style is a positive evaluation. In one definition, the *OED* states that this word refers to '[t]he manner of expression characteristic of a particular writer (hence of an orator), or of a literary group or period; a writer's mode of expression considered in regard to clearness, effectiveness, beauty, and the like', and is hence '[u]sed for: A good, choice or fine style'. In this sense, to talk about a text carrying 'style' is similarly something that could be thought of as positive. In the area of stylistics, however, the word 'style' is not thought of as a necessarily positive term (though admittedly authors tend to analyse texts they find of interest and therefore possibly 'value'; I myself am both a keen reader and analyst of crime fiction). Style is here instead used to refer to 'the way in which language is used in a given context, by a given person, for a given purpose and so on' (Leech and Short, 1981: 10): a perceived distinctive manner of expressing oneself with language, regardless of whether that manner is liked, appreciated, valued or not.

In stylistics, 'style' is interpreted as a property of all texts, as opposed to a property of literary texts exclusively. Besides, as Leech and Short (1981: 1) put it, 'to make progress in understanding style, one has to make use of an explicit understanding of language – not just language in a literary context'. Having said that, it is interesting to note that the *OED* does recognise that, in its figurative sense, style can be seen 'as a symbol of literary composition'. Entitling this book *English Literary Stylistics* therefore enables me to concentrate on introducing features, frameworks and models relevant to the study of literary texts, though that is not to say that these are not applicable or indeed relevant to non-literary ones as well.[1]

As a student of stylistics, I found I had to struggle with a number of questions surrounding this issue of style. I wondered whether style elements were consciously or unconsciously 'inserted' by the writer. In other words, to what extent are writers aware of their linguistic choices? I suspect very little, if at all. Whilst undertaking some research into the metaphors of the criminal mind, I had the pleasure of meeting the crime fiction writer James Patterson,[2] whose work I had examined linguistically. I asked him whether he had consciously used particular megametaphors or sustained metaphors (see Werth 1999) such as CRIMINAL IS A MACHINE[3] and CRIMINAL IS AN ANIMAL when portraying the criminal mind in his own Alex Cross crime novels; interestingly, and perhaps unsurprisingly, he said that he had not. In fact, few if any authors would claim that they are aware of the linguistic nature of their style, whether they can employ the linguistic terminology to describe it or not.

I also wondered whether 'style' is indeed the same as authorial choice. The term 'style' has been applied to the 'linguistic habits of a particular writer ("the style of Dickens, of Proust", etc)' (Leech and Short, 1981: 11), but would it not be simplistic to assume that these 'choices' are merely down to the author? I agree with Short (2005) that '[b]y examining carefully the choices writers make, and comparing them with alternative choices which they could have made, we can relate those choices in a systematic way and detailed way to overall meaning and effect', but is that what style means? Surely one's choices are determined by a number of external as well as internal requirements, and style is not merely a choice between variant items or structures. Are there not a number of norms (say, generic features) that writers often need to conform to when producing literary texts? For instance, crime writers are, at least to some extent, restricted by the need for them to employ such characters as criminal(s), victim(s) and detective(s), not to mention an element of mystery, a surprise ending and so on. Do these choices have anything to do with their style, the authors' idiosyncratic linguistic habits?

I also contemplated whether style is about deviation[4] or the conforming to linguistic norms. Is deviation itself a factor in determining style? Wales (2001: 372) argues that it would be wrong to imply that style itself is deviant in the sense of 'abnormal', and there arises a need to match any text against linguistic norms of genre, period and language as a whole. Accordingly, I argue that style is generated by an interaction between on one hand, a text's sum of deviations from recognisable norms, and on the other, the extent to which it conforms to these norms.[5] For a crime novel to be 'readable', for instance, there would need to be enough features to identify it as a crime novel to start with (say, there needs to be a crime, an investigation, possibly an unknown perpetrator and so on), but also enough features setting it apart from other novels on the same bookstore shelf, novels within the same genre (say, there might be some unexpected twists and turns in the given text's tale, new characters introduced halfway through to complicate the crime case, and so on).

Having dealt with some definitions and issues surrounding style, I next turn to define the field of stylistics. What does it mean to 'do stylistics', and why would anyone want to anyway?

Why should we do stylistics?

Even though stylistic analysis is often framed as a validation of reader intuition, the sort of insight that such an investigation can provide goes a lot further than that. Stylistics was, initially, born of a reaction to the subjectivity and imprecision of literary studies, and in short, attempted to put criticism on a scientific basis (see Fish, 1980; Short, 1982). In other words, literary criticism was thought of as imprecise and subjective, and so stylistics was born in order to objectify claims made about the way in which literary texts carry meaning. Note, however, that stylisticians, such as Wales (2001: 372), claim that stylistics 'is only "objective" (and the scare quotes are significant) in the sense of being methodical, systematic, empirical, analytical, coherent, accessible, retrievable and consensual'. Similarly, Simpson (1993: 3) points out that few stylisticians claim objectivity in their method of textual analysis, and that they 'prefer to recognize instead that all interpretations are in some sense context-bound and are contingent on the position of the analyst relative to the text'. My fascination with crime fiction as a *reader*, for instance, is bound to have an effect over the way in which I analyse such texts as a *stylistician*. Nevertheless, such clarifications fail to prevent literary critics from being suspicious of such an approach to literature, which they assume claims to be a purely 'objective' method of analysis.

'Stylistics, first of all, normally refers to the practice of using linguistics for the study of literature' (Simpson, 1993: 3). In other words, in offering linguistic operable principles to the study of literature, stylistics (hence sometimes called 'literary linguistics') possesses a *kind* of objectivity that literary criticism seems to lack. As Carter (1991: 5) puts it, practical stylistics is a process of literary text analysis, the basic principle of which is that without 'analytic knowledge of the rules and conventions of normal linguistic communication' we cannot adequately validate the readers' intuitive interpretations. Note that Fowler's (1986) term for stylistics is 'linguistic criticism'; stylisticians could be thought of as indeed critics of literature, but engage in this criticism through detailed and explicit knowledge of the workings of language.

Wales (2006: 213) defines 'linguistic stylistics' as those stylistic studies interested in the workings of language and in testing the validity of linguistic models. She opposes this to 'literary stylistics', which is regarded as a branch of poetics, primarily concerned with the classification of the essential properties or conventions of genres, or theories of form. The general understanding about the difference between linguistic stylistics and literary stylistics thus lies in the analyst's interests: whereas the linguist stylistician is primarily interested in language, the literary stylistician is most interested in literature. In several respects, linguistic stylistics is the purest form of stylistics, in that its practitioners attempt to derive from the study of style and language a refinement of models for the analysis of language, and thus to contribute to the development of linguistic theory (Carter and Simpson, 1989: 4). My entitling this book 'literary stylistics' does not reflect my lack of an interest in language, but it does highlight my fascination with literature and its effects, with genres and their conventions.

As Fish (1980: 28) put it, '[e]ssentially, what the method [of stylistics] does is slow down the reading process so that "events" one does not notice in normal time, but which do occur, are brought before our analytical attentions'. In other words, Fish argues that in engaging in stylistic analysis, students replace the question 'What does this sentence/text mean?' with the question 'What does it do?' He says that 'the text's meaning is transformed into an account of its experience', an event, something that happens, an experience the readers themselves actively participate in. Fish suggests that stylistics is the method, the machine which makes these experiences observable or at least accessible – it makes explicit what goes on below the level of 'self-conscious response'. He therefore called for 'affective stylistics', where instead of tracking the meaning of patterns on the page, stylisticians are invited to track understanding of what the reader is doing when encountering those patterns. In fact, Fish's call has received a response with the recent birth of cognitive stylistics or 'cognitive poetics', which, as Stockwell (2002: 1) puts it, 'is all about reading literature'; 'cognition is to do with the mental processes involved in reading, and poetics concerns the craft of literature'. Cognitive poetics is a field that can be subsumed under stylistics and is clearly related to the discipline of literary criticism, as the former evaluates, or rather re-evaluates, the process of literary activity, yet it draws on theories that delineate the various processes of the human mind when interacting with literature. Put simply, cognitive poetics is a field that investigates what happens cognitively when we read. It is a field capable of, say, explaining how exactly twists work in a story, or how the reader is influenced into sympathising with certain personas in a play, and not others.

Fish (1980) also addresses the question, 'If there is a measure of uniformity to the reading experience, how come so many readers argue for a text's differing interpretations?' His response is that such disagreements are not about a response, but about a response to a response: what happens to one informed reader will happen within a range of nonessential variation to another. In other words, Fish argues that varying interpretations are instead variations of the same interpretation, and it is only when readers become literary critics (an experience much removed from the reading experience) that opinions begin to diverge.

Short (1982: 61) has argued that the stylistic method's advantages are accuracy and clarity of presentation, along with that general characteristic of literary critical analysis of showing that superficially unconnected and previously unseen points can all be related in a particular overall analysis. However, he also argued that we ought to use linguistic stylistic analysis primarily as a means of supporting a literary or interpretative thesis, and further added that the analysis is likely to be of service to literary criticism if it follows its general aims and strategies. It is for this reason that stylistic analysis is often used in support of initial impressions about the 'interpretation' of literary extracts. Even though this might point to such analyses being those of specific readings and not analyses of texts, it needs to be kept in mind that this is a method of analysis that takes the reader as an actively mediating presence fully into account, and it is hence that individual reader's responses that it can describe with some precision.

Simpson (2004: 3–4) argues that doing stylistics is an illuminating method of analytic enquiry which sheds light on the very language system it derives from. It enriches our ways of thinking about language, and in telling us about the rules of language, it educates us about the extent to which we can bend or even break them. He suggests that the practice of stylistics conforms to the following three basic principles, cast as the three 'R's: stylistic analysis should be Rigorous (meaning that it should be based on an explicit structured framework or model of analysis), Retrievable (the terms and criteria the analysis is organised through have meanings which are agreed upon by other students of stylistics – there's a consensus on what means what in which context) and Replicable (the methods should be so transparent, that it would be possible for others to verify results, on the same text or others).

Put simply, this is a method that remains faithful to its principles as it talks about experience and focuses on effects. As Short (1996: 349) puts it:

> [l]ooking at writing in this kind of detail helps to reveal important aspects which might otherwise have gone unnoticed, and it also provides detailed and interesting ways of testing out or supporting critical hypotheses about style and meaning which we may have arrived at through our initial reading.

Nevertheless, Carter and Simpson (1989) claim that in the area of interpretation lie problems. Firstly, it is naïve to assume that any application of linguistic knowledge can result in an objective, value-free interpretation of data; since the system of description 'will inevitably be partial (in both senses of the word) ... so accordingly, will be the interpretation' (Carter and Simpson, 1989: 6). They raise further problems. The analyses of stylistics will simply provide the basis on which interpretations might be textually realised (the analyst has to be trusted on their interpretation of results). Also, any description or analysis is only as good as the model it came from. Finally, in describing data, analysts are necessarily interpreting data. It is a difficult if not impossible task for the analyst to engage in an unbiased description.

A further defect of stylistics lies in the absence of any constraint on the way in which we move from description to interpretation, with the result that any interpretation we put forward is arbitrary (Fish, 1980: 73). How do we get from describing, say, a poem as verbless, to the impression of inactivity or inevitability in the poem? Stylisticians therefore run the risk of making interpretative leaps and overgeneralisations, forcing dubious interpretations to particular linguistic patterns/hypotheses. A related danger lies in the stylistician attributing an independent meaning to linguistic facts. To stay with the same example, even if a verbless poem indeed brings out an impression of inactivity, that does not necessarily mean that other verbless texts will produce the same sort of effect. This is problematic; such facts are likely to have different meanings in different circumstances (see Simpson, 1993: 113 for a discussion of the danger in making direct connections between linguistic patterns and a particular world-view).

To add to these problems, in engaging in stylistic procedures, stylisticians run the risk of being rather circular in their argumentation. If stylistics is the means of supporting initial impressions about a literary thesis (Short, 1982), are we not running the risk of finding out exactly what we were looking for regardless of whether it is actually there or not?[6]

There are a number of lessons to be learnt from all these observations, but as Jeffries (2000) put it, we should not throw the baby out with the bathwater. Stylistics could and does work. It is a very useful tool to have to your disposal if you maintain some scepticism and try and be objective.[7] You should also not make the mistake of assuming that a particular linguistic pattern always means something, or that the techniques on offer are only relevant to the study of literary texts. In fact, the same stylistic tricks can be used for different effects, but they will have some common thread of meaning, albeit with the context altering the exact effect. To return to the example of the verbless poem, stylistics surely makes some progress by explaining why the lack of a verb is likely to reduce the consciousness of time in a text, given the structures of English.

The remaining of this book is, rather conventionally, categorised under the major genres of literature: poetry (Chapters 1, 2 and 3), prose (Chapters 4, 5 and

6) and drama (Chapters 7, 8 and 9). Chapter 1 delineates the terminology and features relevant to the study of poetry, while Chapter 2 is concerned with poetic foregrounding devices and metaphor. Chapter 4 outlines the narrative styles, the linguistic point of view indicators, and the speech and thought presentation frameworks relevant to the study of narratives. Chapter 5 introduces Possible World (see Ryan, 1991a, 1991b, 1998) alongside Text World (see Werth, 1999) theory, Emmott's (1997) frame theory, and schema theory, while also touching on frameworks surrounding the telling of stories (such as those by Labov, 1972 and Propp, 1975, 1984). Chapter 7 introduces theories relevant to the analysis of the form and structure of drama, and accounts for the study of dramatic characterisation. Chapter 8 introduces theories relevant to the study of dramatic conversational analysis. Whereas Chapters 1, 2, 4, 5, 7 and 8 introduce theories, the intervening chapters (3, 6 and 9) offer practice through a number of worked examples. The conclusion provides ideas for further stylistic practice.

1 Naming Poetic Parts

1.1 Analysing poetry

When it comes to poetry, stylisticians, much like literary critics, are concerned with explaining how the poem's form and structure contributes to the effects that it generates, and the ways in which the poem expresses the poet's ideas. However shared their tasks, the two sets of different commentators nevertheless operate at rather different levels of abstraction (Leech, 1969: 6). As noted in the previous chapter, a stylistician is more concerned with explaining in objective and reliable terms the way in which the *language* of the poem particularly contributes to its meaning. And it is for this reason that stylisticians often start by outlining their initial impressions of a text, after which they proceed to engage in detailed and systematic linguistic analysis of the art form to justify or explain these original intuitions.

But what makes poetry special or different from other literary art forms? The *OED* defines poetry as the 'composition in verse or some comparable patterned arrangement of language in which the expression of feelings and ideas is given intensity by the use of distinctive style and rhythm'. What appear to differentiate poetry from other imaginative, creative, or indeed fictional literary art forms are the notions of 'intensity' or emotional impact, coupled with 'style' and 'rhythm' in potentially 'verse' form. Therefore, one of the things we should consider is how to go about describing these 'verses', their 'rhythm' and their accompanying 'intensity'.

1.2 Rhythm and metre

'Rhythm' is something we perceive in many things, such as the beating of our hearts, the sound of a machine, or indeed music. It is essentially a pattern of stresses, the perception human beings have of 'on' and 'off' beats, strong and weak ones, correspondingly referred to as the 'ictus' (/) and the 'remiss' (X). In the context of the English language, this rhythm is evident in the amount of time that elapses between the stressed syllables of words. Poetry, as a special linguistic form, 'has more marked, and more complex, rhythmic effects than ordinary language because it has an *extra layer of rhythmic structuring* which is usually called **metre**' (Short, 1996: 127). Metre is a pattern of rhythm which is perceived to be deliberately regular. Metrical feet in poetry are defined on the basis of this regular pattern, and carry only one strong syllable each.

A set of Greek-derived terms have traditionally been used to classify patterns of rhythm into metres that are 'iambic' (that is 'X /', such as the stress in 'before'), 'trochaic' (that is '/ X', such as in 'butter'), 'anapaestic' (that is 'X X /', such as in 'reconstruct') and 'dactylic' (that is '/ X X', such as in 'passenger'). Depending on the number of metrical feet that a poem's lines have, we use the again Greek-derived terms 'monometer' (one-metre line), 'dimeter' (two-metre line), 'trimeter' (three-metre line), 'tetrameter' (four-metre line), 'pentameter' (five-metre line) and 'hexameter' (six-metre line). Let us look at some examples of the various forms.

According to Short (1996: 132), the metrical norm for English poetry, from the fifteenth century onwards, is the iambic pentameter. Michael Drayton's 'Since there's no help, come let us kiss and part' ([1619]; in Woudhuysen, 1993) follows this decasyllabic (ten-syllable) metre. Having said that, lines 9, 10 and 13 are more strained, the latter particularly as it consists of 12 syllables, five of which are stressed:

```
       X    /    X    /    X   /  X  /   X   /
1    Since there's no help, come let us kiss and part,
       X  / X    /    X    / X   /    X  /
2    Nay, I have done: you get no more of me,
       X   / X  /    X    /    X    /   X   /
3    And I am glad, yea glad with all my heart,
       X    /    X / X   / X  /   X   /
4    That thus so cleanly I myself can free.
       X       /    X / X    / X / X   /
5    Shake hands for ever, cancel all our vows,
       X    /    X    /    X / X /    X /
6    And when we meet at any time again
       X / X    /    X / X   /  X   /
7    Be it not seen in either of our brows
```

```
        X  /  X  /  X / X   /   X /
8     That we one jot of former love retain.
        X   / X  /  /  X  /     / X   /
9     Now at the last gasp of Love's latest breath,
          /    X  X  / X   / X    /  X   /
10    When his pulse failing, Passion speechless lies,
        X   /  X / X  / X / X /
11    When Faith is kneeling by his bed of death,
         X  / X  /  X  / X  /  X /
12    And Innocence is closing up his eyes,
         X  / X    /    X  / X   / X  X  / X
13    Now, if thou wouldst, when all have given him over,
         X    /  X / X   /    X  / X /
14    From death to life thou might'st him yet recover.
```

Note, of course, that stresses are not necessarily 'given' in the English language, particularly on one-syllable words. For instance, line 5's 'Shake' remains unstressed in this poem, but that is only due to the impact of a strong rhythmic context, a metre which forces us to stress each line's words in particular ways (for more on word and utterance stress outside the poetic context, see Jeffries, 2006, section 2.4). I shall return to this point a bit later.

Andrew Marvell's 'To his coy mistress' ([c. 1660]; also in Woudhuysen, 1993) is primarily in iambic tetrameters, although there is some variation in lines 1, 5, 8, 10, 12 and 18. Here are the poem's first 20 lines:

```
        /   X  X   /  X /   X  /
1     Had we but world enough, and time,
        X   / X   / X  / X  /
2     This coyness, lady, were no crime.
        X   /  X  /  X   /   X   /
3     We would sit down and think which way
        X /   X  / X  / X   /
4     To walk, and pass our long love's day;
        /   X  X  / X   / X   /
5     Thou by the Indian Ganges' side
        X     / X  / X / X /
6     Shouldst rubies find; I by the tide
        X  / X   / X  /  X /
7     Of Humber would complain. I would
```

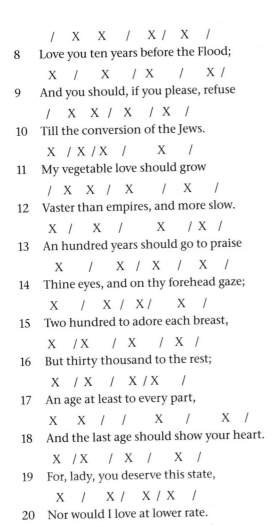

```
      /   X   X   /   X /  X   /
8   Love you ten years before the Flood;
      X   /   X    / X   /    X /
9   And you should, if you please, refuse
      /   X   X /  X   / X   /
10  Till the conversion of the Jews.
      X  / X / X  /    X    /
11  My vegetable love should grow
      /  X   X /  X    /  X   /
12  Vaster than empires, and more slow.
      X  /   X   /    X   / X  /
13  An hundred years should go to praise
      X   /   X / X  / X   /
14  Thine eyes, and on thy forehead gaze;
      X   /   X / X/    X   /
15  Two hundred to adore each breast,
      X   / X   / X   / X  /
16  But thirty thousand to the rest;
      X   / X  /  X / X   /
17  An age at least to every part,
      X   X  / /   X   /    X  /
18  And the last age should show your heart.
      X  / X   / X  /   X   /
19  For, lady, you deserve this state,
      X   /   X / X / X  /
20  Nor would I love at lower rate.
```

Notice how the imposition of a strong metrical scheme adds a rather musical sound effect to the reading of the poem, and how even regular metre has its variations at times, like music itself. This sort of metrical regularity, or background music if you like, is not as typical of twentieth-century poetry as it was of poetry of previous times, a noticeable exception being in the area of children's nursery rhymes, which retain their strong metrical regularity even in recent times (Jeffries, 1993: 40).

Lord Byron's 'The destruction of Sennacherib' ([1815]; in Eliot, 1909) is in anapaestic tetrameters, although lines 6, 8 and 10 start off with an iamb instead. Here are the first 12 lines of the poem:

X X /X   X   / X X / X X /
1   The Assyrian came down like the wolf on the fold,

X X / X   X / X   X / X   X /
2   And his cohorts were gleaming in purple and gold;

X X   / X X   / X X / X X /
3   And the sheen of their spears was like stars on the sea,

X   X /   X X   / X X   / X X/
4   When the blue wave rolls nightly on deep Galilee.

X   X   / X X /X X   / X X /
5   Like the leaves of the forest when Summer is green,

X / X   X / X X / X   X   /
6   That host with their banners at sunset were seen:

X X   / X X /X   X   / X   X   /
7   Like the leaves of the forest when Autumn hath blown,

X / X X   / X X / X   X   /
8   That host on the morrow lay withered and strown.

X X / X X /   X   X / X X /
9   For the Angel of Death spread his wings on the blast,

X   /   X X / X X / X X /
10 And breathed in the face of the foe as he pass'd,

X   X / X X / X   X   / X   X   /
11 And the eyes of the sleepers wax'd deadly and chill,

X X   / X   X   /   X X /X   X   /
12   And their hearts but once heaved, and for ever grew still!

Notice how the 'dididum'ness of the form, brought about by the large number of function[1] monosyllabic words used, reinforces the feel of the galloping of the horse, as the Assyrian rides into battle. Can you find any more such poems where the meaning of the text is reflected in, reinforced by, or even contrasted with the imposed metre? These could be, for instance, poems where the rhythm coincides with references to a train speeding past, hearts beating fast, people and animals running, and so on. Consider whether undertaking a metrical analysis of the poem in fact contributes to your understanding of your original interpretation of it.

As you can see from these examples, those poems that are classifiable under a given metre do not necessarily need to maintain the exact same verse format throughout. Even more so, lines in a poem may repeat the same, even if relaxed, metre, or be combined in entirely different patterns. For instance, let us look at Robert Frost's 'The road not taken' ([1915]1920), a poem which follows the

ABAAB rhyme scheme, and has four stressed syllables per line. To explain the rhyme format, 'A' here corresponds to those lines that end-rhyme[2] in one way, whereas 'B' refers to those that end-rhyme in another; the 'ABAAB' format shows that line 1 (ending in 'wood' in the first stanza) rhymes with lines 3 ('stood') and 4 ('could'), while line 2 ('both') rhymes with line 5 ('undergrowth').

```
        X  /   X /    X X / X   /
1    Two roads diverged in a yellow wood
        X  / X X /   X  / X  /
2    And sorry I could not travel both
        X  / X  / X X  / X /
3    And be one traveler, long I stood
        X   /    X   / X / X X /
4    And looked down one as far as I could
        X   / X /  X X  / X  /
5    To where it bent in the undergrowth;
        X  / X / X X / X /
6    Then took the other, as just as fair
        X  / X  X / X  X / X  /
7    And having perhaps the better claim,
        X / X  X / X  X / X  /
8    Because it was grassy and wanted wear;
         X  / X  / X  / X  /
9    Though as for that, the passing there
        X   /   X  / X X / X  /
10   Had worn them really about the same,
         X  / X  / X /X X  /
11   And both that morning equally lay
        X  / X  / X  / X  /
12   In leaves no step had trodden black.
        X X /  X  / X X/ X  /
13   Oh, I kept the first for another day!
        X  / X  X /   / X X /
14   Yet knowing how way leads on to way,
        X /  X / X  X  / X  X    /
15   I doubted if I should ever come back.
        X /  X / X  /  X X /
16   I shall be telling this with a sigh[3]
```

```
      /    X   /X  X   /X   /
17  Somewhere ages and ages hence:
      X   /   X /    X X  /   X  /
18  Two roads diverged in a wood and I—
      X /  X   /  X   / X  /
19  I took the one less traveled by,
       X  /  X   /  X X  / X X
20  And that has made all the difference.
```

At the start of the poem, the poetic persona faces a dilemma in having to choose between one of two paths. Having chosen one of the two, he thereafter projects himself into the future, where he claims to others that he has chosen the 'less travelled' road. Nevertheless, the ironic undertone suggests that the persona has merely chosen one of two paths, but not necessarily the less travelled one; whichever decision it was that he made at the start, it would have probably made no actual 'difference' to him. Essentially, he would have faced remorse ('I shall be telling this with a sigh') either way.

At first glance, the poem appears to be in iambic tetrameters, although various anapaests appear throughout as well. In fact, there appears to be at least one anapaest per line here. The last line appears to stand out in that its metre and hence rhythm is noticeably different to the rest of the poem, unless we choose to actually stress 'difference' as 'DIfferENCE'. This last line draws attention to itself as a consequence, and invites the reader to concentrate the poem's meaning here.

See Chapter 3, Task A

It is important to note that words in the English language that are made of more than one syllable have a (primary) stressed syllable. For example, 'English' is a two-syllabled word stressed on its first syllable, while 'become' is a two-syllabled word stressed on its second syllable. However, some words have alternative accent positions depending on word class: 'PROgress' is a noun, whereas 'proGRESS' is a verb. Monosyllabic words may or may not be stressed in English, sometimes depending on their verbal context. The monosyllabic *need* would probably be stressed in 'I need you to help me'. In this same example, the monosyllabic 'to' would not, however, be stressed. Furthermore, the way in which we stress words depends on the context, and the sort of meaning we are trying to evoke. For instance, most people would probably stress the phrase 'And what's your name?' something like this 'And WHAT'S your NAme?' or contrastively 'And what's YOUR name?' Words with more than four syllables often have what we call a weaker or secondary stress. The word 'organisation' is primarily stressed on the 'sa' syllable, but also shares a secondary stress, which we could place on the initial 'o'. Try pronouncing monosyllabic and multisyllabic words to test this.

Having made these distinctions, it is important to note that words are often pronounced, and therefore stressed, differently in poetry than in prose. When we read metrical poetry, we are made aware of metre, and allow this to determine the way in which we recite the lines. In other words, a metrical poetic line will invite us to recite it according to metre, as opposed to a prosaic line which invites us to recite it according to the number of syllables, syntax and sense.

Let us return to the first two lines from Drayton's 'Since there's no help', the metre of which invited us to stress the poetic lines as follows:

```
       X    /   X   /   X  / X  / X  /
1    Since there's no help, come let us kiss and part,
      X  / X   /   X   / X  / X  /
2    Nay, I have done: you get no more of me,
```

If we rewrite the lines into prose, we notice that the stress falls on different words:

```
     /    X / X  /   /   / X / X  /
1    Since there's no help, come let us kiss and part,
      /  / X   /   X  / /   X  X /
2    Nay I have done: you get no more of me,
```

In reading these lines as prose, we might choose to stress the (contracted) verb 'is' and the 'come' of the first line, as well as the 'Nay' and 'no' of the second line, possibly relieving stress from the second line's 'more'. Notice that reducing 'is' to the contraction in the poetic context helps reinforce the metre. Poets often manipulate syntactic and morphological constructs in their attempts to impose metre on lines. Return to the poems above and try re-reading them as prose. Does the way you stress the words indeed vary? And of course, there is also the question of whether a 'performance' by an accomplished reader or actor would be capable of resisting the force of a poem's given metre.

Recite the following poem by Christina Rossetti from her *Monna Innominata: A Sonnet of Sonnets* sequence ([1881]; in Fuller's *The Oxford Book of Sonnets*, 2002).

```
      X /    X  /  X / X  /     X  /
1    I lov'd you first: but afterwards your love          A
      X  / X   /    X  / X / X  /
2    Outsoaring mine, sang such a loftier song            B
```

```
     X   /    X  / X  / X  / X  /
3    As drown'd the friendly cooings of my dove.        A
       X   / X  /X  / X  / X  /
4    Which owes the other most? my love was long,        B
     X   / X  / X  / X  / X  /
5    And yours one moment seem'd to wax more strong;     B
     X /  X  / X  / X  / X  /
6    I lov'd and guess'd at you, you construed me –       C
     X  / X  / X  / X  / X  /
7    And lov'd me for what might or might not be          C
     X   /  X  / X  /X  / X  /
8    Nay, weights and measures do us both a wrong.        B
     X  / X/ X  /  X   /  X  /
9    For verily love knows not 'mine' or 'thine;'         D
     X   / X  / X  / X  / X  /
10   With separate 'I' and 'thou' free love has done,     E
     X  / X  / X  / X  / X  /
11   For one is both and both are one in love:            A
     X  /  X   / X  / X / X  /
12   Rich love knows nought of 'thine that is not mine;'  D
     X  / X   / X  / X  /  X  /
13   Both have the strength and both the length thereof,  A
     X  X  / X X  /  X   /  X  /
14   Both of us, of the love which makes us one.          E
```

This romantic poem is primarily in the iambic pentameter format, and tends to force the reader to mostly stress lexical words (such as line 2's noun 'song' and line 1's verb 'loved') rather than function words (such as line 6's preposition 'at' and line 2's article 'a'), much like prose. Nevertheless, the metre of the poem invites us to stress line 6's 'construed' in its first rather than its second syllable, though the *OED* allows both stress possibilities anyway. Similarly, we are invited to stress 'for' in line 7, and to somewhat alter our pace in our pronunciation of 'verily' in line 9 and quicken our pronunciation of 'both of us' and 'of the love' in the poem's final line. This last line may bear four rather than five stresses, thus being in the tetrameter rather that the pentameter format. Furthermore, it appears to follow the anapaest–anapaest–iamb–iamb format as opposed to most of the poem's iamb–iamb–iamb–iamb–iamb format. It is the large number of function words in the final line that forces the reader to adjust the metre and quicken the pace. This poem's rhythm would draw attention to itself in its last line which is therefore shortened and quickened. As a result, the line becomes noticeable for expressive effects, concentrating the meaning of the poem on itself.

It is also often useful to engage in an analysis of the poem's rhyming scheme. In this poem, the ABABB CC BDEADAE rhyme signals that, in a total of 14 lines, there is a relatively small variation of five different sounding line-final syllables, which helps make the poem cohesive, and establish certain connections between the rhyming words. 'Love' here gets connected to 'dove', thereby giving the emotion of love connotations more of peace, tenderness and beauty (as exemplified in the symbolism of the dove) rather than, for instance, passion. Similarly, 'song' rhymes with 'long', 'strong' and 'wrong', juxtaposing lasting love with a feeling of 'immorality', evident in the use of 'wrong'. Also, 'thine' rhymes with 'mine', where the words physically enact the meaning of line 12 itself: 'Rich love knows nought of "thine that is not mine".'

See Chapter 3, Task B

1.3 Poetic sound effects

It is, of course, crucial to relate the relationship of rhythm and rhyme to other poetic patterns. Such poetic patterns include alliteration: that is, the repetition of the same or similar consonant sounds, such as the /l/[4] sound in the last poem's line 4: 'love was long'; assonance: that is, the repetition of the same or similar vowel sounds, such as the /ʌ/ sound in line 14's 'us' and 'love'; and 'onomatopoeia', where the sound of a word itself imitates directly the meaning of it, such as line 3's 'cooing'. In the case of onomatopoeia, language appears to be no longer arbitrary, since the sound of the relevant word actually echoes the sound the word itself expresses (onomatopoeic words include ones such as 'tap' and 'sizzle'). Another related term is enjambment, where the line break occurs at a break in a grammatical clause or phrase, such as the break in the last poem's first two lines which separates the subject 'your love' from the predicator[5] 'outsoaring'. Enjambment essentially creates a poetic tension between the graphology and the grammar of the text.

As Jeffries (1993: 40) puts it, such aspects of the sound of poetry appeal 'to the aesthetic sense without necessarily involving the intellect in interpreting its meaning'. And it is not atypical for iconicity to arise from the whole of the poetic context, as opposed to it being attached to individual lexical items. To borrow some commonly quoted examples, Short (1996: 117) argues that the Wilfred Owen poem 'Anthem for doomed youth' enacts gunfire during the line 'Only the s**tutt**ering rifles' ra**pid ratt**le'. This iconicity is achieved by the high density of stop consonants coupled with short vowels here. Similarly,

Jeffries (1993: 54) suggests that in the poem 'Morning song', 'Sylvia Plath makes effective use of the voiceless fricative / θ/ (and /f/) to suggest the almost imperceptible breathing of a new baby: "All night your moth-breath / Flickers among the flat pink roses"' (for more on the sound of twentieth-century poetry in particular, see Jeffries, 1993: chapter 3). You might want to try to test this theory by writing a sound-symbolic poem of your own. Let's take fricative consonant sounds for example, meaning sounds that allow the flow of air in your lungs to come out in a steady flow. You could employ the fricative sounds /θ/ and /f/ when writing about the wind, the sounds /s/ and /ʃ/ when describing the effect of silence, or the /ð/, /z/ and /ʒ/ sounds when writing about a fly or bee going through a room. In employing the use of words produced using these sounds, you might indeed enact the scene you are describing in each case.

It is quite important, of course, to remember that there is such a thing as free verse, where the poems are not restricted to a particular metre or rhyme. This allows readers to try to establish beats themselves, and therefore experiment with a line's possible realisations. A poet famous for taking free verse to the extreme is William Carlos Williams. In his poem 'To a poor old woman' ([1935]1988), he makes reference to a woman munching plums from a paper bag in the street, and proceeds to say that these plums indeed 'taste good to her'. The poem's third stanza reads as follows:

> You can see it by
> the way she gives herself
> to the one half
> sucked out in her hand

What we have here is very noticeable enjambment, rather extreme 'running-on' of the poetic lines; we normally expect line breaks to coincide with syntactic breaks, but this expectation is not satisfied. The prepositional phrase 'by the way' is interrupted mid-way by the first line break. The second line break interrupts the syntactic clause separating the clause's direct object ('herself') and the indirect object ('to the one half'). 'To give yourself to' something is a common English language idiom. Notice, nevertheless, that 'herself' is a rather unusual thing to give to plums – we would perhaps have expected to see the direct and indirect object roles reversed here instead, that is, 'she gives the one half to herself'. The enjambment at this point draws attention to the unusual use of the idiom itself. The third line break further interrupts the noun phrase 'the one half sucked out in her hand', where the head 'half [plum]' is separated from its postmodifying non-finite clause 'sucked out in her hand'. The unusual line breaks coupled with a lack of punctuation give the poem a rather stream-of-consciousness effect, making it hard for the reader to pick and choose where to pause.

The rhythm of Williams' poetry is difficult to establish, which is why he is often said to write in 'variable metre'. Moreover, his stanzas themselves often interfere with the reciting of his poems, giving us a sense of completion even where the sense and content do not actually give us this completion. In 'Landscape with the fall of Icarus' ([1962]1988), he makes reference to the famous Bruegel the Elder painting that touches upon the Greek myth of the tragedy of Icarus. This is a part of his poetic description of the painting:

a farmer was ploughing
his field
the whole pageantry

of the year was
awake tingling
near

Here, we have enjambment across stanzas as well as enjambment across lines. The object 'his field' is separated from its predicator 'was ploughing', the noun phrase 'the whole pageantry of the year' is interrupted by a stanza break, the complement 'awake' is separated from its predicator 'was' at a line break, and the adverbial 'near' is left dangling at the last line, almost randomly.

Williams was obviously an innovator, breaking rules and behaving very much against tradition. He challenges our perspective of poetic line alignment, rhythm and rhyme (though rhyme can still be found, with 'ploughing' rhyming with 'tingling', not to mention internal rhyme in that 'year' rhymes with 'near'). We could even argue that his unusual use of space leaves a lot of 'space' for imagination; quite a few ambiguities arise from his line-aligning, particularly when his readers attempt to recite the poems. His work appears plain, and yet complicated. He wrote about everyday circumstances and drew on the life of the common people for inspiration. His controlled imagery is, however, also complemented by this entirely new and fresh American poetic form.

See Chapter 3, Task C

1.4 Relating poetic form to poetic meaning

In stylistics, we need to do more than merely describe the form of texts. It is in fact essential to try to relate the textual form to the meaning established in the relevant poems. Since its publication in 1871 as part of Carroll's *Alice's Adventures in Wonderland* series, and more particularly the book *Through the Looking-Glass*, the poem 'Jabberwocky' (see Carroll and Gardner, 2001) is traditionally considered to be 'nonsense', and yet thought to be rather interpretable and meaningful. Using the terminology so far introduced in this chapter, let us analyse its poetic form to explain this generated effect. I have numbered the stanzas for ease of reference.

1   'Twas brillig, and the slithy toves
    Did gyre and gimble in the wabe;
    All mimsy were the borogoves,
        And the mome raths outgrabe.

2   'Beware the Jabberwock, my son!
        The jaws that bite, the claws that catch!
    Beware the Jujub bird, and shun
        The frumious Bandersnatch!'

3   He took his vorpal sword in hand:
        Long time the manxome foe he sought –
    So rested he by the Tumtum tree,
        And stood awhile in thought.

4   And as in uffish thought he stood,
        The Jabberwock, with eyes of flame,
    Came whiffling through the tulgey wood,
        And burbled as it came!

5   One, two! One, two! And through and through
        The vorpal blade went snicker-snack!
    He left it dead, and with its head
        He went galumphing back.

6   'And has thou slain the Jabberwock?
        Come to my arms, my beamish boy!
    O frabjous day! Calloh! Callay!
        He chortled in his joy.

7   'Twas brillig, and the slithy toves
        Did gyre and gimble in the wabe;
    All mimsy were the borogoves,
        And the mome raths outgrabe.

The poem is essentially a parody of an old English ballad of dragon slaying, echoing such poems as the famous *Beowulf* (see Heaney, 1999). The references to the 'claws' and 'jaws' allude to the creature in *Beowulf*, as does the Germaniclooking morphology of many of the words, nonsensical (the first stanza's 'outgrabe' and the second stanza's 'shun') or not (the first stanza's ''twas' and the sixth stanza's 'thou'). Moreover, the poem displays both lyrical and archaic grammar. The emphatic 'did' on the first stanza's second line is somewhat poetic and unnecessary, added so as to engage the necessary rhythm. Similarly archaic is the complement–predicator–subject format evident in the same stanza's 'All mimsy were the borogoves', where in everyday English one would expect the more prosaic subject–predicator–complement 'The borogoves were all mimsy' format, a format typical of a non-poetic, or at least more modern poetic context. Other examples of archaic grammar include the third stanza's subject–predicator inversion of 'so rested he', where in a more modern context we would expect 'so he rested'. See if you can trace all other instances of such poetic and archaic grammar.

Obviously, the poem contains a large number of 'neologisms' or 'nonce' words, such as the first stanza's 'brillig' and 'toves' among various others. Note, of course, the morphological similarity between the poem's 'frumious', 'wabe' and 'galumphing', and the English words 'furious', 'wave' and 'galloping' correspondingly, giving the impression that the nonce words could potentially be seen as misreads or misspellings instead. Also notice that such misspellings often contribute to alliteration ('did **g**yre and **g**imble', 'the **T**um**t**um **t**ree') as well·as assonance (''Twas br**i**ll**i**g', 'D**i**d gyre and g**i**mble'), although alliteration and assonance are also evident where actual English lexicon is employed ('the **c**laws that **c**atch', '**sn**icker-**sn**ack', '**He** left ... **He** went ...'). A particularly notice-able example is the sixth stanza's 'Come to **m**y ar**m**s **m**y **b**eamish **b**oy', where the alliteration adds to the line's vivid effect; the high density of labial conso-nants makes the scene all the more dramatic when reciting the poem out loud, and it also helps reinforce a positive image of the boy as bright and the father as proud.

One of the things often pointed out about this poem is that a reader can pretty much work out its 'meaning' despite the fact that it contains many words not evident in the English lexicon (see for instance Rose, 1995). In other words, the reader can work out that a son leaves home in order to kill a rather dangerous creature referred to as the 'Jabberwock', succeeds in this task and returns home victorious, and therefore receives his father's praise and congrat-ulations. Order is restored in the final stanza, a stanza which is noticeably iden-tical to the poem's first stanza. The exact repetition of the two stanzas reinforces the impression that whatever it was that happened, the readers are essentially now returned to the peaceful and pleasurable state where the story started.

What helps the reader make sense of the poem is the fact that it follows the syntactic rules of the English language, despite the nonsensical words. For instance, the reader can work out that the neologisms 'whiffling', 'burbled', 'galumphing' and 'chortled'[6] are onomatopoeic verbs, and though nonsensical, these are indeed interpretable and hence rather revealing and meaningful. Similarly onomatopoeic are the adjective-looking 'slithy' (first stanza) and 'uffish' (forth stanza), not to mention the fifth paragraph's 'snicker-snack', echoing the sound of the knife as it penetrates the creature's body.

Also, the poem certainly has regularity of rhythm. Each stanza is in iambic tetrameter for the first three lines, while all stanza-final lines are in iambic trimeter instead. An exception to this is the third stanza's 'So rested he by the Tumtum tree' which seems to be a combination of two iambs followed by one anapaest and yet another iamb. This is quite a minor variation though; in poems, short function words such as 'the' are very often 'swallowed' under extreme metrical force. The rhythm of the fifth stanza is particularly striking, as the iambic tetrameter is forced to coincide with the knife going in and out of the creature's body as rhythmically as the line itself: 'One, two! One, two! And through and through / The vorpal blade went snicker-snack.' The readers are almost invited to the scene itself, helping to contribute to the slaying of the dragon in their delivery of the poem in regular metre. The similarly rhythmical iambic trimeter stanza-final line ('He went galumphing back') literally enacts the sound of a horse galloping, returning the hero home, the rhythm additionally giving the impression that the horse is galloping rather fast and heavily in doing so.

Furthermore, each stanza follows its own ABAB rhyming scheme, with the exception of the third stanza's 'hand/tree' and the fifth stanza's 'through/head' word-final lines which, though not rhyming, certainly mirror each other when it comes to their position in the poem itself. As previously noted, 'end-rhyme' is where certain line-final vowel and consonantal clusters match phonologically. There are also a number of instances where this poem displays internal rhyme, meaning rhyme that occurs in positions other than the end of a line. There is internal rhyme in the second stanza's 'The jaws that bite, the claws that catch' (where 'jaws' rhymes with 'claws'), in the third's stanza's 'So rested he by the Tumtum tree' (where 'he' rhymes with 'tree'), in the fifth stanza's 'He left it dead and with its head' (where 'dead' rhymes with 'head'), and in the sixth stanza's 'O frabjous day! Calloh! Callay!' (where presumably 'day' rhymes with 'Callay'). There is, of course, also direct repetition of words coupled with internal rhyme in the fifth stanza's 'One, two! One, two! And through and through.'

The stanzas do not in themselves interfere with our recitation of the poem in that they display end-stopping rather than enjambment. This means that, by and large, the end of the lines coincides with major syntactic boundaries. Exceptions to this are the first stanza's ''Twas brillig, and the slithy toves / Did gyre and gimble in the wabe', and the forth stanza's 'The Jabberwock, with eyes of flame / Came whiffling through the tulgey wood', where the clauses' subjects are separated from the relevant predicators.

See Chapter 3, Task D

1.5 Chapter review

In this chapter, we started by considering what it is that makes poetry different from other literary forms. We defined the notions of rhythm and metre, introduced the relevant Greek-derived terminology for stress patterns in poetic lines, and looked at some examples of the various forms. We also examined how metrical schemes relate to poetic content. We then compared stress patterns across poetry and more prosaic forms, and investigated cases where metrical schemes alter the ways in which prosaic lines are pronounced. It also proved useful to engage in an analysis of poems' rhyming schemes, and try to establish how such schemes contribute to meaning making. We then defined the poetic patterns of alliteration, assonance, onomatopoeia and enjambment, and examined how these features too contribute to our interpretation of the poetic content and effects. Overall, we so far explored how analyses of poetic form can illuminate our understanding of poetic meaning.

In the next chapter, I explore the usefulness of the 'figures and ground' model of prominence, alongside the sort of linguistic foregrounding devices that are typical of poetry: in other words, deviation and parallelism. I also engage in deeper analysis of figurative language in the poetic context.

2 Poetic figures, foregrounding and metaphor

2.1 Figure and ground

'Figure' and 'ground' are terms that relate to the phenomenon of prominence, where things essentially draw *attention* to themselves. As Ungerer and Schmid (1996: 156) put it, '[w]*hen we look at an object in our environment, we single it out as a perceptually prominent figure standing out from the ground*' (authors' italics). Essentially, as human beings, we are capable of seeing what is mobile and foregrounded (that is, the figure) in relation to what is static and backgrounded (that is, the ground) around us. Though figure and ground are concepts originally taken from the visual field, they have equal validity when it comes to looking at the structure of language.

> *The same principle of prominence is valid in the structure of language. For example, in locative expressions like in* The book is on the table *the book is conceptualised as the figure.*

> (Ungerer and Schmid, 1996: 156)

Stockwell (2002: 15) argues that characters are 'figures' of their corresponding novels, as they are mobile in time and place; their movement tends to be stylistically represented through verbs of motion and locative expressions using prepositions. For instance, in prepositions such as 'over', 'into' and 'through', the figure is seen as a moving 'trajectory' that describes a staged 'path' in relation to the grounded 'landmark' (Stockwell, 2003b: 22). In the sentence 'The man walked by the shop', 'the man' is the figure and 'the shop' is the ground; 'the shop' is the grounded feature that is fixed in its location, in contrast to the moving man who stages a path in relation to 'the shop'.

These notions have been confirmed by experimental results on visual fields, but as noted, also have correspondence in the linguistic field of literary text

analysis. Stylistic features distract our attention (so they are known as 'attractors'), and by contrast, the remaining ground is characterised by cognitive
neglect (see Stockwell, 2002: 18). Read the following poetic extract by Picasso
([1943]2004), translated from French by Pierre Joris:

15.5.43
the flute the grapes the umbrella the armor the tree and the accordion the
butterfly wings of the sugar of the blue fan of the lake and the azure waves
of the silks of the strings hanging from the bouquets of roses of the
ladders one and incalculable outsized flood of doves released drunk on the
cutting festoons of prisms fixed to the bells decomposing with its thousand
lit candles the green flocks of wool illuminated by the gentle acrobatics of
the lanterns hanging from each arc string and the definitive dawn

The whole of the poem distracts our attention in its use of multiple noun-phrase
types of figure, such as the flute, the grapes, the umbrella and so forth. Not only
is there a limited use of (only non-finite) verbs here, but there is multiple embedding of noun phrases within the post-modifying prepositional phrases of other
noun phrases, as the analysis of the first few lines below shows (noun phrases are
in square brackets, the embedded ones are indented, and the verb is in italics):

15.5.43
[the flute]
[the grapes]
[the umbrella]
[the armor]
[the tree] and
[the accordion]
[the butterfly wings of   ]
                    [the sugar of   ]
                         [the blue fan of   ]
                                   [the lake]

and
[the azure waves of   ]
                    [the silks of   ]
                         [the strings *hanging* from   ]
                                   [the bouquets of   ]
                                        [roses of [the ladders]

More verbs appear in the second half of the poem, which seems to include, again, multiple embedding of noun phrases, this time within the postmodifying non-finite clauses of other noun phrases (see Table 2.1).

Table 2.1

Head noun	Postmodification
Doves	released drunk on the cutting festoons of
prisms	fixed to the bells
the bells	decomposing with its thousand lit candles
wool	illuminated by the gentle acrobatics of the lanterns
the lanterns	hanging from each arc string

So what essentially makes this a difficult text to process is the apparent lack of a clear ground for all of the figures to be seen or set against. Of course, there is also semantic difficulty in processing the text, as it draws on semantic links which are difficult to process. For instance, 'the butterfly wings of the sugar of the blue fan of the lake' presupposes that the sugar indeed has '(butterfly) wings', the lake has a 'blue fan' and the blue fan itself has 'the sugar', all of which are metaphors we would find difficult to process, not to mention identify the figure/ground of. In an analysis of a similar Picasso poem, Stockwell (2003b: 17) notices that the addition of new lines, new images and new attractors provide new figures emerging from the ground of each previous line, an argument that also rings true of the above poem. As with much surreal art and not just surreal poetry, each figure effectively becomes the ground against which further figures are set, while 'neglect sets in cumulatively as the figuration moves on, with the chained figure and ground giving a cosmetic sense of cohesion' (Stockwell, 2003b: 17).

See Chapter 3, Task E

2.2 Linguistic foregrounding

The 'figure/ground' model closely corresponds to the phenomenon to do with the literary notion of 'foregrounding'. Much like figures and grounds, the notion of foregrounding is a principle originally taken from the visual field, but it certainly has applications in, and relevance to, the verbal field. According to Wales (2001: 157), linguistic foregrounding can be defined as 'the "throwing into relief" of the linguistic sign against the background of the norms of ordinary language'. In other words, in linguistics, foregrounding is essentially a psychological effect relating to the prominence that certain features of language achieve, in contrast to the *background* of everyday, non-prominent language. The notion of foregrounding is, in fact, often used to distinguish poetic from non-poetic language, which is why foregrounding is often seen as having links with the notion of 'literariness'. Essentially, foregrounding is one of the effects often claimed to contribute to literature's aesthetic characterisation.

In the context of text analysis, foregrounding is achieved by a variety of means, which have largely been grouped into two main types, 'deviation' and 'parallelism'. Whereas deviations are essentially violations or departures from certain linguistic norms, parallelism refers to unexpected repetition of such norms.

As I note in Gregoriou (2007a), the early Russian Formalists saw literary language as a set of deviations from a norm, a kind of 'linguistic violence', while the idea that poetry specifically violates the norms of everyday language was much propounded by the Prague School (see for instance Mukařovský, 1970). Therefore, within such contexts, 'literariness or poeticality inheres in the degrees to which language use departs or deviates from expected configurations and normal patterns of language' (Carter and Nash, 1990: 31). To put this simply, they drew on the claim that the more deviant the text is, and the more it departs from linguistic norms, the more poetic it is bound to be. Such a definition of literariness appears to have links to literary language's 'defamiliarising' property, where such language is said to generate new or renewed perceptions of our normal view of things through what we might call 'linguistic disturbance' or 'deviance'. Of course, a development of this view of foregrounding would be to see it not only in relation to some external notion of the 'normal', but also in terms of its prominence to the immediately surrounding text, the proximate verbal context. I return to this point shortly.

However, Carter and Nash (1990: 18) point out that features of language use more normally associated with literary contexts are also found in what are conventionally thought of as non-literary contexts. For instance, prominent or foregrounded language is achieved in newspaper headlines, advertisements and street graffiti as much as in the most clearly poetic context of all, poetry. Therefore, Carter and Nash propose that the term 'literariness' is preferred to any term which suggests an absolute distinction between the literary and the non-literary. They instead suggest that literary language should be seen as a continuum, a cline, with some language uses being marked as more literary than others. There is no such a thing as a clear-cut distinction between literary and non-literary language uses, much as there is no such thing as a clear-cut distinction between informal and formal language uses; it is better, and more appropriate, to think of literariness (and (in)formality) in terms of a more/less cline. Carter and Nash (1990: 35) further argue that one crucial determinant in a text's literariness is whether the reader chooses to read the text in a literary way (as a literary text, as it were). For instance, we might find an informal note, a text message or indeed the Bible literary, if we choose to read these texts as literature (see also Gregoriou, 2007a).

2.2.1 Deviation

In previous work (see Gregoriou, 2007a), and as previously noted, I take 'deviation' or 'deviance' to refer to the difference between what we take to be normal or acceptable and that which is not. Admittedly, in the terms' everyday sense, 'deviance' is used with a rather negative semantic prosody and evokes a defiance or rejection of whatever somebody deems normal, ordinary and perhaps mainstream, whereas 'deviation' is more neutral, and only when it is linked to percentages or other independent factors does it attract a negative (or positive) evaluation. When the two are used as linguistic and/or stylistic terms, however, they have tended to be used synonymously. I follow this tradition here although some writers (for example Leech and Short, 1981) have tried to make a distinction between them (preferring 'deviance' for divergence in frequency from a *norm*).

Deviations can occur at many levels, and stylisticians need to be aware of the level of language at which each deviation occurs, keeping in mind that deviation can occur at more than one level at the same time.

According to Short (1996), deviation can be 'external' if it departs from the norms of the English language, the relevant genre or the relevant period. In other words, we witness external deviance where a text departs from norms external to the text itself, norms imposed outside the boundaries of this piece. For instance, if a writer breaks the rules of the English language by, say, not including any nouns in a poem, they are essentially deviating externally from rules of the language itself. If a poem reads as if it were an advert, a joke or a riddle, it is externally deviating from supposed 'rules' to do with generating the poetic form. A poem would, again generate external deviance if written in antiquated grammar: for instance, where complements precede subjects, as in 'Jabberwocky's 'All mimsy were the borogroves'. Here, as noted, we would perhaps expect the more prosaic or less temporally distant subject–predicator–complement format, 'The borogoves were all mimsy.' Leech and Short (1981: 52) in fact use the term 'deviation of historical period' to refer to the latter sort of external deviation, or similar instances of archaism and/or anachronism in literary texts. Texts could further generate external deviance if they deviate from the norms typical of that particular author.

Short (1996) reserves the use of 'internal' deviation to refer to departures from patterns established in the text itself. Jokes have a tendency to generate this type of internal deviance a lot. Let us take the following example of a joke, which echoes the well-known 'This little piggy'[1] nursery verse:

> There were three pigs.
> The first pig went to a bar, ordered a drink and gulped it down, before going to the lavatory and then leaving.
> The second pig went to the same bar, ordered a drink and gulped it down, before going to the lavatory and then leaving.
> The third pig went to the same bar, ordered a drink and gulped it down. He was just about to leave, when the bartender asked if he was going to the lavatory before leaving. The third little pig said 'No, I'm the little pig that goes wee wee wee all the way home.'

This rather terrible joke's effect depends on generating internal deviance; a pattern gets established *internally*, within the context of the joke itself, and then the pattern gets broken. On the first two occasions, the pigs arrive, order and gulp down their drink, before visiting the lavatory and then leaving. The pattern is being firmly established and even reinforced on the third occasion, where a third pig enters, orders and again gulps down their drink. The pattern, however, is subsequently broken on this last occasion because this third pig fails to visit the pub's facilities before leaving, and so prompts the bartender's query whether he actually intends to do so. Foregrounding is generated because we reach the narrative peak at the internally deviant story point at the joke's end, which coincides with the third pig's direct speech presentation. We are, of course, discussing a 'content', rather than a 'stylistic' norm here, but the point can be extended to the use of certain linguistic features, as I shall illustrate later.

Short (1996) further differentiates between linguistic deviation that is 'discoursal', 'semantic', 'lexical', 'grammatical', 'phonological' and 'graphological'.

Discoursal deviation refers to a text deviating from the sort of discourse typical of its genre and/or subgenre. For instance, in reading a third-person narrative, readers expect characters to interact with each other, but they would not expect the author to interact with the characters, or indeed address the readers directly, using second-person narration. Where authors engage in such interaction, they can be said to discoursally deviate, or depart from the norms typical of third-person narratives.

The band names 'Here Are the Facts You Requested', ' James, What Are We Gonna Call Our Band?' and 'Not Now I'm Naked' are similarly discoursally deviant. We expect band names to take the form of noun phrases (such as Red

Hot Chili Peppers and Bob Marley and the Wailers). Here Are the Facts You Requested is a full declarative clause instead, and reads much like a formal email extract or post-it note, the sort we associate with formal and impersonal work-like interaction. James, What Are We Gonna Call Our Band? is in the interrogative clausal form, echoes a casual utterance between band members, and therefore appears to be inappropriate genre-wise; again, we would expect a noun phrase in reference to a band rather than an interrogative to do with asking one's opinion on the naming matter. Not Now I'm Naked is a clause and is, again, casual-utterance like, and appears to echo the sort of thing that a teenager would say in response to their mother knocking on their bedroom door.

Semantic deviation refers to illogical or paradoxical meaning relations between words, such as with the use of metaphor. Such deviation can be found in Shakespeare's line 'in black ink my love may still shine bright' from Sonnet 65 ([1609] see e.g. Shakespeare, 1911). Here, it is illogical or nonsensical to read the sentence in its literal sense; it is impossible for love, an abstract concept, to literally 'shine'. The reader, however, assumes appropriacy in the use of such wording and therefore draws on metaphor to interpret the line; our love can be encapsulated or concretised in the form of a poem, which could in turn give the emotion a sort of permanence that human life itself lacks. The names of the bands Ambitious Vegetables, Dancing Cigarettes and The Celery Stalkers are also semantically deviant, as these all suggest absurd semantic connections: vegetables cannot be ambitious, cigarettes cannot dance, and stalkers are not made of and/or cannot pursue celery. In the case of the last example, 'celery' can be taken to be a descriptor of the stalkers, like 'angry' in 'The Angry Stalkers', or alternatively, indicate the object of the stalking, like 'teenager' in 'The Teenager Stalkers'. This could also be taken as a pun on a stick/stalk of celery, of course. In whichever case, the meaning relationship is incongruous.

Lexical deviation is to do with the use of words inappropriate for their context, the conversion of word classes, or neologising: that is, the making up of new words. 'Jabberwocky', which we analysed in Chapter 1, includes a large number of 'nonce' words, such as 'whiffling', an invented verb, and 'mimsy', an invented adjective. A taboo word could also prove inappropriate, say in a very formal context, and therefore generate lexical deviation. The names of the bands 'Diet Christ', 'Evil Side of Math' and 'Fatal Sneeze' are also lexically deviant. Diets are not the sorts of things we find relevant to religion, we do not associate maths with evil and neither do we associate an everyday harmless action such as sneezing with death. We could even argue that these band names in particular are not only lexically but also semantically deviant. We not only react to finding these words in strange contexts or unusual collocation, but they also consequently express rather illogical semantic relationships.

Grammatical deviation is to do with deviation either at the level of a word's individual make-up or at the level of syntax. The former deviation can be described as 'morphological', and the latter as 'syntactic'. Morphological deviation can take the form of atypical word structure, unusual bound morpheme suffix endings, odd compounding or extraordinary spellings, whereas syntactic deviation can take the form of unusual or reversed word order, strange phrase structure or the breaking of any other syntactic rule of the English language.

Have a look at the following extract from Lewis Carroll's ([1865] 2001) *Alice's Adventures in Wonderland*.

> 'Yes, we went to school in the sea, though you mayn't believe it –' ... 'I only took the regular course.'
> 'What was that?' inquired Alice.
> 'Reeling and Writhing, of course, to begin with,' the Mock Turtle replied; 'and then the different branches of Arithmetic – Ambition, Distraction, Uglification, and Derision.'

The words 'reeling', 'writhing', 'ambition', 'distraction' and 'derision' are all lexically deviant. Though these are all words indeed found in the English language, they are here found out of context, in strange collocation. Note that these in fact resemble words that would have been appropriate for the context, correspondingly the words 'reading', 'writing', 'addition', 'subtraction' and 'division'. The word 'uglification', though also a pun on 'multiplication', is an invented one, and also a morphologically deviant one. Here, the actual adjective 'ugly' is converted to the invented verb 'to uglify' (following such verbs as 'to quantify' or 'to specify'), and the verb is then converted to the invented noun 'uglification' (following such nouns as 'quantification' and 'specification').

The band names Likk, Newlydeads and Popemobile are lexically deviant in that these are neologisms, and they are also morphologically deviant; Likk appears to be a deviant phonological misspelling of the word 'lick', Newlydeads appears to be a deviant misread of 'newlyweds', while Popemobile is an unusual compound noun. Having said that, Popemobile was indeed used a lot to describe the car designed for the Pope after he was shot at – an analogy with Batman's Batmobile perhaps.

'Man Is the Bastard' is a slightly syntactically deviant band name, in that the definite article does not introduce 'given' or known information here. 'Me First and the Gimme Gimmes' is also grammatically deviant; not only are some words morphologically deviant (that is, 'gimmes') but the word order is also unusual. 'The the' and 'This' are also syntactically deviant band names in that we do not expect to find determiners repeated, or determiners in isolation, without accompanying head nouns to form noun phrases.

Phonological deviation includes such things as unusual sound effects, alliteration, assonance, the altering of normal spelling to represent particular accents and dialects, and the phonetic misspelling of words. Harrison's 'Them & [uz]' [1984] (1995), draws on such deviation particularly on the following line:

I chewed up Littererchewer and spat the bones

In this poem, Harrison aligns himself with the working class of Britain. The line is deviant in that it misspells 'literature' to give the phonological impression of a connection with the 'chewing of litter', a metaphor for the mindless and pointless energy that reading literature supposedly requires. 'Literature', a rather abstract concept, is here concretised and presented as if it were some sort of animal (in that it has 'bones') which the poetic persona chose to eat or chew on in the past; the line therefore portrays semantic deviance also. Of course, 'chewed' and 'chewer' are also very alliterative, and along with 'spat', are onomatopoeic here, re-enacting the actual action described.

Suxx and Goo Goo Dolls, along with the previously analysed Likk, are morphologically as well as phonologically deviant band names (the Suxx example particularly being a pun on the word 'sucks'). Three Meter Peter is also a phonologically deviant band name in that it adopts both rhyme and assonance.

Graphological deviation includes unusual layout and use of space, strange word and letter arrangement, as well as altered punctuation. Essentially, anything that is visually unusual constitutes graphological deviation. The title of Roger McGough's 'COMECLOSE and SLEEPNOW' poem is graphologically deviant in the use of capital letters and the omission of the gaps between some of the words. The capital letters could allude to two individuals, one saying 'Come close' and the other saying 'Sleep now'. We might even be forced to read the title with the verb 'come' and adverb 'close' strung together, the words themselves mirroring the closeness they are inviting. Similarly, we might pronounce the words 'sleep' and 'now' quickly, in the form of a two-syllabled word, to echo the quickness with which the addressee is invited to fall asleep.[2]

Roast P07a70 and *.fat (pronounced 'star dot fat') are graphologically deviant band names, in their use of letters among numbers and other symbols to spell out words. Equally graphologically and phonologically deviant is the band name Phatlip, with its use of phonetic misspelling (of 'fat') and, along with band names such as Likehell and Oysterhead, its omission of the space between the words.

See Chapter 3, Task F

Having introduced the deviation aspect of the model of foregrounding, let us return to poetry and undertake an analysis of a poetic text before turning to consider the parallelism aspect of the foregrounding model. Have a look at the following opening extract from Kay's (1991) *The Adoption Papers.*

1	I never thought it would be quicker
2	than walking down the mainstreet
3	I want to stand in front of the mirror
4	swollen bellied so swollen bellied
5	The time, the exact time
6	for that particular seed to be singled out
7	I want to lie on my back at night
8	I want to pee all the time
9	amongst all others
10	like choosing a dancing partner
11	I crave discomfort like some women
12	crave chocolate or earth or liver
13	Now these slow weeks on
14	I can't stop going over and over
15	I can't believe I've tried for five years
16	for something that could take five minutes
17	It only took a split second
18	not a minute or more.
19	I want the pain
20	the tearing searing pain
21	I want my waters to break
22	like Noah's flood
23	I want to push and push
24	and scream and scream.
	...

This is the opening of the first chapter (named 'The seed') of a book-long auto-biographical poem to do with a young black girl's adoption by a Scottish couple. It is graphologically deviant in its use of different fonts (here, Stone

Sans and Stone Serif), to correspondingly express the adoptive mother's as well as the birth mother's perspectives in parallel form. Notice that this duality would have proved confusing and incoherent had the same font been used throughout. The duality of the poetic personas also constitutes the poem as discoursally deviant.

Lines 1–2, 5–6, 9–10, 13–14, and 17–18 appear to give the words of the birth mother, with the remainder of the lines being taken from the adoptive mother's perspective. This alignment suggests that the poem could be read in two ways. We could read all lines in actual sequence, something that could potentially prove cognitively difficult to process. Alternatively, we could choose to separate the two voices, and attach the string of lines from each persona to two distinct sequences. Try reading the poem in different ways, to work out which reading is most effective.

There is some internal deviance from line 19 onwards. Until line 19, the two voices take turns and occupy a two-line stanza each, a pattern that is broken when the adoptive mother's voice occupies three two-line stanzas rather than one (lines 19–24), after which the pattern appears to be abandoned altogether. This may bear some significance; the merging of the voices from that point onwards could give the implication that anyone could be in the position of either of the two personas.

The poem additionally draws on semantic (and maybe even pragmatic?) deviance in its expression of the adoptive mother's needs, wants and cravings. We do not normally expect people to crave swollen bellies, tearing pains or discomfort. It is also unusual for anyone to express a need to 'push' and scream. In other words, even though this persona wants a swollen belly, wants to lie on her back at night, and wants to experience pain and discomfort, what the reader understands is that she actually wants to experience pregnancy. Further semantic deviance is evident on lines 10 and 22 in the use of similes, and in line 12, in reference to women craving 'earth', something paradoxical, especially in contrast to the less conceptually difficult references to women craving 'liver' or 'chocolate' during pregnancy. The biblical reference to Noah's flood could also be taken to be a form of lexical deviance, as the words are out of context, meaning that they are found in unusual collocation.

There is also exophoric reference (designation to things outside the text itself), along with semantic and syntactic deviance in the various referents the reader is invited to work out the antecedents of. That is:

'it' refers to 'adoption' in line 1
'the time' refers to 'the time of conception' in line 5
'that particular seed' refers to 'the seed of conception' in line 6
'all others' refers to 'all other seeds' in line 9
'something' refers to 'having a child' in line 16

'it' refers to 'giving your child up for adoption' in line 17, and
'the pain' refers to 'the childbirth pain' in line 19.

The antecedents are not absolutely clear, and the readers have to start thinking along the lines of pregnancy to make sense of them. Note also that the normally transitive verb 'push' is here used intransitively,[3] a use of the verb which is actually acceptable in the context of childbirth, so it is in fact syntactically non-deviant.

Readers are, overall, invited to activate their schematic expectations in reference to pregnancy (which involves swollen bellies, pregnant women sleeping on their back, wanting to pee all the time, feeling uncomfortable, craving chocolate and so on) and childbirth (which involves waters breaking, and women pushing and screaming) in order to work out what it is that this female persona is actually craving (for an introduction to 'schema theory', see Chapter 5, section 5.2).

Chapter 6 ('The telling part') of the same long poem introduces yet another voice, that of the adopted girl:

1	Ma mammy bot me oot a shop
2	Ma mammy says I was a luvly baby
3	Ma mammy picked me (I wiz the best)
4	your mammy had to take you (she'd no choice)
5	Ma mammy says she's no really ma mammy
6	(just kid on)
7	It's a bit like a part you've rehearsed so well
8	you can't play it on the opening night
9	She says my real mammy is away far away
10	Mammy why aren't you and me the same colour
11	But I love my mammy whether she's real or no
12	My heart started rat tat tat like a tin drum
13	All the words took off to another planet
14	Why
	...

This part of the poem builds on the discoursal and graphological deviance of the opening extract, in the use of the same alternating fonts, yet this time in differentiating the adoptive mother's voice from that of the adopted girl. The content of the two sets of lines helps the reader work out which line corresponds to each persona. What further helps the reader differentiate the personas is the use of phonological, morphological and syntactic deviance in lines 1–6, 9, 11 and 14. The use of non-standard grammar[4] ('she'd no choice' for 'she had no choice', 'she's real or no' for 'she is real or not'), along with the phonetic misspelling of words ('ma' for 'my', 'mammy' for 'mummy', 'oot' for 'out of', 'luvly' for 'lovely', and 'wiz' for 'was') clearly alludes to the perspective of a child. Interesting morphological deviance is found on line 6, where 'just kid on' refers to 'just kidding', yet the reader is forced to notice the use of the word 'kid' along with the adverb 'just' to further link the conversation to the subject of adoption.

The adoptive mother's lines (lines 7–8, 10 and 12–13) are more standard in their grammatical and lexical nature. Some semantic deviance is evident in the use of simile ('telling your child they are adopted' is likened to an actor rehearsing a part well, yet feeling that they cannot play it on the opening night) and metaphor (the personification of the words taking off to 'another planet' on line 13). Some phonological deviance is also evident in line 12, where the onomatopoeic words 'rat tat tat' allude to the fast beating of the adoptive mother's heart at the time of 'the telling'. An exception to this is line 10, a line that is given in the font ascribed to the adoptive mother, and yet appears to be from the perspective of the child ('Mammy why aren't you and me the same colour'). Here, the adoptive mother perhaps quotes the child relating this question back to her (hence the heart racing on line 12), and therefore prepares herself to disclose the fact that the child is in fact adopted.

The spacing of the poem is also graphologically internally deviant. There is a two-line stanza pattern across the first three stanzas, a pattern which is broken on line 7, with the fourth stanza being significantly longer than the rest. Finally, the poem is even further discoursally deviant in that the characters are not interacting directly with each other; the adopted child speaks to other, non-adopted children ('your mummy had to take you'), while the mother appears to either be speaking and/or thinking to herself or a close friend/counsellor, similar to the sort of discourse pattern encountered in the poem's opening chapter.

See Chapter 3, Task G

2.2.2 Parallelism

In the earlier section, we considered deviation (unexpected irregularity) as a form of foregrounding, and yet also mentioned parallelism (unexpected regularity) as an alternative or accompanying form of foregrounding. Parallelism has so far been defined as the unexpected repetition of norms, whether these are norms that are linguistic, generic or norms of a particular historical period and/or author. Like deviation, parallelism can occur at more than one linguistic level at the same time.

Short (1996: 67) introduced the 'parallelism rule' according to which '[w]hen readers come across parallel structures they try to find an appropriate semantic relationship between the parallel parts'. In other words, if words in a text are structurally paralleled, through the same or similar sound, meaning or positioning in a syntactic structure, readers seek either some sort of equivalence or oppositeness in the meaning relation that these words have. Have a look at the version of Auden's poem 'Funeral blues'[5] (in Auden and Isherwood, 1936) reproduced below:

1	Stop all the clocks, cut off the telephone,
2	Prevent the dog from barking with a juicy bone.
3	Silence the pianos and with muffled drum
4	Bring out the coffin, let the mourners come.
5	Let aeroplanes circle moaning overhead
6	Scribbling on the sky the message He is Dead.
7	Put crepe bows round the white necks of the public doves,
8	Let the traffic policemen wear black cotton gloves.
9	He was my North, my South, my East and West,
10	My working week and my Sunday rest,
11	My noon, my midnight, my talk, my song;
12	I thought that love would last forever: I was wrong.
13	The stars are not wanted now; put out every one,
14	Pack up the moon and dismantle the sun,
15	Pour away the ocean and sweep up the wood;
16	For nothing now can ever come to any good.

This poem displays a lot of syntactic and semantic parallelism, in its expression of the loneliness and overwhelming grief that comes with the death of a lover. The first half of the poem is written in the imperative form, with the third stanza adopting the declarative format, and the final stanza being a combination of both syntactic formats.

The opening stanza further employs syntactic parallelism in its combination of imperative verbs (as predicators) and objects. I have inserted the poetic lines in Table 2.2 to highlight the parallelism, and also demonstrate the slight syncopation which happens when the clauses no longer match the poetic alignment.

Of course, this stanza also employs semantic parallelism in drawing on a number of actions or events that are noisy (a clock ticking, a phone ringing, a dog barking and so on), to express the poetic persona's need for silence, isolation and mourning, possibly surrounding the event of the funeral. If the poem

Table 2.2

Adverbial	Predicator	Object	Adverbial
	1. Stop	all the clocks	
	cut off	the telephone	
	2. Prevent	the dog from barking	With a juicy bone
	3. Silence	the pianos	
with muffled drum	4. Bring out	the coffin	
	let	the mourners come	

is taken to be about the *loss* rather than actual *death* of a lover, it could further be said to be semantically deviant in its metaphorical use of the LOSS IS DEATH metaphor.

Equally semantically deviant is the whole of the third stanza, where the poet conceptualises the lover in logically paradoxical ways, and invites the reader to interpret the metaphors used, so as to understand what it was that the persona actually feels deprived of. This stanza is further effective in (a) its parallel use of a large number of grammatical complements and (b) the lexical links between the complements themselves, seeing that they collectively cover the whole spectrum of directions (line 9), days (line 10), and time (line 11) (see Table 2.3).

The poem, of course, overall adopts the AABB rhyme, so it draws on phonological parallelism as well. Particularly noticeable is the semantic connection that 'overhead'/'Dead' (lines 5–6) draws on, raising the idea that the dead are watching the living from up above, a possible reference to heaven.

See Chapter 3, Task H

2.3 Metaphor

'Figurative or metaphorical meaning', in semantics, describes a word's extension of meaning, which is in contrast to a word's literal, basic or conceptual meaning (Wales, 2001: 151). Surfing, for instance, has the basic definition of 'the sport or pastime of surfboarding' (*OED*), but also the metaphorical or figurative meaning of 'the act of using the internet' (*OED*), when used with reference to computing. Cognitive linguists such as Gibbs (1994) and Lakoff and Johnson (1980) see figu-

Table 2.3

Subject	Predicator	Complement	Object
9. He	was	my North	
		my South	
		my East	
		my West	
		10. My working week	
		and my Sunday rest	
		11. My noon	
		my midnight	
		my talk	
		my song	
12. I	thought		that love would last forever
I	was	wrong	

rative language as an integral part of human categorisation, one that has traditionally been seen as 'reaching its most sophisticated forms in literary or poetic language' (Saeed, 1998: 302). Metaphor is often seen as the central form of figurative language use (others being idioms, phrasal verbs, similes and proverbial phrases). When words are used in metaphoric senses, one field or domain of reference is mapped onto or carried over another on the basis of some perceived similarity between the two fields (Wales, 2001: 250). The starting point or described concept is often called the 'target' domain, while the comparison concept or the analogy is called the 'source' domain. In Richards' (1936) terminology, the former is called the 'tenor' and the latter the 'vehicle'. Metaphors are traditionally introduced in linguistics using small capitals. Where metaphors are sustained or extended across large segments of texts or indeed across texts, these can be referred to as 'megametaphors' (see Werth, 1999).

Read the following two lines from Sylvia Plath's ([1959] 1981) poem 'Metaphors', keeping in mind that the poet may have thought that she was pregnant when she composed this piece:

[I'm] An elephant, a ponderous house,
A melon strolling on two tendrils.

In these lines, Plath adopts the genre of a riddle in order to get the reader guessing what it is that she is referring to, while also allowing the reader access to her feelings and overall frame of mind. The poet conceptualises herself (as target) metaphorically as an elephant, a house and a melon, all sources or ways of expressing her discomfort, unsettledness and unease with her condition. Note that all of these sources or vehicles are in fact denoting large or indeed the largest entities within their corresponding categories. An elephant is a big animal, a melon a big fruit, and the house is in fact 'ponderous', all perhaps correlating to the sense of her being large within her own category as well: that is, a large person, indeed a large woman.

Cognitive linguistics models the process of understanding metaphor as a mapping of the properties between the two spaces or domains, and it is this 'blended space' that represents the new emergent understanding (Stockwell, 2002: 107). In the case of Plath's two lines, as an elephant, she feels large and probably moves slowly and with difficulty. As a house, she feels that she is protecting and 'housing' her baby, which might also correlate to her feeling somewhat used or exploited in this process. In reference to the melon 'strolling on two tendrils', she probably more particularly refers to her belly being as swollen, bloated and big as a melon, and hence heavy and uncomfortable to carry around. Note that this fruit, personified by its collocation with 'strolling' here (as 'strolling' is a verb requiring an animate subject), is particularly womb-like in its contents, while carrying connotations of nurturing sweetness at the same time. This line further draws on the MY LEGS ARE TENDRILS metaphor to indicate that her legs are thin, weak and fragile, probably unable to sustain the weight of her big round belly.

'Metonymy' is a notion closely linked to metaphor, and describes a referential process where a speaker refers to an entity by naming something associated with it instead of referring to it directly. We can refer, for instance, to a sports team by reference to its country of origin, by saying sentences like 'Greece beat England in today's match'. Closely linked to metonymy is the semantic part–whole relation of 'meronymy', evident in 'Lend me a hand, will you?' where the speaker indeed requires someone's entire bodily help, and not just the use of the other's hand. In the following line from Plath's 'Metaphors':

O red fruit, ivory, fine timbers!

the 'red fruit', 'ivory' and 'fine timbers' metonymically as well as meronymically refer to the previous lines' 'melon', 'elephant', and 'ponderous house' respectively, as a way of extracting further meaning from the metaphors. The 'red fruit' directly evokes associations with nurturing, while the ivory raises connotations of preciousness and value. The timbers are similarly the essence of the house, what holds it up and in turn constitutes this belly as a shelter for the baby.

The metaphors that these lines evoke are unusual, special, poetic, literary ones, in contrast to those metaphors that Lakoff and Johnson (1980) describe as 'cognitive' or 'conceptual' metaphors. Cognitive metaphors are pervasive in everyday language and thought, and so less obvious and transparent than 'literary' or 'creative' ones. For instance, the cognitive metaphor THE MIND IS A MACHINE can be found in everyday language, such as 'After the meeting, I was suffering from information overload.' Here, the mind is conceptualised as a computer that might crash if it is given more information to process than it can handle. Such metaphors, further categorised as structural, orientational and ontological, indeed play a central role in the way in which we structure our experience and conceptualise the society we live in. THE MIND IS A MACHINE is an ontological metaphor, a grouping of metaphors that concerns ways of viewing events, activities, emotions, ideas as entities and substances.

Plath concludes her 'Metaphors' poem with the line:

Boarded the train there's no getting off

In contrast to the earlier Plath lines, which are self-consciously literary, this last line draws on the structural LIFE IS A JOURNEY metaphor, defined as structural because it involves one concept being metaphorically structured in terms of another. Here, the conception itself or the decision to have the baby is conceptualised as much like the decision to board a particular train. To draw on the same structural metaphor, the female persona has taken a particular turn and path, from which she feels she can no longer swerve. Once you board a train, it is too late to get off it, much like pregnancy, which is too difficult to undo or turn your back on. Orientational metaphors are those which involve a projection of our experience of spatial orientation on a variety of abstract concepts. GOOD IS UP and BAD IS DOWN are, for instance, orientational metaphors found in 'I'm on a *high* today' and 'He's been *down* with the flu all week.' (For more on figurative thinking, see Chapman, 2006: 112–14; for more on similes and metaphors, see Clark, 2007: 116–18.)

See Chapter 3, Task I

2.4 Chapter review

In this chapter, we started by considering the terms 'figures' and 'ground', terms which relate to visual and verbal features being prominent in relation to the background within which they operate. We considered the argument that characters are the figures in novels in relation to the ground or the landmarks they move around. Prepositions, verbs of motion, and locative expressions stage the characters' movement in relation to features grounded in terms of their location. This framework proved useful in considering surreal poetry, poetry which, much like other surrealist art forms, challenges the standard notions of perspective, offering instead alternative dream-like views of life itself.

The notion of foregrounding also proved to have applications to the verbal field. This 'prominence' effect was said to be achieved either by deviation or parallelism. Deviation, Short (1996) argues, can be external or internal, and it can take place at the levels of discourse, grammar, lexis, semantics, graphology and phonology. We looked at examples of various deviations and parallelisms (in both poetry and other genres), noting that these can indeed occur at more than one level at the same time. Finally, we explored semantic deviation further, particularly with reference to metaphors (literary and conceptual) and metonymies.

Chapter 3 offers practice with the stylistics of poetry, while Chapters 4 and 5 are concerned with the stylistics of prose. Chapter 4, in particular, considers various narrative styles, analyses the notions of viewpoint and mind style, and finally outlines frameworks to do with the analysis of speech and thought presentation in fiction.

Stylistics of Poetry Practice

Task A

Try to work out the metre of the two William Blake ([1793]1925) poems below. How does this sort of analysis relate to your impression of the poems?

Little Fly

Little Fly,
Thy summer's play
My thoughtless hand
Has brushed away.

Am not I
A fly like thee?
Or art not thou
A man like me?

For I dance
And drink and sing,
Till some blind hand
Shall brush my wing.

If thought is life
And strength and breath,
And the want
Of thought is death,

Then am I
A happy fly
If I live
Or if I die

The sick rose

O rose, thou art sick!
  The invisible worm,
That flies in the night,
  In the howling storm,

Has found out thy bed
  Of crimson joy,
And his dark secret love
  Does thy life destroy.

Comments on Task A

Little Fly

    / X /
1   Little Fly,

    X / X   /
2   Thy summer's play

    X   /   X   /
3   My thoughtless hand

    X   /   X /
4   Has brushed away.

    / X /
5   Am not I

    X / X   /
6   A fly like thee?

    X / X /
7   Or art not thou

    X /   X /
8   A man like me?

    / X /
9   For I dance

    X   /   X   /
10   And drink and sing,

    X   /   X   /
11   Till some blind hand

    X   /   X   /
12   Shall brush my wing.

```
     X   /   X  /
13   If thought is life
     X    /   X    /
14   And strength and breath,
      X  X   /
15   And the want
     X   /   X  /
16   Of thought is death,

      /  X  /
17   Then am I
     X /  X  /
18   A happy fly
     / X /
19   If I live
     X /  X /
20   Or if I die
```

This poem follows the ABCB rhyme. There are two stressed syllables in each line, possibly with the exception of line 15. The poem appears to be in the iambic dimeter format, with the exception of almost all of the stanza opening lines (that is, lines 1, 5, 9 and 17), which appear to ellipse the opening off-beat. In other words, these are 'dumdedums' rather than 'dedumdedums'. A slight pause is forced when opening the new stanza, as the preceding stanza's final on-beat is followed here by yet another stanza-opening on-beat. A similar exception occurs mid-stanza, on line 19. Omitting the opening remiss here gives a slight pause that splits the final stanza in two. All in all, the poem's dimeter structure gives it a very nursery-like feel. This impression correlates to the poem's simplistic theme of saluting a fly, an impression also reflected in the relevant poetic collection being entitled *Songs of Innocence and Experience*.

The sick rose

```
     X  /   X  X   /
1    O rose, thou art sick!
     X  X  / X X   /
2    The invisible worm,
      X  /  X  X   /
3    That flies in the night,
     X  X   /  X   /
4    In the howling storm,
```

```
   X   /   X   X   /
5  Has found out thy bed
    X  /   X   /
6  Of crimson joy,
    X   X   /   X X   /
7  And his dark secret love
    X   X   /   X  /
8  Does thy life destroy.
```

This poem follows the ABCB rhyme scheme, and has two stressed syllables per line. Nevertheless, the total number of syllables per line varies from four to six. Having analysed the poem's metrical scheme, I have highlighted the iambs to signify the patterned arrangement:

iamb, anapaest
anapaest, anapaest
iamb, anapaest
anapaest, **iamb**

iamb, anapaest
iamb, **iamb**
anapaest, anapaest
anapaest, **iamb.**

Overall, the combination of iambs and anapaests here is certainly not as random as it might originally appear to be. In fact, each stanza is very much patterned, with the first and last line being mirror images of each other, and the middle lines revealing a very structured arrangement of the given metres. The structured playfulness adds to the directness with which the addressee speaks to the rose, which is said to be 'destroyed' by the 'dark secret love'.

The study of metre is, admittedly, a complicated and difficult matter. Identifying a poem's metrical scheme, if it indeed has one, is far from an exact science, and it is possible for different analysts to identify different metrical readings or realisations of the same poem. There is not necessarily a single correct metrical analysis of a poem. One of the factors that might generate some analytical variation is whether we choose to analyse a poem on the page, as written work, as opposed to a spoken recitation. The analysis of a particular performance is likely to yield much less analytical disagreement with respect to the stressing of certain words, or the metrical scheme that has been imposed on the reading of the poem.

What is more, it is difficult for the analyst to be sure of the precision of the analysis, or the meaningfulness of a metrical feature, not least in order to be able to engage an interpretation that is not dubious. As Short (1996: 128) puts it, 'metrical structure is the level of poetic organisation which is least directly-connected with meaning', this being one of the reasons why there are still a number of disagreements among experts on rhythm and metre about fairly basic aspects of their study.

Task B

Tony Harrison is a British poet interested in the subject of linguistic equality. In 'Them & [uz]' [1984] (1995), the poet recalls his schooldays at Leeds Grammar School, where he was among a minority of boys with a local accent. He here expresses his feelings in relation to his Yorkshire dialect, a dialect which he felt was getting in the way of his education. Use the terminology introduced in Chapter 1 to talk about the poetic form, and explain the effects that this particular extract generates.

9   All poetry (even Cockney Keats?) you see
10 's been dubbed by [ʌs] into RP,
11 Received Pronunciation, please believe [ʌs]
12 your speech is in the hands of the Receivers.
13 'We say [ʌs] not [ʊz], T.W.!' That shut my trap.
14 I doffed my flat a's (as in 'flat cap')
15 my mouth all stuffed with glottals, great
16 lumps to hawk up and spit out ... *E-nun-ci-ate!*

Comments on Task B

This poem makes effective use of phonological, graphological and poetic features. Here is a metrical analysis of this particular extract:

```
    X / X X  / X  / X    /   X  /
9   All poetry (even Cockney Keats?) you see

       X   /   X  /  / X X/
10  's been dubbed by [ʌs] into RP,

    X /    X X X/ X   /   X / X
11  Received Pronunciation, please believe [ʌs]

    X  /  X X X  /  X  X  X/ X
12  your speech is in the hands of the Receivers.'
```

```
     X   X   /   X   /  X /   X    /   X   /
13   'We say [ʌs] not [ʊz], T.W.!' That shut my trap.

     X   /    X   /  /   /  X   /   /
14   I doffed my flat a's (as in 'flat cap')

     X    /   X   /    X    / X    / X
15   my mouth all stuffed with glottals, great

      /    X  /   X   X   X   /    X /   X / X
16   lumps to hawk up and spit out ... E-nun-ci-ate!
```

In this poem, young Harrison's non-standard accent is being ridiculed by his former teacher. Harrison's regional voice is evident in his use of Yorkshire lexis (that is, 'trap', 'doffed'), informal grammar (the reduction of 'has been' to ''s been' on line 10) and his references to Yorkshire accent ('flat 'a's, glottals). This is contrasted with his teacher's more standard language, reflected in the authoritative tone in the inverted commas of line 13 (that is, notice the term of address 'T. W.' in reference to Tony Harrison's first and middle name initials). Harrison conceptualises words as food that people 'stuff', 'hawk up' and 'spit', much like with certain approaches to education, whereby they are 'fed' information, and expected to merely deliver it right back (as opposed to processing the information, and being empowered to think for themselves). We could even argue that Harrison's poem is onomatopoeic in this respect, something also particularly evident in the use of words such as 'glottals', 'hawk' and 'spit'. The poem has an angry tone, and Harrison appears to be reacting against this childhood schooling of his; despite his education and academic achievements (notice the references to Keats and Received Pronunciation), he feels judged negatively on the basis of his regional accent. The underlying message is that he wishes he could maintain both his Northern identity and his academic credibility, regardless of his accent.

Even though Harrison's poem appears to employ small patterns of mostly iambs and anapaests which stay for a line or two, these are then disrupted. Seeing that he makes much more strict or regular use of metre in his other poetry, this is perhaps here particularly noticeable, at least to those readers who are familiar with the rhythm of his other work. This adds to the impression that Harrison is, at least to a certain extent, against the literary establishment. What adds to this anti-establishmentarian impression is the fact that the poem unusually incorporates phonetic symbols to represent the sound of words.

Finally, lines 9 to 16 of the poem are in rhymed couplets, and there is a lot of alliteration (that is, 'all' and 'glottals' on line 15, and the various stops on line 16's 'lumps to hawk up and spit out') and assonance (that is, 'Receive' and 'believe' on line 11, 'flat cap'[1] on line 14). The high number of stops in particular gives a rather abrupt effect to the piece, an effect which complements the sense of the poet as discontent with his childhood experiences. Similarly, the assonance on line 11 invites the reader to see the words 'receive' and 'believe' as connected or perhaps even contrasted in meaning. Overall, the high repetition of the same or similar sounds adds a density not only to the 'sounding' but also to the 'meaning' of the poem.

Task C

Find enjambment, alliteration, assonance and onomatopoeia in the following poems by William Wordsworth ([1807/1815/1827]1888), and comment on their effect.

Composed upon Westminster Bridge, Sept. 3, 1802

1 EARTH has not anything to show more fair:
2 Dull would he be of soul who could pass by
3 A sight so touching in its majesty:
4 This City now doth, like a garment, wear
5 The beauty of the morning; silent, bare,
6 Ships, towers, domes, theatres, and temples lie
7 Open unto the fields, and to the sky;
8 All bright and glittering in the smokeless air.
9 Never did sun more beautifully steep
10 In his first splendour, valley, rock, or hill;

11 Ne'er saw I, never felt, a calm so deep!
12 The river glideth at his own sweet will:
13 Dear God! the very houses seem asleep;
14 And all that mighty heart is lying still!

Surprised by joy – impatient as the wind

1 SURPRISED by joy – impatient as the Wind
2 turned to share the transport – Oh! with whom
3 But Thee, deep buried in the silent tomb,
4 That spot which no vicissitude can find?
5 Love, faithful love, recalled thee to my mind –
6 But how could I forget thee? Through what power,
7 Even for the least division of an hour,
8 Have I been so beguiled as to be blind
9 my most grievous loss? – That thought's return
10 Was the worst pang that sorrow ever bore,

11 Save one, one only, when I stood forlorn,
12 Knowing my heart's best treasure was no more;
13 That neither present time, nor years unborn
14 Could to my sight that heavenly face restore.

Scorn not the sonnet

1   SCORN not the Sonnet; Critic, you have frowned,
2   Mindless of its just honours; with this key
3   Shakspeare unlocked his heart; the melody
4   Of this small lute gave ease to Petrarch's wound;
5   A thousand times this pipe did Tasso sound;
6   With it Camoens soothed an exile's grief;
7   The Sonnet glittered a gay myrtle leaf
8   Amid the cypress with which Dante crowned
9   His visionary brow: a glow-worm lamp,
10 It cheered mild Spenser, called from Faeryland

11 To struggle through dark ways; and, when a damp
12 Fell round the path of Milton, in his hand
13 The Thing became a trumpet; whence he blew
14 Soul-animating strains – alas, too few!

Comments on Task C

The three poems share an almost identical format. They all have an opening ten-line long stanza, followed by a second four-line stanza. Iambs predominate, and there is certainly rhyme throughout all three of the poems, though this is not rigid and identical across all three. Also evident is the predominance of initial capital letters in the line-opening words, a feature typical of the poetic form, if rather archaic now. The poems also share similarities with respect to content, in that they feature a poetic persona moved by his emotions. Wordsworth was one of the defining members of the English Romantic movement, and his work is obviously influenced by the sights and scenes of his surroundings (see first poem), engrossed with emotion about his loved ones (see second), and informed by respect and knowledge of his predecessors' work (see third).

The first poem's opening eight lines constitute a single sentence. In this single sentence, there is enjambment on lines 2–3 and lines 4–5 (where the phrasal verb 'could pass by' is separated from its object 'A sight ...', and the predicator 'wear' is separated from the object 'the beauty ...'), and on lines 6–7 (where the predicator 'lie' is separated from the complement 'open'). This contributes to the stream-of-consciousness effect, where the poetic persona expresses his amazement at the scenery; the running-on of lines somewhat mirrors the running-on of thoughts going through the poet's mind as he writes. There is end-stopping in the second stanza instead.

Some assonance is evident in line 2's 'he be' (/hi: bi:/), line 12's 'sweet will' (/swi:t wɪl/, with /iː/ and /ɪ/ both being front vowels), and 'line 13's 'seem asleep' (/ siːm 'sliːp/). There is also some alliteration in line 2's 'sight more-touching', line 6's 'Ships, towers, domes, theatres, and temples lie' (which employs a number of plosives or stops) and again line 13's 'seem asleep'. There is also some phonaesthesia in line 8's use of 'glittering', a word whose initial 'gl' cluster carries connotations of brightness, light and shiny glossiness (much like the word 'glossiness' itself, as well as such words as 'glamour', 'glow' and 'glisten'). The sound of the poem is rather evocative, reflecting a poetic persona that is moved by his environment's magnificence, something also evident in the personification of the sun, the houses, the river, the buildings and the city itself throughout.

The second poem expresses the poet's guilt over a moment of happiness, as it demonstrates to him that he momentarily forgot about his child's death ('But how could I forget thee?'). This poem is in a fairly strict iambic pentameter. The metrical scheme invites the second line's fourth stress to fall on 'Oh', hence re-enacting the poetic persona's sighing and surprise at imagining his daughter next to him.

The poem has an instance of enjambment on lines 9–10, where the subject 'That thought's return' is separated from the predicator and complement 'Was the worst pang'. Interestingly, this is one of the most emotional lines of the poem, where the poet recalls the overwhelming sense of loss for his daughter's death, and the enjambment draws attention to this; the grammar and line-aligning cause a pause which itself evokes the heart-stopping moment for the narrator. Another enjambment is found on lines 13–14 ('neither present time, nor years unborn / Could to my sight that heavenly face restore'), where the subject is separated from the remainder of the clause, the long lines reflecting the eternity which the lines themselves refer to. We could argue that the delayed main verb is also iconic of the narrator's wishing and waiting here (for more on grammatical iconicity, see Jeffries, 1993, chapter 6).

There is some assonance, such as in line 3's 'But Thee, deep, buried' (/ði: di:p 'berɪd/ , again with /iː/ and /ɪ/ both being front vowels) and line 12's 'no more' (/nəʊ mɔʊr/, as is there some alliteration, such as in line 5's 'my mind', line 8's 'Have I been so beguiled as to be blind?' and line 10's 'Was the worst'. There is also onomatopoeia in line 10's use of 'pang', a word that refers to sharp physical pain, and also echoes the shooting impact of a weapon against someone's body. The irrevocable emotional pain experienced at the loss of the child here hence takes on physical dimensions.

The third poem tracks the history of the sonnet through the ages. This poem has more enjambment with noun phrases being split across line endings (such as in 'the melody / of his small lute' on lines 3–4), predicators separated from objects ('crowned / His visionary brow' on lines 8–9, and 'he blew / Soul-animating strains' on lines 13–14), and subjects separated from predicators ('a damp / Fell round' on lines 11–12). There is also enjambment across stanzas, with the predicator-adverbial 'called from Faeryland' (line 10) being separated from the (again adverbial) clause 'To struggle though dark ways' (line 11).

Instances of assonance include line 2's 'with this key' (/wɪð ðɪs ki:/), and line 8 and 9's 'crowned / His visionary brow'. Alliteration is found in the title itself, 'Scorn not the sonnet', and on line 5's 'Tasso sound', while the use of the phonaesthetic 'glittered' on line 7 and 'glow' on line 9 also contributes to the sound symbolism and overall phonological effects. For instance, the alliteration in the title invites the reader to work on establishing a meaning association between 'scorn' and 'sonnet', even though we do not commonly associate the 'sonnet' form with disrespect or ridicule. The sonnet is here conceptualised as a key, a lute, a pipe, a leaf, a lamp, and a trumpet among others, to express its usefulness over the centuries.

Task D

Through an analysis of the poetic form of John Keats' 'Bright star!' ([1838]1850), justify the initial impressions you have of the poem's meaning.

Bright star! Would I were stedfast

1　Bright star, would I were stedfast as thou art –
2　Not in lone splendour hung aloft the night
3　And watching, with eternal lids apart,
4　Like nature's patient, sleepless Eremite,
5　The moving waters at their priestlike task
6　Of pure ablution round earth's human shores,
7　Or gazing on the new soft-fallen mask
8　Of snow upon the mountains and the moors –
9　No– yet still stedfast, still unchangeable,
10　Pillowed upon my fair love's ripening breast,
11　To feel for ever its soft fall and swell,
12　Awake for ever in a sweet unrest,
13　Still, still to hear her tender-taken breath,
14　And so live ever – or else swoon in death.

Comments on Task D

Keats' poem appears to be addressed to a 'bright star' in the sky. The poetic persona points out that the star is secure and fixed in its position in the world. The star is separated, isolated, motionless ('would I were stedfast as thou art') and sleepless ('with eternal lids apart'), stripped of any human features. The persona wishes he shared this position in eternity, so as to enjoy his relationship with his beloved for the rest of time. There is religious imagery throughout (such as line 4's 'eremite', line 5's 'priestlike task', and line 6's 'ablution'), as well as implicit references to sex (that is, line 10's 'ripening breast' and line 12's 'sweet unrest'). There is ambiguity in the use of the word 'still' throughout also; it is unclear whether this is taken to mean 'motionless', 'always', or maybe even both. What adds to this ambiguity is the repetition of the words 'still' and 'ever' right through the poem.

The 14-line long sonnet is in the iambic pentameter and follows the ABAB CDCD EFEF GG rhyming scheme. The rhyme not only contributes to the poem's phonological patterning, but it also establishes meaning connections between the rhyming words. For instance, here 'art' rhymes with 'apart', to stress that the star's separateness is connected to its being unwavering. Also, 'night' rhymes with 'eremite', to personify the sleepless star in its likening to a sleepless hermit in the night. Similarly 'breast' rhymes with 'unrest' to add a sexual undertone to the poet's relationship with the beloved. Finally, 'breath' rhymes with, and is here contrasted to, 'death'.

There is enjambment throughout. For instance, the noun phrase 'The moving waters at the priestlike task / Of pure ablution round earth's human shores' is split across lines 5 and 6. Similarly, the noun phrase 'the new soft-fallen mask / Of snow ...' is split across lines 7 and 8. The enjambment gives the poem stylistic fluidity, both in terms of the grammatical structures cutting across the lines, and in terms of the thoughts running through the poem itself. It is hard to identify the opening and the closing of sentences and clauses though; in fact, there appears to be only one 'sentence' here, signified by the full stop at the poem's end, though this is not to say that poems need follow sentence-like prosaic structures. In other words, we bring certain expectations to poetic texts, one of which is that these are unlikely to be 'sentenced' in an 'ordinary' way.

There is noticeable alliteration particularly on line 7's 'soft-fallen mask', on line 8's 'the mountains and the moors', on line 9's 'still stedfast, still unchangeable', on line 10's 'fair love's ripening breast', on line 11's 'To feel for ever its soft fall and swell', and on line 13's 'tender-taken breath'. The high density of the fricative /f/ in lines 7 and 11, and of the approximant /r/ on line 10, adds sensuality and softness to the reading of the lines, both of which are echoed in the meaning of the lines themselves; the alliteration here is rather iconic. Similarly, the persistence described on line 9 is mirrored in the persistent repetition of the /st/ phonemic cluster. There is, finally, some assonance, such as on line 13's 'her tender-taken' (/ hər 'tɛndər 'teikən/), which again invites the reader to concentrate some density of meaning here also.

Task E

Use the figures and ground model to analyse the following poetic extract by Picasso ([1939]2004), translated from French by Pierre Joris.

> 25.12.39 [11]
> good evening monsieur good evening madame and good evening children big and small damasked and striped in sugar and in marshmallow clothed in blue in black and in lilac mechanically malodorous and cold pug nosed one-eyed irascible and filthy on horseback on crutches potbellied and bald made of sententiousness sliced very fine by the machine to make terrified rainbows just good to be thrown in the frying pan tell me my dears my loves my little piggies have you ever counted by holding your nose until 0 and if not repeat with me the list of losing of all the lotteries

Comments on Task E

This poem appears to take the form of a speech, as it directly addresses the readers or audience as 'monsieur', 'madam' and 'children big and small', figures that stand against an unknown ground. The remainder of the text is essentially a very long-winded post-modification of these children, who are said to be damasked, striped, then clothed and so on. Thereafter, the children are very much grounded, as their 'sententiousness' is objectified and, like a figure, becomes sliced by the grounded machine to make 'terrified rainbows'. The rainbows are next themselves 'figured' and thrown in the grounded frying pan. The poem ends much like it started, with a direct address to the poetic persona's figured 'dears', 'loves', and/or 'little piggies', who are strangely perhaps asked whether they ever counted by 'holding their nose until 0'. Finally, the poetic persona himself is figured as someone who is part of the action, someone who speaks and asks to be repeated: 'repeat with me the list of losing of all the lotteries'. Much as with the other Picasso poem analysed in Chapter 2, it is the multiple grammatical embedding of phrases within phrases and/or within clauses that make it hard for the reader to work out not only what is happening, but also what is figured against the ground.

  Much as in Picasso's visual art, the artist resists the standard notions of perspective. In more conventional realistic visual art forms, there is the tendency, for instance, for objects in the foreground of paintings to be proportionately larger than similar-sized objects in the background of paintings. Picasso's surreal verbal and visual art, in the latter periods of his work at least, rejects such restrictions, and suggests alternative, dream-like perspectives of life itself.

Task F

What sorts of linguistic deviation do the following advertising slogans employ?

1   'A great big hug in a mug.' (Bachelors Cup-A-Soup)

2   'Dogs go wacko for Schmacko's.' (Schmacko's)

3   'For bonzer car insurance deals girls get on to Sheila's Wheels.' (Sheila's Wheels)

4   'It's not insurance, it's RIASurance.' (RIAS)

5   'It's your O2. See what you can do.' (O2)

6   'Kwik Fit'll fix it.' (Kwik Fit)

7   'Put Knorr in, get more out.' (Knorr)

8   'Train2Plane' (First Capital Connect)

9   'You name it. We label it!' (Easy2Name.com)

Comments on Task F

1 The 'A great big hug in a mug' slogan is phonologically deviant (in the use of the 'hug'/'mug' rhyme) as well as semantically deviant. One cannot literally be hugged 'in' or 'by' a mug – the advertising campaign alludes to the feeling of cosiness and comfort (that is, 'hug') that the product would bring (that is, 'mug'). The slogan takes the form of a noun phrase that describes the product, rather than the expected whole clause, so one could argue that it is perhaps syntactically deviant also.

2 The 'Dogs go wacko for Schmacko's' slogan is phonologically deviant (in the use of the 'Wacko'/'Schmacko' rhyme) but also lexically and/or morphologically deviant in the use of 'wacko'. There is also semantic deviance in the

suggestion that dogs will literally 'go wild or crazy' for the product, meaning that they will actually merely enjoy it.

3 The 'Sheila's Wheels' slogan is, again, drawing on rhyme ('deals' rhymes with 'wheels') and is hence phonologically deviant. We also have semantic deviance in the metonymic use of 'get on to Sheila's Wheels' to refer to 'signing with this particular insurance company', as opposed to actually 'entering (the woman named) Sheila's car'. Of course, 'wheels' is also metonymically used in reference to 'car'. Finally, the use of 'bonzer' is lexically deviant as it is a particularly Australian slang expression of approval, used to mean 'excellent' or 'very good', and adds to the whole campaign's Australian theme. The direct address to the target audience 'girls' could also be said to be overtly informal and so discoursally deviant.

4 RIAS's slogan 'It's not insurance, it's RIASurance' draws on graphological, semantic and phonological deviance. Firstly, the slogan rhymes ('insurance'/'RIASurance'). Also, the phonological respelling of 'reassurance' into the graphologically deviant 'RIASurance' creates semantic correlations between the company and a sense of renewed or restored confidence about its quality, beyond the sort of credibility one would assign to just any insurance company.

5 The O2 phone company's slogan 'It's your O2. See what you can do' manages to create a correlation between the company and 'oxygen', 'breath' or even 'wellbeing'. There is hence semantic deviance in the metonymic use of 'O2' to refer not to what one needs in order to survive, that is, oxygen ('It's your O2' has clear connections with the 'It's your life' expression), but what one could do with owning the product (in that 'It's your O2' also means 'It's your phone'). The slogan is also phonologically deviant in the use of the 'O2'/'do' rhyme.

6 The name of the Kwik Fit company itself is morphologically, phonologically and lexically deviant, with its phonetic respelling of 'quick' into 'kwik'. The slogan is further phonologically deviant in the alliteration (particularly of the plosives /k/ and /t/, and the fricative /f/) and assonance (of /ɪ/): /kwɪk fɪt l fɪks ɪt/. One could also argue that there is semantic deviation here, in the metonymic use of the company's name Kwik-Fit to actually refer to the product and/or service of 'fixing' whatever the problem is.

7 The Knorr advertising slogan ('Put Knorr in, get more out') is phonologically deviant in its use of the 'Knorr/more' rhyme, establishing a link between the product and 'excess'. The slogan, of course, depends on the familiar phrase 'put more in, get more out'. It is also semantically deviant in the metonymic use of 'Knorr' to refer to the actual stock cube one might use in their cooking.

8 The 'Train2Plane' slogan is graphologically and syntactically deviant. It makes unusual use of rebus ('2' for 'to') and space on the line, and it is rather

elliptical in terms of its syntactic nature. It is effective in that it essentially communicates what it is that the company offers – a service to take you to the airport by train.

9 The 'You name it. We label it!' slogan is phonologically deviant, again, with its use of direct repetition and hence rhyme of 'it'. It also is semantically deviant in the ambiguous use of the 'You name it' expression, which could either be taken to mean 'Whatever you want' or, alternatively, 'Whatever you choose to name'.

Task G

Analyse the following poetic endings from Benjamin Zephaniah's (a) 'White comedy' (from *Propa Propaganda*, 1996), and (b) 'De rong song', in terms of linguistic deviance and parallelism.

a) Caught and beaten by de whiteshirts
   I waz condemned to a white mass,
   Don't worry,
   I shall be writing to de Black House

b) Your tea is
   Dry
   Your ice is
   Hot,
   Your head is
   Tied up in a
   Not,
   Don't worry
   Be happy.

   You worry
   Because
   You're hurrying,
   And hurry
   Because
   You're worrying,
   Don't happy
   Be worried.

Comments on Task G

a) The title of the relevant poetic series, *Propa Propaganda*, employs both phonological and morphological deviance, in that there is alliteration of the /pr/ opening phonemes as well as phonetic misspelling of 'proper' into 'propa', so as to represent the writer's actual accent. We get the same sort of deviance evident in the use of 'waz', the respelling again alluding to the Caribbean persona's actual accent.

The title of the poem, 'White comedy', is lexically deviant in the use of the word 'white', where one would expect the word 'black'. There is such a thing as 'black comedy', to refer to dark, morbid or sick humour, but we here find the word 'white' in unusual collocation. Similarly lexically deviant is the use of 'whiteshirts' and 'white mass', in that the morpheme 'white' is again used where one would expect the morpheme 'black'. In this sense, the poem draws on lexical and semantic parallelism as well. The poet effectively draws the reader's attention to the fact that we attach negative connotations to the use of the 'black' morpheme ('blackshirts' being a distinctive reference to fascists, and 'black mass' being a mass for the dead and/or Satanism), and that this negative image may be attached, by extension, to black people themselves.

The use of 'Black House' at the poem's last line is internally and lexically deviant, since the poet actually engages in the exact opposite process so far employed; rather than replacing the expected 'black' morpheme with 'white', the poet replaces the expected 'white' morpheme with 'black' to protest against there not having ever been a black American president. The second to last line can also be said to be internally and discoursally deviant in the use of an ironic, yet direct, imperative address to the reader, whereas the poet had so far used declaratives. The poem's ending is indeed effective in that it breaks the patterns it itself established, to draw on prominence through foregrounding.

b) This poem, inspired by Bobby McFerrin's 'Don't worry, be happy' song, details the misfortunes of a persona who, despite their lack of luck, is invited to put aside their worries and 'be happy'. It could therefore be said to be externally generically and discoursally deviant, in its reliance on the reader's familiarity with the song it ironically echoes. There is direct lexical repetition of the two-line imperative 'Don't worry / Be happy' at the end, and sometimes the middle, of each stanza. In this sense, the poem draws on lexical parallelism.

The second to last stanza draws on semantic deviance in that it makes reference to impossible semantic or contradictory relationships: between dryness and liquid tea, heat and ice. Notice that the occurrence of various contradictions itself draws on semantic parallelism. There is phonetic misspelling and so graphological and phonological deviance in the use of 'not' for 'knot' in the same stanza. Similar deviance is, of course, evident in the use of 'rong' for 'wrong' and 'de' for 'the' in the song's title, the latter being also phonologically deviant in its representation of the poetic persona's Caribbean accent.

There is also grammatical parallelism in the repetition of the 'Your X is Y' (subject–predicator–complement) structure in this stanza (Your tea is / Dry / Your ice is / Hot, / Your head is /Tied up in a / Not), as is there parallelism in the use of single-word lines (Dry / Not / Hot), the last two of which rhyme and hence draw on phonological parallelism / deviance as well.

The final stanza makes use of further deviance and parallelism. The 'You X because you Y' grammatical structure ('You worry / Because / You're hurrying') is subsequently reversed and mirrored in the 'You Y because you X' structure of the following lines ('You hurry / Because / You're worrying'), drawing on the lexical parallelism of 'hurrying' and 'worrying' in a circular relationship, and hence a 'Catch 22' situation, where the former causes the latter and vice versa.

The poem draws on internal deviance at its very end by yet again repeating the grammatical structure of 'Don't worry, be happy' of the previous stanza endings, but this time with the invented word of 'happy-ing' replacing the 'worrying' and vice versa. There is grammatical deviance in the use of the verbless 'Don't happy' line, mirroring the 'be' verb omission typical of certain Black English varieties. Or this could merely be seen as an example of conversion[2] or zero-derivation, whereby the adjective 'happy' is 'verbed'. There is also phonological foregrounding in the use of the 'worry'/'hurry' rhyme, the 'hurrying'/ 'worrying' rhyme, the alliteration and assonance of '**hurry**' and '**happy**' (notice the /ha/ sound, despite the spelling of the words here), and of course, lexical parallelism in the repetition of the 'worry' and 'hurry' morphemes throughout.

The underlying message is that there are important things for people to be worried about, as there are unimportant things which are not worth worrying about. The point is that the reader needs to work out what is and what is not important, before worrying, and to also be aware of the circularity that certain emotions have.

Task H

What sorts of linguistic parallelism do the following poetic rhymes employ?

a)   Star light star bright
     The first star I see tonight,
     I wish I may, I wish I might
     Have the wish I wish tonight

b)   Half a pound of tupenny rice
      Half a pound of treacle
      That's the way the money goes,
      Pop! Goes the weasel,

      Up and down the City road,
      In and out the Eagle,
      That's the way the money goes,
      Pop! Goes the weasel.

c)   Rock a bye baby on the tree top,
      When the wind blows the cradle will rock,
      When the bough breaks the cradle will fall,
      And down will come baby, cradle and all.

Comments on Task H

The poems obviously are very rhythmical and employ full rhyme, hence they display multiple forms of phonological parallelism. A form of phonological parallelism lies in the use of internal rhyme (that is, 'light'/'bright' in the first), onomatopoeia ('pop' in the second) and alliteration (that is, 'bye baby', 'tree top' and 'bough breaks' in the third), although these can also be classified as forms of deviation as well.

There is also lexical parallelism in the repetition of the same or similar words. In the first rhyme, 'wish', 'star' and 'tonight' are repeated. In the second rhyme, there is direct repetition of not only the 'half a penny of' expression, but also of the 'That's the way the money goes / Pop goes the weasel' lines. In the third rhyme, we have repetition of the verb 'will', and the nouns 'baby' and 'cradle'.

The rhymes also display forms of syntactic parallelism. The first rhyme starts with a paralleled direct address to a star, referred to as 'star light', 'star bright' and 'the first star I see tonight'. There follows a subject–predicator format ('I wish') with a series of further paralleled embedded clauses, the most complex of these being 'I wish I may ... have the wish I wish tonight'. The second rhyme repeats the 'Half a pound of X' format across the first two lines, and the combined and paralleled prepositional phrases 'up and down the City road' and 'in and out the Eagle' across lines 5 and 6. Finally, the third rhyme has syntactic parallelism in the use of the 'When X Y, the cradle will Z' structure across lines two and three ('When the wind blows the cradle will rock' /'When the bough breaks the cradle will fall').

It is typical of nursery rhymes to employ a lot of phonological patterning and lexical repetition which can be very pleasurable to young babies, despite the babies not being able to actually process the meaning of the rhymes themselves at an early language acquisition stage. The high level of repetition is particularly useful as nursery rhymes often help in children's vocabulary development, along with their developing musical appreciation. The persistent parallelism on the syntactical level adds rhythm and musicality to the reciting of the verses, which can be sang to children not only when engaging in play, but also when putting them to sleep.

Task I

Analyse Shakespeare's 18th sonnet ([c. 1592]; below from 1911), in terms of its use of figurative language.

1   Shall I compare thee to a summer's day?
2   Thou art more lovely and more temperate:
3   Rough winds do shake the darling buds of May,
4   And summer's lease hath all too short a date:
5   Sometime too hot the eye of heaven shines,
6   And often is his gold complexion dimm'd;
7   And every fair from fair sometime declines,
8   By chance or nature's changing course untrimm'd;
9   But thy eternal summer shall not fade
10   Nor lose possession of that fair thou owest;
11   Nor shall Death brag thou wander'st in his shade,
12   When in eternal lines to time thou growest:
13   So long as men can breathe or eyes can see,
14   So long lives this, and this gives life to thee.

Comments on Task I

Shakespeare's romantic poem fits into the sonnet form in that it expresses a single main idea, consists of 14 decasyllabic lines, and follows the iambic pentameter and the ABAB CDCD EFEF GG rhyming pattern, all of which are typical features of the Shakespearian sonnet form. The last two lines break the rhyming pattern established by the poem itself and hence draw on internal deviance; these lines are foregrounded or made to look prominent. It is here that the reader's attention is drawn and that the implied author expresses the poem's essence and point.

Shakespeare's sonnet starts by posing a question drawing on a simile. The addressee is figuratively (yet directly) likened to a summer's day, compared to which she or he is thereafter deemed to be lovelier and more pleasant. The poem therefore builds on the metaphorical conceptualisation of YOU ARE A SUMMER'S DAY, which invites a mapping to do with relaxation, pleasure and warmth. The poem then proceeds to answer the question it posed on line 1, and so elaborates on the mapping further. On line 3, May's flowers are said to be shaken by the rough winds, while the summer is said to not last nearly as long as the addresser would like it to. These suggest that, in contrast to the summer itself, the addressee will remain unharmed by life and somewhat eternal. The heaven's eye is the target domain for the source domain of the sun from line 5 onwards, the sun here being said to bring too much heat, while it is personified as a human whose complexion is often dimmed (probably by summer clouds). The addressee's inner 'summer' is, on line 9, said to manage to maintain its beauty. This line implicitly draws on the conceptual metaphors WARMTH IS GOOD and COLD IS BAD, also to be found in everyday metaphors such as 'She has a warm character' and 'He gave her the cold shoulder.' Here, in contrast to the addressee, the summer itself is said to fade and eventually cease. Finally, on line 11, death itself is personified as a man who would want to drag the addressee into the shade of death, drawing here on the conceptual metaphors LIFE IS SUNSHINE/LIGHT and DEATH IS SHADE/DARKNESS. Note that these metaphors are also quite common and found in everyday expressions such as 'He is in the twilight of his life.'

From line 12 onwards, the addressee is said to be captured in the poetic lines that are metaphorically conceptualised as a container within which the addressee is allowed to live and grow. And the poem itself, personified as a living entity, will survive and live for many years to come, and in extension, give life to the addressee. The beloved would therefore in turn be immortal, unlike the summer which cannot physically last forever.

Narrators, Viewpoint, Speech and Thought

4.1 Narratives: some introductory terminology

Narratives code experience and can be said to be constructions of reality. We often use narratives to recount personal experiences or construct fictional ones, in order to inform and/or entertain. They help us relate to others and build various bonds among us, express our feelings and deal with situations around us, in the course of our everyday lives.

Oral narratives differ from written narratives in a number of ways. Some oral narratives are indeed fictional (such as jokes), but by and large, oral narratives tend to relate personal experience and are in fact chronologically ordered (see Labov, 1972; Labov and Waletsky, 1967). On the other hand, even though some written narratives are also based on personal experiences (such as autobiographies), most literary written narratives are fictional and said to be the non-temporarily ordered discourse of an explicit or implicit narrator who tells us about events in a so-called 'world'. It is for this reason that analysts have consistently persisted in making a distinction between 'plot' and 'discourse'.

> The term plot is generally understood to refer to the basic story-line of the narrative; in other words, the sequence of elemental, chronologically-ordered events which generate a narrative. Narrative discourse, by contrast, encompasses the manner or means by which the plot is narrated. Narrative discourse, for example, is often characterised by stylistic devices such as flashback, prevision and repetition – devices which all disrupt the basic chronology of a story.
>
> (Simpson and Montgomery, 1995: 141)

In short, 'plot' is the crude story-line material which the writer moulds into an artistic narrative design, the discourse. The Russian Formalists (notably

Shklovsky, 1925) introduced the alternative pair of terms, 'fabula' and 'sjužet', in the 1920s. Similarly to 'plot' and 'discourse', fabula refers to the logical ordering possible of the events, whereas sjužet describes the actual sequence of events as narrated: deep versus surface structure, so to speak. In simple narratives, fabula and sjužet coincide. In orally recounting a situation that took place yesterday, we are likely to follow the logical ordering possible of events, rather than attempt a complex artistic design of going back and forward in time.

According to Culler (1975: 213), for a sequence to count as plot, we must have 'aspects of the movement from the initial situation to the final situation which help to produce a contrast between a problem and its resolution'. In other words, every narrative may be said to integrate a succession of events structured around some sort of problem and its solution. It is on the same trail of thought that Brémond's (1966: 62–3) classification of 'narrative cycle' lies, according to which narrative events can be classified into two categories of elementary sequences: amelioration and degradation, referring respectively to states that either favour or oppose a human project. At the beginning of a narrative, either a state of deficiency or a satisfactory state exists. The narrative goes through at least one cycle, ending with either a satisfactory state or a state of deficiency. Put simply, readers most often need to be presented with a problem, so that there is a force that drives them into reading the story in the first place.

For instance, in the reading of a traditional or classic romance novel or film, we tend to witness unrequited love. Such narratives tend to be structured around one person's desire for or love for another, a love which, for one reason or another, is left either unreciprocated or somehow otherwise unfulfilled. Such narratives are oriented toward the resolution of this problem, and the lovers very often come together in the end.

See Chapter 6, Tasks A and B

4.2 Types of narration

A primary distinction to be made is that between first and third-person narrators. Genette (1980) uses 'homodiegetic' narration to refer to the choice of a first-person narrator; here, the 'I' is also a primary character in the story. According to Leech and Short (1981: 265), it is a type of narration that often 'convert[s] the reader to views he would not normally hold for the duration of the story'. Third-person or 'heterodiegetic' narration (Genette, 1980) is where the narrator is not a character in the fictional world and so reference to characters in this world involves the use of third-person pronouns. Such a narration further implies the merging of the author and the narrator, although as Short (1996: 258) argues, there is no *necessary* reason for this to be the case. It is for this reason that Short adds a further layer of discourse structure, which involves an 'implied author' and an 'implied reader'. Whereas the notion of implied author refers to that author implied by our understanding of the text, an implied reader is the reader we have to become in order to read and react sensitively to the text; or as Leech and Short put it, 'a hypothetical personage who shares with the author not just background knowledge but also a set of presuppositions, sympathies and standards of what is pleasant and unpleasant, good and bad, right and wrong' (1981: 259). Such a 'mock' (Booth, 1961) or 'implied' reader is hence ostensibly guided towards particular judgements of characters and events.

In the case of reading a crime series, the implied reader is the one who shares background information as to the characters on which the series is based, as well as some awareness of the generic nature of the series at hand. Expectations of this sort guide the reader in making predictable judgements and reacting aptly to the information presented.

The extract below comes from Michael Connelly's *The Poet* (1996), a story of the hunt for the serial killer William Gladden, who travelled across the country kidnapping and murdering children, before uploading photos of his so-called 'work' on an Internet bulletin board accessed by fellow paedophiles. In the extract below, Gladden is reading an extract from such a board, written by a paedophile called the Eidolon:

> Gladden looked at the words on the screen. They were beautiful, as if written by the unseen hand of God. So right. So knowledgeable. He read them again.
>
> They know about me now and I am ready. I await them. I am prepared to take my place in the pantheon of faces. I feel as I did as a child when I waited for the closet door to be opened so that I could receive him. The line of light at the bottom. My beacon. I watched the light and the shadows each of his footfalls made. Then I knew he was there and that I would have his love. The apple of his eye.
>
> We are what they make us and yet they turn from us. We are cast off. We become nomads in the world of the moan. My rejection is my pain and motivation. I carry with me the vengeance of all the children. I am the Eidolon. I am called the predator, the one to watch for in your midst. I am the cucoloris, the blur of light and dark. My story is not one of deprivation and abuse. I welcomed the touch. I can admit it. Can you? I wanted, craved, welcomed the touch. It was only the rejection – when my bones grew too large – that cut me so deeply and forced on me the life of a wanderer. I am the cast off. And the children must stay forever young.

(Connelly, 1996: 299)

The real author here is Michael Connelly himself, but the implied author, the persona created by the reader and the real author, is one who not only approves of but also practises paedophilia. However, we should not presume that implied author views can be extended to the actual author;[1] it would, in fact, be quite horrific to make this presumption here. The first person character-narrator of this text is the Eidolon, and the character-narratee is Gladden. The implied reader is one who would sympathise with the view here expressed, and who is, most likely, a paedophile. It is this clashing of views between the implied reader and the real reader (the latter here also corresponds to you and I) that makes this such a difficult and uncomfortable read. We, as the real readers, are likely to be resisting this positioning, whereas Gladden himself seems quite appreciative and accepting of it.

The following non-literary excerpt, taken from the Michael Connelly official website, deals with this same issue:

> I was at a book signing not unlike the many before it and the many that would come after. In fact, I don't remember what bookstore I was at or even which city I was visiting. But the man who approached my table asked a question I had never been asked by a reader.
> 'You don't have children, do you?'
> I looked at him and smiled politely, the tired smile you see when you've just been thrown a curve ball and all you really want to do is quietly sell a pile of books and then get on to the next bookstore in the next city.
> 'What makes you say that?' I asked.
> 'Because of your book,' he said. 'A father wouldn't have written it.'
> He, of course, had been right.
>
> (Connelly, 1997)

It is clear that this exchange refers to *The Poet*. The author admits, 'I felt as if though he were accusing me of a crime .... His advice was to stay clear of children – in the literary sense, I assumed.' *The Poet* is the only novel Connelly has written in which chapters allow consistent access to the criminal consciousness, and that, he felt, was held against him. Having since become a father, Connelly re-read *The Poet* and saw the point the man was trying to make; 'He was right. A father would not have written it. It cut too close to the bone.' What the man at the desk did was address the implied author/real author level of Connelly's fiction. He assumed that it would be difficult to write from the perspective of a dangerously deviant criminal mind, without experiencing a certain amount of discomfort, and this would become impossible for someone, like a parent, so close to the story's victims.

See Chapter 6, Tasks C and D

4.3 Point of view

A further distinction that needs to be made is that between the internal and external narrative events: 'Internal narrative is mediated through the subjective viewpoint of a particular character's consciousness, whilst in an external narrative events are described *outside* the consciousness of any participating character' (Simpson, 1993: 39). Whereas the sentences in (a) are a form of external narration, those in (b) are in internal narration.

(a) Maria was sitting in a bar. While she was waiting for him, John was on his way, running. He came to join her a bit late. They ordered some food. Maria didn't have any dessert. John ordered a coffee but didn't drink it.

(b) Maria was sitting in a bar, worrying while waiting for John. He finally came to join her. He was running all the way there, so felt warm by the time he arrived. They were very hungry. After having some food, she said she didn't want any dessert. John felt he shouldn't have any either, so he ordered coffee instead. It tasted awful so he didn't drink it.

Pretty much the same sequence of events is communicated in (a) as in (b). We do not get access to any of the two characters' consciousness in (a). The narrator merely tells us what happened in an external third-person type of narration. In (b), however, we get a sense of both of the characters' consciousnesses. The 'worrying' allows us access to Maria's feelings, while the 'finally' gives us a sense of her relief and maybe even frustration. There is a viewpoint shift in the third sentence of (b), where we switch into John's consciousness – he felt 'warm'. Their shared viewpoint is expressed in '[t]hey were very hungry', while we go back into Maria's perspective in her expressing her wants to John, in the form of indirect speech. The final extra information we get in (b) is that John chose not to have any dessert *because* Maria would not have any herself, and did not drink his coffee *because* it tasted awful. John's decisions are, again, communicated through his thoughts, perceptions, and therefore viewpoint.

In the case where readers get information to which they would not ordinarily have access, namely the thoughts and feelings of the characters (as in (b)), the narrators are additionally described as 'omniscient', because they take on absolute knowledge and control of the narration of the events. Such narrators involve readers in a personal relationship with characters, manipulate sympathies and cause bias. The choice of one of these types of narration over another will influence the reader's reaction and judgement over the events described. In (b), that we as readers have access to the two characters' consciousnesses adds information to their characterisation. As readers we might assume, for instance, that Maria is a worrier or expects John to be punctual, whereas John gets warm from running (perhaps is less fit than he would like), is accommodating (for not having pudding on his own) and probably fussy about coffee. Note that the narration in (a) does not allow readers to make the same sorts of assumption.

The particular angle or perspective from which *fictional* worlds are presented, or the so-called 'point of view', 'concerns all features of orientation', including 'the position taken up by the speaker or author, that of the consciousness depicted by the text, and that implied for the reader or addressee' (Fowler, 1986: 9). By focusing on the stylistic choices that signify particular and distinctive outlooks of the world (see Short, 1996: 286),we can gain insight into the nature of the character–character and character–narrator relationships, as well as come to an understanding of how the author manipulates the readers' sympathy towards the characters. Linguistic indicators of point of view include (a) evaluative lexis, (b) expressions of certainty/uncertainty, (c) indicators of characters' thoughts/perceptions, and (d) (cognitive) deixis. (See Jeffries, 2006: 190–1 and Chapman, 2006: 122–4 for brief discussions on deixis, and Short, 1996: 286 for a detailed checksheet on the subject.) The different viewpoint types are worth defining here.

Groups of indicators can be linked together interpretatively, namely in terms of 'spatio-temporal', 'psychological' and 'ideological' viewpoint (see Simpson, 1993: 11). Spatio-temporal viewpoint 'refers to the impression which a reader gains of events moving rapidly or slowly, in a continuous chain or isolated segments' (Fowler, 1986: 127). It is the viewing position – as in the visual arts – that the readers feel themselves to occupy; the position from which their chain of perceptions seems to move. Such perspective is often communicated through adverbs (such as 'here' and 'there'), demonstrative pronouns in noun phrases (such as 'this week' and 'that room') and others (see Jeffries, 2006: 96–7, for more on demonstrative determiners).

Psychological or perceptual viewpoint refers to the way in which narrative events are mediated through the consciousness of the 'teller' of the story: 'It will encompass the means by which a fictional world is slanted in a particular way or the means by which narrators construct, in linguistic terms, their own view of the story they tell' (Simpson, 1993: 11–12).

Finally, ideological viewpoint, or world-view, refers to the set of values, or belief system, communicated by the language of the text and shared by people from similar backgrounds to the speaker. In this case, 'viewpoint has less to do with an individual's spatio-temporal location in some particular sense, but with a generalised mind-set or outlook on the world that a person, often as a representative of a group of people, might have' (Short, 1996: 277).

To illustrate this distinction, let's look at an extract from the opening of Jim Thompson's *The Killer Inside Me* [1952] (2002):

I'd finished my pie and was having a second cup of coffee when I saw him. The midnight freight had come in a few minutes before; and he was peering in one end of the restaurant window, the end nearest the depot, shading his eyes with his hand and blinking against the light. He saw me watching him, and his face faded back into the shadows. But I knew he was still there. I knew he was waiting. The bums always size me up for an easy mark.

(Thompson, 2002: 1)

Here, we share the first-person narrator Lou's perspective. Lou's spatio-temporal perspective is communicated through the adverb 'when', through the freight coming in a few minutes 'before' the time the story proper starts, while he apparently sees the other character from *inside* the restaurant window. His ideological perspective is communicated through his calling the other a 'bum', a collection of people supposedly 'always' (notice the certainty) sizing him up 'for an easy mark'. His psychological perspective comes across through the verbs of perception ('saw') and knowledge ('knew'), both of which indicate access to Lou's consciousness exclusively here. Everything we know about the so-called bum is communicated through Lou's perception and knowledge. We do not know through the bum himself that he stays there waiting for Lou, for instance. We only have this information through Lou, who 'knew' (perhaps more accurately, presumed) that the bum was indeed still there, waiting for him.

See Chapter 6, Task E

Simpson (1993) has proposed another linguistic framework for the analysis of point of view in fiction, one that is closely linked with the notion known as modality. Modality is the study of attitudinal features of language, and is concerned with the attitude and stance people have toward the propositions they express. Modal verbs (such as 'could', 'would' and 'should') are just one realisation of this, others being modal adverbs (such as 'possibly', 'certainly', 'preferably' and so on), evaluative nouns (such as 'terrorist'), adjectives (such as 'beautiful') and adverbs (such as 'horribly'), lexical verbs (such as 'need to', 'have to', 'ought to' do something), verbs of knowledge, prediction and evaluation (such as 'understood', 'knew', 'believed' and so on), and generic sentences (such as 'We all know what modality means') (see also Fowler, 1986; Jeffries, 2006: 116–21; Clark, 2007: 151–3).

Simpson further argued that these linguistic features can be grouped together into four main modal systems:

- **Deontic**: This is the modal system of obligation, duty and commitment, expressed in sentences such as 'You *may* sit down', 'You *should* come to class on time', 'You *must* submit essays by the deadline.'

- **Epistemic**: This is the modal system of knowledge, belief and cognition, which deals with certainty/uncertainty. This is expressed in sentences like 'She *might/will possibly* come along.' The strongest statements are epistemically non-modal (such as in 'She *will* come').
- **Boulomaic** (closely related to deontic): This is the modal system of desire and wishes, expressed in sentences such as 'I *wish he would/hope he will* come along.'
- **Perception** (closely related to epistemic): The modal system communicating certainty/uncertainty through perception, such as in 'He *will obviously/ apparently* come along.'

A fifth modality type that could be added to the list is:

- **Ability**: This concerns the use of *can/could* meaning physical ability (such as in 'I *can* ice-skate. When I was younger I *could* ice-skate for hours without falling').

See Chapter 6, Task F

A number of issues are worth noting here. First, straightforward mental processes such as 'I saw him' and 'I heard him' do not count as perception modality. Compare these examples with the modalised 'He *seems* happy' and 'He *sounds* OK' respectively. *Seems* and *sounds* here communicate a certain degree of commitment through perception, which is why they are classified as modalised, as opposed to the first two examples which merely communicate perception.

Second, some modals can perform more than one job. For instance, whereas 'You *may* leave the table' expresses permission (and is therefore a form of deontic modality), 'You *may* pass the exam' expresses possibility (and is therefore a form of epistemic modality). Similarly, 'I *should* finish the essay tonight' could be interpreted in two ways: either as an epistemically modalised expression (meaning 'I *will possibly* finish the essay tonight') or as a deontically modalised expression (meaning 'I *have to* finish the essay tonight'). Of course, the surrounding verbal context would normally disambiguate such instances.

Finally, the unmodalised categorical expressions are always strongest. Compare the certainty communicated through the Guinness slogan's 'Good things come to those who wait' with the uncertainty that would have been communicated through the epistemically modalised alternative, 'Good things *may* come to those who wait' or the deontically modalised alternative, 'Good things *should/have to* come to those who wait.'

Simpson (1993: 55) further seeks to reveal the prevailing point of view of texts by isolating their *dominant* modality. He classifies narrative types as follows:

Deontic + Boulomaic systems = 'POSITIVE' modality
Epistemic + Perception systems = 'NEGATIVE' modality
Texts displaying no dominant modality = 'NEUTRAL'.

He additionally differentiates between Category A narrators (who are essentially first-person narrators), and Category B narrators (who are third-person narrators). Category B narrators are further classified into two types: 'narratorial' mode, where the narrator is external, and 'reflector' mode, where the narrator is internal and hence privy to the thoughts, feelings and opinions of any one or more characters.

Here is an extract from Paul Auster's *The Book of Illusions*:

Everyone thought he was dead. When my book about his films was published in 1988, Hector Mann had not been heard from in almost sixty years. Except for a handful of historians and old-time movie buffs, few people seemed to know that he had ever existed. *Double or Nothing*, the last of the twelve two-reel comedies he made at the end of the silent era, was released on November 23 1928. Two months later, without saying good-bye to any of his friends or associates, without leaving behind a letter or informing anyone of his plans, he walked out of his rented house in North Orange Drive and was never seen again. His blue DeSoto was parked in the garage; the lease on the property was good for another three months; the rent had been paid in full. There was food in the kitchen, whiskey in the liquor cabinet, and not a single article of Hector's clothing was missing from the bedroom drawers. According to the *Los Angeles Herald Express* of January 18, 1929, *it looked as though he had stepped out for a short walk and would be returning at any moment*. But he didn't return, and from that point on it was as if Hector Mann had vanished from the face of the earth.

(Auster, 2002: 1)

This extract takes the form of first-person narration, as the narrator here is a participating character in the story. Hence the narration is Type A. The extract features negative shading because of the uncertainty communicated through epistemic and perception modality ('few people <u>seemed</u> to know that he had ever existed', 'it *looked as though* he had stepped out for a short walk and would be returning at any moment', 'it was <u>as if</u> Hector Mann had vanished'). According to Simpson (2004: 127), such shading gives the impression of a 'bewildered' narrator, in that (s)he relies on external signals and appearances to sustain a description. Such shading, Simpson adds, often characterises 'existentialist' or 'Gothic' styles of narrative fiction.

See Chapter 6, Task G

4.4 Mind style

The notion of 'mind style' was developed by Fowler (1977: 76) to refer to 'cumulatively, consistent structural options, agreeing in cutting the presented world to one pattern or another', giving rise to 'an impression of a world-view'. Since mind style is a realisation of narrative viewpoint that *deviates* from a common-sense version of reality, it is a necessary notion to consider in an analysis of extracts allowing access to deviant characters' consciousness. It is where the fiction writer, though not compelled to take on a single character's viewpoint, voluntarily 'limits' his or her omniscience to those things that belong to a particular character's worldview, that the notion needs to be considered. This limitation is often referred to as a form of focalisation, a term originating from the work of Genette (1980), and which Bal (1985: 100) adopted to refer to 'the relations between the elements presented and the vision through which they are presented'. In a more recent article, Bockting (1994: 159) offers the following definition of mind style: 'Mind style is concerned with the construction and expression in language of the conceptualisation of reality in a particular mind.'

As I argue in Gregoriou (2007a), I use 'mind style' more specifically to refer to the way in which a particular reality is perceived and conceptualised in cognitive terms. It may now be related to the mental abilities and tendencies of an individual, traits that may be completely personal and idiosyncratic, or ones that may be shared, for example by people with similar cognitive habits or disorders. One such mind is that of the autistic person.

Mark Haddon's discourse structure in *The Curious Incident of the Dog in the Night-Time* (2003) conflates the narrator with the character, as it takes the form of first-person homodiegetic narration, a narration which, by definition, provides readers with a biased version of events. The 15-year-old character-narrator Christopher Boone seems to have a form of 'high-functioning' autism known an Asperger's syndrome, and decides to write a novel revolving around the murder of his next-door neighbour's dog, Wellington. The novel that Chris, as the implied author, writes is *The Curious Incident*. Here, the real author Haddon attempts to genuinely represent the workings of an autistic mind and so features a linguistically deviant discourse; the story is narrated through the mind of a cognitively disabled child and therefore the version of the world we encounter often requires decoding. Chapter 7 opens with the following paragraphs:

This is a murder mystery novel.

Siobhan said that I should write something I would want to read myself. Mostly I read books about science and maths. I do not like proper novels. In proper novels people say things like, 'I am veined with iron, with silver and with streaks of common mud. I cannot contract into the firm fist which those clench who do not depend on stimulus'.[1] What does this mean? I do not know. Nor does Father. Nor do Siobhan or Mr Jeavons. I have asked them.

Siobhan has long blonde hair and wears glasses which are made of green plastic. And Mr Jeavons smells of soap and wears brown shoes that have approximately 60 tiny circular holes in each of them.

But I do like murder mystery novels. So I am writing a murder mystery novel.

[1] I found this book in the library in town when Mother took me into town once.

(Haddon, 2003: 5)

Chris frames the novel as a murder mystery one, but highlighted here is his tendency to digress, which is generically unexpected. Whereas keen readers of crime fiction expect detail, that detail is normally interpretable as potentially important and relevant to the solving of the crime – Chris's detailing is not. The linguistic deviance is highlighted in the simple and concise nature of Chris's sentences, his lexical repetitiveness ('murder mystery novel' is repeated three times, 'proper novels' is also repeated), his inability to linguistically decode the metaphorical expressions in the excerpt he quotes, and his over-preciseness. For instance, Chris tells us that he has asked people what the excerpt means even though this assertion is unnecessary as it has already been implied. Similarly, the detail in the other characters' description is unnecessary. It is this linguistic deviance alongside Chris's social eccentricity (he is the kind of character that would obsessively count the number of tiny circular holes in someone's shoes) and his digressing tendency that makes the character abnormal, and his mind style peculiar.

The range of non-standard characters who exhibit mind style can be widened to include those that are cognitively primitive, psychologically impaired or emotionally troubled. We could even borrow this same sense of mind style in reference to the criminal persona and mind (see Gregoriou 2002b, 2003a, 2003b, 2007a and 2007b). Even though I would not go to the extent of marking criminality as a mental disorder, it can surely be taken to be an idiosyncratic tendency certain people are prone to, regardless of whether they are born with it or have come to adopt it later on in life.

See Chapter 6, Task H

4.5 Speech and thought presentation

Stylisticians are interested in the choices that authors have available to represent character speech and thought, and how these choices affect meaning and viewpoint. According to Leech and Short (1981) and Short (1996, 2005), all sentences in fiction are either direct address to the reader, or narration, or the representation of character speech and/or character thought. Characters' speech and thought can be slotted into a number of categories (for a speech and thought presentation diagram, see Short, 1996, 2005; also see Clark, 2007: 123–6).

NRS is narrator's representation of speech (such as in 'They spoke for a while'), where we are merely told that speech took place.[2] NRSA is narrator's representation of speech act (such as 'He apologised to her'), which refers to acts performed by saying something, after Austin (1962) and Searle (1969). Short additionally indicates that such NRSA presentations may give us some indication of the subject matter (as in 'He apologised for his behaviour'). IS is indirect speech (such as 'He apologised for shouting at her the previous day'), and reflects the state of affairs expressed in the utterance but in the narrator's words. FIS is free indirect speech (such as 'He was very sorry for shouting at her yesterday'), which contains a mixture of DS or character-appropriate features ('very', 'yesterday') and IS or narrator-appropriate features ('he', 'was', 'her'). DS is direct speech (as in '"I'm very sorry for shouting at you yesterday", he said'), and includes a reporting clause, as well as a reported clause in quotation marks, the two separated by a comma. FDS is free direct speech (such as 'I'm very sorry for shouting at you yesterday'), a subtype of the direct speech category which, much like DS, contains the actual words the character uttered, but excludes the quotation marks or the reporting clause, or both. Both DS and FDS carry the flavour and vividness of the original, and feature no filtering of the utterance through the narrator, which is why these are classed as belonging to the narrator's end of the scale. The further we get from the original utterance, the more control the narrator claims over the speech report.

According to Short (2005), the same categories of presentation are available to an author representing the thoughts of characters. These categories – narrator's representation of thought (NRT), narrator's representation of thought act (NRTA), indirect thought (IT), free indirect thought (FIT), direct thought (DT) and free direct thought (FDT) – can be defined in exactly the same way linguistically as the equivalent speech presentation categories.

NRT: He thought for a while.
NRTA: He pondered over the state of his job.
IT: He wondered whether he should look for another job.
FIT: Should he look for another job?
DT: He wondered, 'Should I look for another job?'
FDT: Should I look for another job?

Overall, whereas direct presentations claim to contain the actual words and grammatical structures the character used in the original utterance (whether speech or thought 'utterance'), indirect presentations refer to the propositional content of that utterance, but in the words of the narrator. Free indirect presentations, on the other hand, represent a 'semantic halfway house' (Short, 1994: 186) between the faithfulness claims of direct and indirect presentations. It is therefore difficult, and often impossible, to work out whether the words and structures represented are those of the narrator or the character. It is for this reason that Short argues that the semantic indeterminacy opens up myriad possibilities for the manipulation of point of view. This mixing or merging of narratorial indirectness and characterological directness through 'free indirect discourse'[3] has been endorsed as a powerful mode of representing characters in an (allegedly) authentic/realist way.

Short (2005) argues that the DS mode is popularly taken to be the norm insofar as speech presentation is concerned, and therefore a movement towards the narrator's end of the scale (that is, towards FIS) would produce the contradictory qualities of control and vividness. In the previous FIS example, 'He was very sorry for shouting at her yesterday', the narrator both maintains command over the speech event's report, while giving us readers a flavour of the original, making the scene come alive for us. This, Short adds, is why FIS is often used as a vehicle for irony, though admittedly such an effect can be generated by other means too. To stay with the same example, by employing the FIS category to represent the speech, the narrator could be said to cast doubt over the sincerity attached to the apology and therefore communicate the speech event with a layer of mistrust.

Short (2005) continues that the IT mode is taken to be the norm in thought presentation,[4] and therefore a movement away from the narrator's end of the scale (that is, towards FIT) would produce the sense that the readers are getting a more vivid and immediate representation of the character's thoughts as they happen. This, Short adds, produces a sense of *empathy*. He (2004) later came to create another category between straightforward narration (N) and narrator's representation of thought (NRT), that of internal narration (NI). He gave arguments in favour of NI being part of narration rather than the thought presentation scale. Part of the difficulty in the placing of this intermediate category lies in 'thought' being a difficult notion to define and understand in the first place. For instance, one of the questions to be asked is whether thought is part of cognition or not. The ambiguity of certain examples which can be classified as straightforward narration *or* as FIT lies at the heart of this discussion.

Consider the following short example:

They sat along the side of the river. It was a beautiful day. He loved her.

Would you classify 'He loved her' as FIT (translatable as '"Oh how I love you,"' he thought' in DT and as 'He thought about his love for her' in NRTA), or is this straightforward narration? How do we know? Is it the narrator giving us a statement about the internal world of the male character, or is this the character communicating to us his subconscious thoughts? In some such cases, the surrounding verbal context would help us decide between the two; if the extract is followed by more clear FIT, then we are more likely to come back to classify 'He loved her' as FIT also. But not all such instances are easily disambiguated by the surrounding verbal context.

Let us apply Short's speech and thought presentation model to an extract from Ben Elton's *Blast from the Past*.

(1) It was 2.15 in the morning when the telephone rang. Polly woke instantly. Her eyes were wide and her body tense before the phone had completed so much as a single ring. And as she woke, in the tiny moment between sleep and consciousness, before she was even aware of the telephone's bell, she felt scared. It was not the phone that jolted Polly so completely from her dreams, but fear.

(2) And who could argue with the reasoning powers of Polly's subconscious self? Of course she was scared. After all, when the phone rings at 2.15 in the morning it's unlikely to be heralding something pleasant. What chance is there of its being good news? None. Only someone bad could ring at such an hour. Or someone good with bad news.

(3) That telephone was sounding a warning bell. Something, somewhere, was wrong. So much was obvious. Particularly to a woman who lived alone, and Polly lived alone.

(4) Of course it might be no more wrong than a wrong number. Something bad, but bad for someone else, something that would touch Polly's life only for a moment, utterly infuriate her and then be gone.

(5) 'Got the Charlie?'

(6) 'There's no Charlie at this number.'

(7) 'Don't bullshit me arsehole.'

(8) 'What number are you trying to call? This is three, four, zero, one ...'

(9) 'Three, four, zero? I'm awfully sorry. I think I've dialled the wrong number.'

(10) That would be a good result. A wrong number would be the best possible result. To find yourself returning to bed furiously muttering, 'Stupid bastard,' while trying to pretend to yourself that you haven't actually woken up; that would be a good result. Polly hoped the warning bell was meant for someone else.

(Elton, 1999a: 9–10)

This extract takes the form of heterodiegetic internal third person narration, as the events are mediated through the character Polly's consciousness. The first paragraph takes the form of narration. We are told about actions that took place ('the telephone rang', 'Polly woke instantly'), and given information about the character's emotional reaction to the events ('she felt scared', 'It was not the phone that jolted Polly so completely from her dreams, but fear').

The second paragraph, however, features some thought presentation, particularly in the form of interrogatives/questions. 'And who could argue with the reasoning powers of Polly's subconscious self?' takes the form of FIT, as it features Polly's thinking process. While some of this wording is narrator-appropriate ('Polly' is used rather than 'my'), the thought takes the form of an interrogative which is character-appropriate. 'What chance is there of its being good news?' is also FIT for the same reason. However, we could argue that the whole of this second paragraph, as with many FIT instances, is ambiguous with narration. Short (2005) notes that typically we tend to feel in the course of reading that DT is the representation of conscious thought on the part of the character, whereas FIT feels more like the representation of subconscious thought. This seems to be affirmed here, as we not only sympathise with the character, but also get the sense that Polly might not be as conscious of her thoughts at this stage as we are.

The third and forth paragraph feature narration ('The telephone was sounding a warning bell', 'Polly lived alone') and FIT ('Something, somewhere, was wrong. So much was obvious. Particularly to a woman who lived alone', 'Of course it might be no more wrong than a wrong number'), which again carry a subconscious element.

From paragraph 5 until 9, we get a series of what we would initially classify as FDS instances; all of these include reported clauses in quotation marks, but lack a reporting clause. The lack of the reporting clause is, here, significant. The nature of the short discussion is indicative of the first speaker being the caller and the second speaker being Polly, but we have no indication who the caller is. We therefore share Polly's concerns at this stage – she knows no more about the caller than what we do, which adds to the effect of suspense.

It is not until paragraph 10 that we come to realise that paragraphs 5–9 are not instances of speech presentation after all, but are instead instances of speech embedded within a hypothetical scenario that Polly herself constructs in her thoughts. Short's speech and thought presentation framework, however, does not anticipate the need for such double coding; something cannot be classified as speech and thought at the same time. However, if within someone's thoughts, someone is speaking, such double coding is needed.

From paragraph 10 onwards, we not only reclassify paragraphs 5–9 (we scrap the story out and start all over, as it were), but switch to FDT instances 'That would be a good result. A wrong number would be the best possible result', classified as free because linguistically it is character-appropriate; there is no reporting clause, the propositional content is given, and 'would' is appropriate to the character at this stage. We get yet another instance of DS embedded within Polly's free direct thought processes: 'To find yourself returning to bed furiously muttering, "Stupid bastard," while trying to pretend to yourself that you haven't actually woken up', classified as free direct due to the language's characterological directness.

This complexity in the presentation of the various categories is very effective in this piece. It indeed helps put us readers into the mind of a character who is very suddenly disturbed from sleep, and deals with various conscious and subconscious thoughts, concerns and wishes going through her mind in the few moments it takes her to actually answer the phone.

See Chapter 6, Task I

4.6 Chapter review

In this chapter, we looked at the basic distinctions between oral and written narratives, alongside plot and discourse, before considering Brémond's narrative cycle as a very simple model accounting for a narrative sequence generating plot. Having made further distinctions between homodiegetic and heterodiegetic narrators, internal and external narrative events, we made correlations between certain narrative style choices and the manipulation of reader sympathy, alongside a potential cause for bias. We looked at the various viewpoint types and relevant linguistic indicators, and considered the notion of modality alongside Simpson's modal grammar of point of view, a model for slotting texts into type, depending on the dominant modality evident. We then explored the notion of mind style, which was here linked to the representation of autistic and criminal characters in particular, especially where the texts allow readers access to the relevant characters' consciousness. Finally, we considered the speech and thought presentation categories, along with the effects that particular choices within these categories generate.

In the next chapter, I introduce the notion of possible worlds and text world theory, followed by frame and schema theory, and also consider various models relevant to narrative storytelling analysis.

Narrative Worlds, Schemata and Frames

5.1 Possible worlds and text world theory

Possible worlds, though originally associated with the disciplines of philosophy and logic, have also found their way to the literary and even linguistic analyses of fictional text. According to Semino (1997: 57), such studies of fiction include the logical properties of sentences of (and about) works of fiction, the ontological status of fictional entities, the definition of fiction, and the nature of the worlds projected by the different types of fictional and/or literary texts. Often associated with the work of Ryan (1991a, 1991b, 1998), possible worlds are essentially 'conceivable states of affairs'. Wales (2001: 310) asserts that the word 'world' is therefore used metaphorically, and there lies the question; what exactly is the relationship between the real (or actual) world we inhabit, possible worlds and fictional worlds?

Ryan (1991a) proposes that fictional worlds are alternative possible worlds which function as the actual world of the universe projected for the text's storyline. In other words, Ryan suggests that the actual world is only one of a multitude of possible or conceivable ones, and that the 'real' world of the text is in effect the 'text actual world'. He goes on (1991a: 87) to describe possible worlds as different versions of the fictional world (text actual world) which may correspond to characters' beliefs ('knowledge worlds'), expectations ('prospective extensions of knowledge worlds'), plans ('intention worlds'), moral commitments and prohibitions ('obligation worlds'), wishes and desires ('wish worlds'), and dreams or fantasies ('fantasy universes').

Stockwell (2002: 94–5) slightly adapts Ryan's typology as follows:

- He uses 'epistemic worlds' (for Ryan's 'knowledge worlds') for what characters know/believe to be true in their fictional worlds.
- He uses 'speculative extensions' (for Ryan's 'prospective extensions of

knowledge worlds') for characters' speculations, anticipations and hypotheses.

- He keeps Ryan's use of 'intention worlds', in reference to what characters plan to do to effect change.
- He keeps Ryan's use of 'obligations worlds' for the characters' world versions filtered through their moral commitments, senses and values.
- He keeps Ryan's use of 'wish worlds' for the characters' wishes and what they imagine different.
- He uses 'fantasy worlds' (for Ryan's 'fantasy universes') in reference to the characters' visions, dreams, hallucinations and any actual imaginations they compose themselves.

Ryan (1991a: 20) argues for there being a situation of equilibrium (see also the discussion of Brémond's narrative cycle in Chapter 4) where there is perfect correspondence between the text actual world on one hand and all possible worlds in the fictional universe on the other. In other words, if everyone is content, knowledge is shared and wishes are fulfilled, the characters are all in a state of bliss.

He goes on, however, to argue effectively that a conflict between these sorts of worlds is necessary to get a plot started; if there is no conflict between characters' possible worlds (including internal conflict in one character and conflicts with the text actual world), there would also be no need for action, and therefore no plot. It is for these reasons that we often see narrative plots where characters want who or what they have not got (a conflict between the text actual world and their wish world) or face moral dilemmas in their course of actions (a conflict between their obligation world and their intention world perhaps). Equally, there are many narrative plots where different characters' expectations (or speculative extensions) clash, or where their knowledge and plans differ in some way. Also, various fantasy novels, science fiction narratives and fairy tales are surrounded by phenomena that oppose our natural laws, and therefore the text actual world by definition is in conflict with the real world the readers inhabit.

The following is an extract from the opening of Ben Elton's *Inconceivable*, a story about a couple struggling to come to terms with the fact that they have problems conceiving a child:

Dear ...?
Dear.
Dear Book?
Dear Self? Dear Sam.
Good. Got that sorted out. What next?
Lucy is making me write this diary. It's a 'book of thoughts'. 'Letters to

myself' is how she put it, hence the 'Dear Sam' business, which of course is me. Lucy says that her friend, whose name escapes me, had a theory that conducting this internal correspondence will help Lucy and me relax about things. The idea is that if Lucy and I periodically privately assemble our thoughts and feelings then we'll feel less like corks bobbing about on the sea of fate. Personally, I find it extra-ordinary that Lucy can be persuaded that she'll become less obsessed about something if she spends an hour every day writing about it, but there you go. Lucy thinks that things might be a whole lot better if I stopped trying to be clever and started trying to be supportive.

(Elton, 1999b: 7)

Those reading the first few paragraphs of this book immediately become aware that the two characters share a problem they are currently trying to solve. In fact, the story is based on the initial conflict between the two characters' joint intention world to have a child and the text actual world where they are unable to conceive one and become increasingly agitated by this. This conflict is, therefore, in need of action which in turn generates a plot.

Sam follows Lucy's advice to write a 'book of thoughts', although the ironic tone of the extract suggests that he does not believe that it will help ease his anxiety or contribute toward the solving of their problem in any way. We hence have another contrast between his belief or knowledge world and Lucy's.

There is also a slight conflict between the two characters' knowledge worlds, in that Sam cannot remember Lucy's friend's name whereas Lucy presumably can. Another conflict of knowledge worlds lies in the fact that Lucy believes that Sam is going along willingly with writing in the diary, whereas he feels forced into it or perhaps obliged to conform to her wish that he do it (in the latter case, his obligation world is in conflict with his knowledge world). Another conflict arises between Lucy's wish world, where Sam stops 'being clever' and starts 'trying to be supportive', and the text actual world implied, where Sam is neither serious nor supportive enough.

See Chapter 6, Tasks J and K

The cognitive linguist Paul Werth borrowed possible world theory terminology in his attempts to put together a theory of how humans process discourse, accounting for the particular textual elements that activate this process. The cognitive, pragmatic and experiential theory of reading he devised is known as text world theory.[1] Werth died before completing his monograph *Text Worlds: Representing Conceptual Space in Discourse*. The book was nevertheless edited from the manuscript by Mick Short, and became available in 1999.

In the context of text world theory terminology, and in accordance with possible world theory terminology, 'real world' refers to the world we – us real people – live in, whereas 'possible world' features as a term for various versions of conceivable worlds, inclusive of the text actual or fictional world. Werth, however, further used the term 'discourse world' to refer to our use of language to refer to such worlds (whether real, fictional or possible ones), while 'text world' is the term he uses to refer to the story depicted by the language of the text. Essentially, Werth suggests that we can draw text worlds on paper, since:

> [w]e can think of a text world as a blank form with questions on it: where does this take place? When? Who is taking part? What objects are there? What are the relationships between any of these entities? What qualities do these entities possess?

> (Werth, 1995b: 55)

To start with, he distinguishes two types of elements: 'world builders' and 'function advancers'. World building elements are essentially the scene setters. These constitute the background against which the action will be portrayed, giving us readers a sense of time and place within which to set events, and an idea of the sorts of objects and characters involved. On paper, world builders are presented in the form of an annotated list, marked 't' for time, 's' for space (or 'l' for location), 'c' for characters and finally 'o' for objects.

Function advancing propositions are, as the name suggests, the set of propositions that propel the story forward. Any sorts of states, actions, events and processes described are essentially function advancers, including the various arguments and predictions made about the characters. On paper, function advancers are presented as various kinds of 'paths' or arrows. Vertical arrows are known as pathways, and these are material actions and events in terms of their transitivity. Actions are essentially 'doing' verbs with animate participants such as people ('She *bought* a book') whereas events are action verbs with inanimate participants ('The record *played*'). Horizontal arrows are known as modification relationships, and these are relational or attributional predications in the transitivity model.[2] The sentences 'Jake *is* smart' and 'Mary *owns* a car' are relational processes, in that they express processes of being and having respectively.

Consider the following simple opening to a story:

Maria and John were sitting in the kitchen.
Mike came in.
He had a long coat on.

In terms of world builders, we have two characters to start with, Maria and

John, before Mike joins them. They are located in the kitchen in terms of space, though no reference is made to objects, and neither do we get a specific sense of time, other than the fact that events are situated in the past ('were sitting'). Nevertheless, we can presume that they are sitting on chairs, probably in front of a table, while the reference to the coat gives us an indication of the weather conditions and, therefore, the nature of the season (more likely winter or autumn than spring or summer). An explanation of these presumptions could arise through a *schematic* analysis of the same lines (see below for discussion of schema theory).

The reference to Maria and John sitting down is function advancing, as is the reference to Mike joining them, and his having a long coat on. The first and last of the three advancers are modification relationships (horizontal arrows), as these merely express the state of the scene. The middle function advancer ('Mike came in') indicates movement, however, and would therefore be classified as a pathway (a vertical arrow).

The text world diagram would look like Figure 5.1.

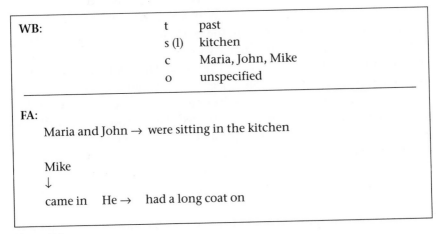

Figure 5.1

Werth introduces the term 'sub-worlds' to refer to alterations to the world builders of the story line. He divides these sub-worlds into three types. He uses the term 'temporal alternations' to refer to flashbacks, flash-forwards or instances of direct speech, all of which indicate a change to the temporal parameters of the story line, 'spatial alternations' to refer to changes in terms of space (of the 'meanwhile, back in the living-room' sort), and 'modalised propositions' for anything remotely modalised, including expressions of speculation and desire (see Chapter 4 for an outline of a modality framework). Stockwell (2002: 140–1) instead prefers the term 'deictic sub-worlds' for

Werth's temporal and spatial alternations collectively, and splits Werth's modalised propositions category into two sub-types: attitudinal sub-worlds, which are alternations as a result of desire, belief or purpose (constituting respectively desire worlds, belief worlds and purpose worlds), and epistemic sub-worlds, which are 'the means by which text world theory handles the dimension of possibility and probability'.

So how would we draw sub-worlds? On paper, since these various paths (or groups of paths) form part of another text world, one with different world builders, these paths are projected and enclosed in separate rounded rectangles which extend from the main text world.

Read the following extract from *Talking with Serial Killers: The Most Evil People in the World Tell their Own Stories*, a collation of interview-informed narratives, put together by the investigative criminologist Christopher Berry-Dee:

> It was 24 September 1974 and early morning in Minneapolis. The sun was up and patrolmen Robert Nelson and Robert Thompson were cruising along 1841 E 38th Street when they spotted the 1968 black-over-pea-green Chevrolet Caprice. It was parked across the road from a diner. Thompson made a slow circuit of the block, while his partner checked the police bulletin details issued the day before.
>
> 'That's it,' said Nelson. 'That looks like the car. All we gotta do is find the driver. He's a big guy and, according to this, he's built like a gorilla.'
>
> The two officers peered through the Caprice's window and scrutinized the interior. Sure enough, there was the red plaid car rug, pornographic magazines, and a bible. By the gearshift, they noticed several packs of Marlborough [sic] cigarettes; all items that had been detailed by a previous rape victim of the man the police were searching for.
>
> (Berry-Dee, 2003: 10)

In the text's first paragraph, we have a number of world builders relating to time ('24 September 1974', 'early morning') and location ('Minneapolis', '1841 E 38th Street'), all giving the impression that we are here dealing with a representation of actual events that took place in a certain place and time in the factual past. The characters are the two patrolmen, while a number of objects are mentioned (the Chevrolet Caprice, the police bulletin boards and others). Collectively, these are the stationary elements that initially frame the story.

A number of function advancers are mentioned in this first paragraph: (a) the police men were cruising, (b) they spotted the Caprice, (c) the Caprice was parked across the road, (d) Thompson made a slow circuit of the block, and (e) his partner checked the police bulletin details. Whereas (a), (d) and (e) indicate change and motion and are therefore classified as pathways (vertical arrows), (b) and (c) are expressive of states or mental/relational predications and are therefore classified as modification relationships (horizontal arrows). This new information gives the text its point and helps advance the plot.

In this same paragraph, the mention of 'the day before' triggers a deictic sub-world, triggering a temporal alternation or flashback to an event taking place the previous day. The 'issuing of the police bulletin' is another function advancer, this time a pathway (vertical arrow), since it denotes an alternation or variation from one state to another.

The second paragraph features direct speech and hence another temporal alternation. Within this direct speech presentation, Nelson forms an intention sub-world ('All we gotta do is find the driver'), though modalised sub-worlds are also formed ('That looks like the car', 'according to this ...'). These modalised propositions can be described as epistemic; they feature epistemic modality. Attributional predications ('He's a big guy', 'he's built like a gorilla') also feature, and these would take the form of horizontal arrows; they are modification relationships.

In the third paragraph, we return to the original text world which frames the two characters peering through the car's window and noticing objects, featuring verbs expressing further modification relationships ('peered', 'noticed'). A number of objects enter the scene in the form of relational modification relationships within the mental processes ('there was the red plaid car rug, the pornographic magazines, and a bible', 'they noticed several packs of Marlborough cigarettes'). Another temporal alternation features at the end, which takes us to flashbacks of a previous rape victim 'detailing' items of the man the police were 'searching' for, both of these expressing pathways.

Even though actually drawing the text world may help us identify patterns here, the analysis is here revealing in itself. Overall, it shows that readers do not get access to each of the two characters' consciousness, but only to their joint perception and Nelson's speech. The temporal alternations build up the plot and add to the suspense, though the epistemic and intention sub-worlds give us a sense of uncertainty and yet good will. The absence of many pathways indicates that not much action and movement is taking place.

But why is this analysis worth doing? Text world analysis can help us readers keep track of our mental processes in comprehension (much like frame theory: see below). While explaining how we map worlds when reading, text world analysis can further help us understand ambiguity as well as multiplicity in meaning, and it can enable us to investigate the ways in which unreliable narrators work (for relevant analyses, see Gavins, 2000, 2001a, 2001b, 2003; Hidalgo Downing, 2000a, 2000b, 2003).

See Chapter 6, Task L

5.2 Schema theory

The general term 'schema theory' covers a range of work, from as early as the work of the philosopher Kant (1963) at the end of the eighteenth century, to psychological experiments by Bartlett (1932), to recent cognitive psychology. Central to the development of the theory is the work of Roger Schank (Schank and Abelson, 1977; Schank, 1982a, 1982b, 1984, 1986), while the framework has itself been set out by Semino (1997: 119–233), Culpeper (2001: 63–86, 263–86), Stockwell (2002: 75–89), and Clark (2007: 157–62). As Stockwell puts it:

> [e]ssentially, the context that someone needs to make sense of individual experiences, events, parts of situations or elements of language is stored in background memory as an associative network of knowledge. In the course of experiencing an event or making sense of a situation, a schema is dynamically produced, which can be modelled as a sort of script based on similar situations encountered previously. New experiences and new incoming information are understood by matching them to existing schematic knowledge.
>
> (Stockwell, 2003a: 255)

Stockwell argues that although there is a wealth of empirical evidence that suggests such a mechanism may be in operation, it is schema theory itself that has gone on to provide analytical detail to account for the workings of the process.

The term 'schema', then, refers to skeletal organisations of conceptual knowledge; connected bits of general cultural information based on verbal and non-verbal experience are stored as packages or schemas (the plural is sometimes given as schemata), which although stereotypical, are continually 'updated' (Wales, 2001: 351). As Cook (1994: 9) puts it, schema theory's basic claim is that a new experience is understood by comparison with a stereotypical version of a similar experience held in memory. The new experience is then processed in terms of its deviation from the stereotypical version or conformity to it. Short (1996) uses the helpful analogy of a filing cabinet. Having described schemata as bits of information stored in the form of packages, he suggests that:

> [w]hen we come across a reference to a situation we have come across before, we access the relevant 'file' in the 'filing cabinet', which consists of an organised inventory of all the sorts of things related to that situation which we have previously experienced. These schemas get updated from time to time as new information comes at hand.
>
> (Short, 1996: 227)

Since schemata are abstract cognitive structures which incorporate generalised knowledge about objects and events, containing slots which are filled with specific information bits as a text or message is processed, these are bound to vary depending on the culture and overall personal background and experience that each one of us has had.

Let us take a pub or bar as an example. Given a message about a 'pub' or 'bar' when in Britain, adult readers activate the relevant and possibly well-developed 'pub' schema. They will anticipate references to, and specific information about, barstaff and barstools, draught beer, lager and various bottled alcohols, special offers, seating areas, and some sort of a crowd. Those familiar with bars in the Mediterranean might instead or additionally expect a waiter or waitress, a menu, free popcorn and nuts, and certainly background music.

Schema theorists make a useful distinction between two types of information stored, that which is ordered *sequentially* (in a sort of narrative) and that which is not. Non-sequentially ordered information is said to be stored as 'frame', and sequentially ordered information as 'script'. Note that the use of 'frame' here differs from the use of the same term in Section 5.4.

To take the example of 'a restaurant', my frame assumptions include the fact that there will be tables, chairs, waiters, chefs, menus, plates, forks and knives and so on. My script assumptions are that when you enter a restaurant, someone approaches you to ask how many people are to join your party. Your waiter or waitress takes you to your table before offering you the menu and then asking for your drinks order. The server is also likely to tell you about any special offers or the 'dish of the day' at this point. Once your drinks are served, you are likely to be asked whether you have chosen what you want to eat. You are likely to wait a while before your meal is served. Once you have started eating, the server is likely to come to ask whether everything is fine with your meal. Once finished, you are offered coffee or dessert. You pay for your meal having finished any dessert, and are likely to be given a receipt on your way out. Note that your restaurant frame and script might be different from mine, but they are more than likely to certainly share many of the features I mentioned.

See Chapter 6, Task M

Schema analysts make certain distinctions in relation to what can happen to all of these associative networks of background memory in response to various sensory and linguistic experiences.

For one, schemata can be disrupted, where conceptual deviance offers a challenge to the reader's knowledge structure or schema. For example, if you enter a restaurant that has no menu, your restaurant schema is likely to be 'challenged' or 'violated'.

Schemata can also be 'refreshed', whereby a schema is revised and its membership elements and relations are recast (Stockwell, 2002: 80). I moved to Britain in the mid-1990s, but can still remember the day I realised that if someone offers to buy you a drink in the UK they expect it to be a reciprocal arrangement. On that occasion, my schema was changed for good, particularly in relation to pub outings in this particular country.

Schemata can further be 'reinforced', where new incoming facts strengthen and confirm schematic knowledge. For example adverts directed at women tend to rely on and confirm stereotypical assumptions about them, rather than challenging such assumptions; the schema of the older woman wanting to look younger or of the young woman wanting to look beautiful or lose weight is often hence strengthened in advertisements, a concept similar to that of 'schema preserving', which is to do with schemata being confirmed. (For more on schema affirmation, literature and cultural multilingualism, see Jeffries, 2001.)

Stockwell (2002: 79) further notes schema 'accretion', where new facts are added to an existing schema, enlarging its scope. As from the summer of 2006, pubs in Britain are allowed to stay open after 11 o'clock at night, and so people's pub schema in Britain is likely to have changed as a result. As from the summer of 2007, a restaurant schema in Britain is likely to no longer contain a 'smoking section', seeing that smoking has been banned in public places like restaurants in the UK. On such occasions, the relevant schemata can be said to have been added to.

In a literary environment, Stockwell (2002: 80) makes a distinction between three different fields in which schemata operate: 'world schemata' (content schemata), 'language schemata' (appropriate forms of linguistic patterning and style in which we expect a subject to appear), and 'text schemata' (our expectations of the way world schemata appear in terms of sequencing and structural information). World schemata essentially relate to how the world works, language schemata relate to the sort of language and style deemed appropriate for the text and context, and text schemata relate to the nature appropriate for the text types in question.

What is odd about the following text? What type of schemata does it violate?

She went to the restaurant at 4. She paid and left. By 4:15, she was home and absolutely starving.

Script-wise, there appears to be a problem here. You expect the character to pay having finished her meal, unless the restaurant in question is a take-away restaurant, something not directly mentioned here. If we assume that the character had already eaten the meal by 4:15, there is also a bit of a disruption to our world schema, in that readers would not expect someone to be hungry if she has just eaten.

See Chapter 6, Tasks N and O

5.3 Telling stories

5.3.1 Labov's oral narratives model

In his study of the Black English Vernacular (BEV) narrative form, Labov (1972) developed a widely employed analytical model. He essentially attempted a structural description of his BEV informants' *oral* narratives of personal experience, yet along with his collaborator Waletzky (Labov and Waletzky, 1967), he came to develop a model made applicable to the analysis of *written* narratives, and also narratives produced in languages other than English.

Labov defines 'narrative' as:

> [o]ne method of recapitulating past experience by matching a verbal sequence of clauses to the sequence of events which (it is inferred) actually occurred [...] With[in] this conception of narrative, we can define a *minimal narrative* as a sequence of two clauses which are *temporarily ordered*: that is, a change in their order will result in a change in the temporal sequence of the original semantic interpretation.
>
> (Labov, 1972: 359–60)

From the dozens of stories collected, he proposed the following narrative categories (1972: 363):

1 Abstract.
2 Orientation.
3 Complicating action.
4 Evaluation.
5 Result or resolution.
6 Coda.

Even though many story-tellers dispense with one or more of these ingredients, according to this model, a well-formed or complete narrative would not. In addition, each of these categories could overlap with anything from a single sentence to a stretch of several clauses. The categories listed above are arranged in the sequence in which they are expected to occur, with the exception of evaluation, which is situated outside the pattern and can be inserted at any stage during a story. (For more on narratology and Labov's model, see Clark, 2007: 118–22.)

Let's look at a short story, to investigate the function and form of the various elements.

You're never going to believe what happened to me yesterday! I went to this bar to have a quick drink after work. I was on my own, looking for some peace essentially, to wind down after a very stressful day at the office. This woman walks up to me and starts yelling at me for absolutely no reason whatsoever. 'Leave me alone,' I said. She would not go away. Eventually, the barman had to ask her to leave. I tell you, that's the last time I'm going somewhere on my own, ever again!

The abstract is meant to signal that a story is about to begin, and draws the attention of the listener, giving some idea of what the story will be about. This is normally a short statement, provided before the narrative proper commences, of the sort 'You are never going to believe what happened to me yesterday!', and functions as an advertisement for the addressee to attend to the narrative.

The orientation is meant to help the listener identify the time, place, persons, activity and situation involved (that is, the 'who, what, when and where' of the story). This often takes the form of past tense verbs, along with adverbs of time, manner and place. In the story above, the first person narrator is on his (let's call it a 'him') own in the bar to start with, probably in the course of an early weekday evening ('after work'). Unlike Labov's argument in relation to the temporal sequencing of the story, we also get a momentary flashback to the narrator's 'stressful day at the office' here, as a way of justifying his need for a quiet drink.

The complicating action is essentially the core narrative category, providing the 'what happened' story element, realised by narrative clauses which are temporally ordered and normally have a verb in the simple past. The story-teller above goes into a bar, after which the woman walks up to him and starts yelling at him. We then get some direct speech presentation, which essentially is here part of the action (though some would argue that, on certain occasions, speech presentation is evaluative instead[3]), which is followed by the yelling woman's refusal to go away (classified as either free indirect speech if taken to mean something along the lines of 'She replied, "I'm not leaving"', or alternatively as mere narration).

The resolution recapitulates the final events of a story (that is, the 'what finally happened' element), and overall comprises the last of the narrative clauses which began the complicating action. In the story above, this takes the form of 'Eventually, the barman had to ask her to leave.'

The evaluation functions to make the point of the story clear and ward off responses of the 'so what?' nature. This is marked by a number of different linguistic forms, which include evaluative comments (such as 'a quick drink' and 'a stressful day' in the story above), embedded speech (as noted, the characters' conversation could be classed as evaluative here), or comparisons with unrealised departures from basic narrative grammar such as modals, negatives, intensifiers and explicatives (such as 'looking for some peace', 'to wind down', 'for absolutely no reason whatsoever' in the story above).

Finally, the coda is meant to signal that a story has ended, while bringing listeners back to the point at which they entered the narrative. No specific linguistic features mark codas, although these frequently take the form of a generalised statement which is timeless in character, such as the above story's 'I tell you, that's the last time I'm going somewhere on my own, ever again!' (For analyses of how social background impacts on the structuring of narratives of personal experience, see Lambrou, 2003; 2007.)

See Chapter 6, Tasks P and Q

5.3.2 Propp's morphology of the folktale

A particularly influential model used for the analysis and description of story content – that is, the development of plot – was created by Russian Formalist Vladimir Propp (1975, 1984). This is known as the morphology of the folktale. Note that here, the term 'morphology' is used in its more general, biological sense of the study of the forms of things, as opposed to the study of the internal patterning of words. (For more on the latter, see Jeffries, 2006, Chapter 3.2.)

According to Propp's model, characters vary, but actions and what he refers to as 'functions' are constant. They can be categorized according to the role they play in progressing the events of the story. However, regardless of the number of optional actions a tale may contain, the order of those actions that are included is always the same. Essentially, while not all so-called functions are present, he found that all the tales he analysed displayed the functions in unvarying sequence.

In Propp's model, individual actions are seen as representations of particular functions. There are only 31 functions, some obligatory, others optional. With this model, Propp was able to analyse and describe a large collection of Russian folktales in a comprehensive way, and therefore claimed that he discovered certain general laws of narrative, although his ambition was to describe the general laws of the wonder tale only.

After the initial situation is depicted, Propp argues that the tale takes the sequence of the following 31 functions:

1   A member of a family leaves home (the hero is introduced).
2   An interdiction is addressed to the hero ('don't go there', 'go to this place').
3   The interdiction is violated (the villain enters the tale).
4   The villain makes an attempt at reconnaissance (either the villain tries to

find the children/jewels and so on, or the intended victim questions the villain).

5   The villain gains information about the victim.

6   The villain attempts to deceive the victim to take possession of victim or victim's belongings (trickery; the villain, disguised, tries to win the confidence of the victim).

7   The victim is taken in by deception, unwittingly helping the enemy.

8   The villain causes harm/injury to a family member (by abduction, theft of magical agent, spoiling crops; or causes a disappearance, expels someone, casts a spell on someone, substitutes a child, commits murder, imprisons/detains someone, threatens forced marriage, provides nightly torments). Alternatively, a member of family lacks something or desires something (such as a magical potion).

9   Misfortune or lack is made known (the hero is dispatched, hearing a call for help; alternatively, the victimised hero is sent away, or freed from imprisonment).

10   The seeker agrees to, or decides upon, counter-action.

11   The hero leaves home.

12   The hero is tested, interrogated, attacked and so on, preparing the way for his/her receiving the magical agent or helper (donor).

13   The hero reacts to actions of the future donor (withstands/fails the test, frees a captive, reconciles disputants, performs a service, uses the adversary's powers against them).

14.   The hero acquires use of a magical agent (directly transferred, located, purchased or prepared; or it spontaneously appears, and gets eaten/drunk, while help is offered by other characters).

15   The hero is transferred, delivered or led to whereabouts of an object of the search.

16   The hero and the villain join in direct combat.

17   The hero is branded (wounded/marked, receives ring or scarf).

18   The villain is defeated (killed in combat, defeated in contest, killed while asleep, or banished).

19   The initial misfortune or lack is resolved (object of search distributed, spell broken, slain person revived, captive freed).

20   The hero returns.

21   The hero is pursued (the pursuer tries to kill, eat, undermine the hero).

22   The hero is rescued from pursuit (obstacles delay the pursuer, the hero hides or is hidden, transforms unrecognisably, is saved from the attempt on his/her life).

Many tales end here, with the marriage of the hero to the girl, if there is one. But most have another misfortune in store, and a new 'story' is created.

23 The hero, unrecognised, arrives home or in another country.
24 The false hero presents unfounded claims.
25 A difficult task is proposed to the hero (such as trial by ordeal, riddles, test of strength/endurance).
26 The task is resolved.
27 The hero is recognised (by a mark, brand or thing given to him/her).
28 The false hero or villain is exposed.
29 The hero is given a new appearance (is made whole, handsome, is given new garments and so on).
30 The villain is punished.
31 The hero marries and ascends the throne (is rewarded/promoted).

In addition to the various functions, Propp argues that the dramatic personae can be slotted into the following categories:

Hero (also the seeker or victim)
Villain
Donor (from whom the hero gets some magical object)
Magical helper (the character that helps the hero in the quest)
Dispatcher (the character that makes the lack known)
False hero (the character who takes credit for hero's actions)
Prince/princess (person the hero marries)
Victim (person harmed by the villain if not the hero)

We can apply this framework to, for example, modern crime fiction. In the case of Michael Connelly's Harry Bosch crime series, the detective Harry is certainly the hero, seeking villains and often enduring suffering in doing so, whereas each killer takes the form of the villain who harms the victims. The investigative team (medical examiners, forensic scientists and so on) take the form of the magical helper(s) or donor(s), while those who witness the murder or find the corpse are the dispatchers. The princess is each female persona who, at any one time, is romantically involved with the detective, while the false heroes are the characters who eventually turn out to have committed crime(s), characters probably known to us readers from the start. For instance, as I argue in Gregoriou (2007a), in the context of Connelly's *Angels Flight* (1999), the real murderer of a 12-year-old girl turns out to be her father who has been sexually abusing her, while Bosch's fellow police officers appear to have tortured the girl's wrongly suspected rapist and murderer when he was in their custody. Similarly, in *The Concrete Blonde* (1995), Mora, Bosch's fellow police officer who specialises in the porn industry, turns out to be a perverted man who is in fact involved in child pornography. Such characters could easily be classified as false heroes.

It can be interesting to see how powerful the narrative structures of folk mythology are, and how they are continually reinserted into modern popular culture. How applicable are dramatic persona categories to American television series such as *Buffy the Vampire Slayer, Angel* and *Charmed*?

See Chapter 6, Task R

5.4 Emmott's frame theory

Emmott's (1997) theory of narrative comprehension provides yet another analytical framework that hypothesises about the mental stores and inferences that are necessary to create and keep track of contexts and characters when reading a narrative text. According to Emmott's model, the reader turns any situation encountered into a contextual frame which restricts (that is, 'frames') their expectations and mental representation of the circumstances containing the current content. The reader then accordingly monitors the group of characters in particular places, times and circumstances.

Emmott distinguishes between two sorts of information about characters and scenes, which she describes as 'episodic' and 'non-episodic'. Episodic information is likely to change in the course of the narrative, and proves immediately relevant. What a detective understands or knows about the case (s)he investigates is, at any one point, episodic. Non-episodic information is not immediately relevant, and is likely to remain unchanged. Background information to do with where each victim was born and raised, for instance, is unlikely to be thought of as hugely relevant to the solving of a case. Note, however, that the effectiveness of much crime fiction lies in readers classifying episodic information as non-episodic. We might be misled into considering important information relating to certain characters as initially irrelevant, only to later find out that it functioned as a clue that we might have noticed. Whether episodic or non-episodic, the information is still meant to make its way into what Emmott calls the 'central directory', a term referring collectively to all of the information readers get, allowing them to re-track processing of the clues at a later time.

Emmott argues that there are various ways in which we can monitor a contextual frame, and these fall under the categories of 'binding', 'priming' and 'overtness'. Characters can be bound in a 'room' frame if, for instance, they enter the room, are born, wake up or somehow otherwise gain consciousness in it, while they can be bound out of a 'room' frame by leaving the room, falling asleep, collapsing or even dying in the room. When a frame moves into primary focus, it is said to be primed, yet where the reader's attention is taken elsewhere, the given frame is said to be unprimed. When, in reading a story, we move from say, the kitchen to the living room, the kitchen frame gets unprimed while the living room frame gets primed. Textually overt characters are those actually mentioned, bound and primed, whereas textually covert characters are those not directly mentioned yet still bound and primed into scenes. If the character John moves from the kitchen to the living room frame with us, and then we are told that 'Clare is watching television in the living room', at that point Clare gets overted and bound into the now-primed living room, while John, now bound out of the kitchen frame and bound into the living-room frame, gets coverted.

Any changes in terms of frames' binding, priming or overtness are described as modifications. Frame switches refer to moves from one frame to another, while frame recalls refer to the return to a previously primed frame; 'Where a frame switch occurs over a short or parallel period of time, the unprimed frame is potentially available for frame recall' (Stockwell, 2002: 157). To stay with the same example, when we have switched to the living room where Clare watches television, the unprimed kitchen frame is still available for us to recall. In other words, as readers, we are capable of keeping track of who is where doing what, regardless of where we ourselves 'are' at any given point. Frame switches and recalls can either be instantaneous or progressive. Fleeting frame switches into such things as thoughts or passing memories are said to constitute frame mixes instead. What characters believe to be true about the nature of frames instead forms part of their 'belief frames', while 'enactors' refers to different versions of the same character evident in the narrative.

The 1998 film *Sliding Doors*, directed by Peter Howitt and starring Gwyneth Paltrow, could be used to illustrate these concepts. In the film, the character of Helen is undervalued in her job while, unknown to her, her boyfriend is cheating on her. One day, she tries to catch a train on her way back from work, at which point the whole of the narrative, and in turn her character, splits in two.

In one version, she catches the train only to return home and find her boyfriend in bed with his mistress. Helen and her boyfriend break up, but with the support of her friends, Helen rebuilds her life and becomes quite successful in her new career in PR. She even falls in love with a new man, James, only for her to die in a tragic accident at the story's end. In the second version of the narrative, Helen does not catch the train, and returns home after the mistress is gone. Her life becomes very complicated as she tries to hold down two jobs, and she does not find out about her boyfriend's cheating until the very end. It is then that she again meets James, and the two narratives eventually merge to some extent into one.

The film portrays two enactors of Helen, each of them sharing different belief frames pretty much throughout the two narratives. In the first narrative, Helen knows about her boyfriend's cheating, whereas in the second she does not. Frame switching takes place throughout the film, allowing readers to keep track of each of the two parallel narratives. While the viewers attend to one narrative, the other remains available for recall.

Similarly, we have different enactors of both protagonists in the 2004 feature film *Eternal Sunshine of the Spotless Mind*, directed by Michel Gondry. Here, the two main characters keep meeting up and falling in love, although they both go to extreme measures to physically erase memories of each other, over and over again. Viewers need to keep track of the changing belief frames of the various enactors for the film to make sense.

Emmott (1997: 225) uses the term 'frame repair' to refer to instances where 'a reader becomes aware that they have misread the text either through lack of attention or because the text itself is potentially ambiguous'. What the reader faces is therefore a 'miscuing' of the signals needed in order to understand the episodic information offered (Emmott 1997: 160). As Emmott suggests, such repairs force readers not only to replace the erroneous frame when they discover the problem, but to also reread or reinterpret the text with the correct frame from the point at which the switch should have taken place. This process has also been referred to as 'schema refreshing' (see Semino, 1997; Cook, 1994). If the reader/viewer has deliberately been misled over a long stretch of text, the repair could instead be classified as major and hence more of a 'frame replacement'. Emmott draws on detective fiction extracts herself, to stress that this function does in fact appear with extreme formulaic regularity in this specific genre.

Such repairs and replacements often take place in films. In the 1999 film *Sixth Sense*, directed by M. Night Shyamalan, the child psychologist Crowe is trying to cure a young boy who has the unfortunate gift of seeing dead people (who do not know they are dead). He spends a lot of time with the boy, despite his wife's annoyance. The viewers do not learn (for certain, though some might guess earlier) that Crowe has been dead all along until the film's very end, at which point this new-found knowledge of the character as a ghost constitutes more of a frame replacement, forcing us readers to (whether literally or not) re-watch the film to correct the frame from the point at which the switch should have taken place. The film, in fact, helps us in doing so, by re-showing in quick sequence all the frames that essentially the viewers would need to adjust in order for the narrative to be correctly restored.

Similarly, the 1997 film *The Fifth Element*, directed by Luc Besson, features such a repair or replacement at the end, where we find out that the man in the recurrent dream and memory of the young Korben Dallas (played by the actor Bruce Willis) is none other than the adult Korben Dallas. Frame replacement enables us to restore the narrative at this point, as well as thereafter keep track of the varying Korben enactors being bound into the same frame.

Watch the 2005 film *Derailed*, directed by Mikael Hafstrom. Can you use frame theory to spot and explain the multiple plot reversals here?

See Chapter 6, Tasks S and T

5.5 Chapter review

In this chapter, we outlined possible world theory terminology, and related it to Werth's text world theory. These are both models that try to account for story processing in relation to various sorts of 'worlds'. Employing such analysis of reading comprehension helps literary text analysts to explain ambiguity and multiplicity of meaning, not to mention overall text complexity and its relevant processing difficulty. We then outlined schema theory, which relates to and accounts for different readings of the same text. Labov and Propp offered models for the analysis of story-telling, accounting for the type of characters evident, the nature and ordering of various functions and elements, and the prototypicality of certain story types. Emmott's frame theory offered us yet another analytical framework for keeping track of characters' whereabouts and beliefs, along with the readers'/viewers' knowledge change in the course of plot development.

Chapter 6 offers practice in the stylistics of prose. Chapters 7 and 8 are concerned with the stylistics of dramatic texts. In Chapter 7, I start by considering the structure of dramatic (and everyday) conversation, along with the text/production/performance distinction, before outlining characterisation distinctions relevant to the analysis of such texts.

6 Stylistics of Prose Practice

Task A

Consider the generic parameters of a detective/crime story. Do such stories' plot and discourse coincide? What is the effect of this convention? Also, how does Brémond's narrative cycle apply to the reading of a crime novel?

Comments on Task A

Moretti has argued that detective fiction is a genre that is not only distinct from novelistic works but, even more so, is 'anti-novelistic' or 'anti-literary':

> the aim of the narration is no longer the character's development into autonomy, or a change from the initial situation, or the presentation of plot as a conflict and an evolutionary spiral, image of a developing world that it is difficult to draw to a close.

> (Moretti, 1983: 137)

Moretti here points out that, contrary to his so-called 'aim of narration',[1] detective fiction's objective is to 'return to the beginning', as the individual initiates the narration not because he lives – but because he dies. He goes on to add that detective fiction's ending is its end indeed – its solution in the true sense – and further states that, in the terms of the Russian Formalists, it is the criminal that produces the sjužet whereas the detective provides the fabula (Moretti, 1983: 146). Whereas the former term, attributed to the criminal, refers to the story as shaped and edited by the story-teller, the latter, attributed to the detective, refers to the story as a mere chronology of events. Besides, it is the detective who reinstates the relationship between the clues and their meaning, who comes to reconstruct events so as to bring us back to the very beginning of the story. Moretti further argues that the criminal embodies the literary pole, and the detective the scientific.

The plot of crime stories usually does not coincide with the discourse, and the effect of this generic convention is important. The pleasure of reading prototypical crime fiction (where the actual discourse starts post-death) depends on being unfamiliar with the actual plot throughout; knowing all of what has happened in chronological order would eliminate the element of surprise. This pleasure of delayed recognition at the end is in fact where the largest attraction of the genre lies.

As I argue in Gregoriou (2007a), in the reading of a crime novel specifically, the initial satisfactory state is interrupted by a state of deficiency whereby an event of murder takes place. Such narratives go through at least one cycle, where the state of content-ness is reinstated by the resolution; the murderer is discovered and brought to justice. It is therefore the enigma of 'who did it?' that forms a structuring force. The readers are invited, therefore, to organise the text in light of this question, so that they are eventually able to answer it by the time they reach the novel's end.

Task B

How would you apply these concepts to Tolkien's [1968] (1991) *The Lord of the Rings*? Is Brémond's narrative cycle applicable here? Is there a difference between the story's plot and discourse?

Comments on Task B

In reading this trilogy, we notice that the story goes through two major cycles (or, we could argue, one major circle with a number of embedded ones). What is perhaps unusual about this story is that its main character, the young hobbit Frodo, wants to destroy something, unlike many stories where the main character wants to get hold of something/someone. Although there are a number of minor stories, here is one way of outlining the overall two-cycle storyline:

Equilibrium: At the story's very start, Frodo faces no problems. In fact, the setting of the first scene is a pleasant village birthday party.

Disequilibrium: In order for Frodo to save the world from the dark Lord Sauron, he must return the mythical ring (a kind of wedding ring between world and evil) to Mount Doom, where it was forged.

Equilibrium: Frodo forms a coalition with races of Middle Earth (elves, dwarves, other hobbits and so on) to help him battle the armies of Sauron.

Disequilibrium: Their journey south forces the fellowship to split, some characters get lost and some are killed.

Equilibrium: They eventually succeed and the ring is destroyed. They all return home, some get married and some retire.

Even though the overall *Lord of the Rings* story is given in chronological order, it begins with several events that take place in Tolkien's other works (*The Hobbit*, 1974, and The *Silmarillion*, 1977), and it therefore somewhat assumes knowledge of the author's larger fictional world of Middle Earth. Hence, the *Lord* discourse proves disruptive of the possible chronological ordering of events, in encompassing stories that are interdependent, interrelated and consistent to this fictional context (much like the work of the Greek Homer), but not ones that are narratively given in their chronologically natural order. The first book in the trilogy, *The Fellowship of the Ring*, in fact opens with a party hosted by Bilbo, a hobbit who also centrally features in *The Hobbit*.

Also, in the second book of the trilogy, once the Fellowship group is separated, we move from one subgroup to another, attending to a series of events that happen simultaneously. In fact, in *The Two Towers* the first and second parts take place at the same time, which is where the discourse and plot structure stop coinciding. In the first part, the ring-bearers Merry and Pippin are captured by orcs, while the remaining members of the fellowship go to their rescue. In the second part, we join Frodo and his servant Sam who, at the same time, make their way to Mordor to destroy the ring once and for all.

Task C

Who is the implied reader of the advert whose text is reproduced below?

Forget agony aunts, your mother and your best friend. We'll work day and night to get you a man.

(a magazine advert for a cream for facial blemishes)

Comments on Task C

The language of the advert is indicative of a most probably female heterosexual audience who share an interest in 'getting a man' but currently do not have one. The reference to the mother and the best friend is also indicative of the audience being young, most likely teenagers. The text additionally presupposes that the reader (a) has spots, (b) wants to treat spots, (c) has problems finding a boyfriend, (d) has made a connection between their spotty face and their lack of a boyfriend, and (e) has tried to or has thought about solving their problem by speaking to their mother and best friend, and by writing to or reading agony aunts' columns. The implied reader is basically one who would accept and react favourably to this positioning rather than resist it.

Task D

Identify the real author, real reader, implied author, implied reader, narrator and narratee of this extract from Jim Thompson's *The Killer Inside Me* [1952] (2002):

> So, on a Saturday night, April 5th, 1952, at a few minutes before nine o' clock, I ...
> But I guess there's another thing or two to tell you first, and – but I will tell you about it. I want to tell you, and I will, exactly how it happened. I won't leave you to figure things out for yourself.
> In lots of books I read, the writer seems to go haywire every time he reaches a high point. He'll start leaving out punctuation and running his words together and babble about stars flashing and sinking into a deep dreamless sea. And you'll figure out whether the hero's (sic) laying his girl or a cornerstone. I guess that kind of crap is supposed to be pretty deep stuff – a lot of the book reviewers eat it up, I notice. But the way I see it is, the writer is just too goddam (sic) lazy to do his job. And I'm not lazy, whatever else I am. I'll tell you everything.
> But I want to get everything in the right order.
> I want you to understand how it was.
>
> (Thompson, 2002: 161)

Comments on Task D

The extract above is in the form of first-person narration (the narrator is a character in his own story), though it also engages in second-person address to the reader and also features third-person pronouns. The non-standardness of the narration is deliberate, to add to the effect of vividness. The real author is Thompson, and the real readers are you and me. The implied author expresses certain views about writers who choose to 'go haywire' every time their stories reach a narrative peak. This same implied author considers such writers to be lazy, their writing to be unworthy ('that kind of crap'), and some book reviewers easily manipulated by these same lazy writers. Note that the views of the real author, Thompson, do not necessarily match the views of the implied author, though they indeed might.

The first person narrator-protagonist is the character Lou, who is about to tell us his own story of having murdered a woman. The second-person declarations ('And you'll figure out ...' and 'I'll tell you everything') and instances of negation ('I won't leave you to figure things out ...' and 'I'm not lazy') presuppose that the implied reader has certain capabilities and expectations. This implied reader is meant to be capable of working out certain things that are left unsaid, and actually wants the teller to tell them everything. The presuppositions embedded in the negative statements give us further information about the implied reader and narratee, personas who would assume that the actual narrator could possibly leave many things unsaid in laziness, and who would stall at the narrative peak for effect. The narratee or implied reader, therefore, is presented here as having made a number of assumptions about the narrator and murderer. Note that the implied reader's views need not match the real reader's views. Having said that, this type of narration manipulates the real readers into converting to views they do not actually have, even if that is only for the duration of the story. In other words, for the purposes of this particular story, you and I are likely to take the implied reader's position and accept, for instance, that the said manipulative and lazy writers indeed exist, for us to make sense of the story we are presented with here.

Task E

Identify the linguistic indicators of spatio-temporal, psychological and ideological perspective in the extract below from James Patterson's *Cat and Mouse*. We here get access to criminal Gary Soneji's perspective, when he is getting ready to shoot detective Alex Cross while the latter is picking up his children from school.

> *Alex Cross is a dead man. Failure isn't an option.*
> Gary Soneji squinted through a telescopic sight he'd removed from a Browning automatic rifle. The scope was a rare beauty. He watched the oh-so-touching affair of the heart. He saw Alex Cross drop off his two brats and then chat with his pretty lady friend in front of the Sojourner Truth School.
> *Think the unthinkable*, he prodded himself.
> Soneji ground his front teeth as he scrunched low in the front seat of a black Jeep Cherokee. He watched Damon and Janelle scamper into the schoolyard, where they greeted their playmates with high and low fives. Years before he'd almost become famous for kidnapping two school brats right here in Washington. Those were the days, my friend! Those were the days.

For a while he'd been the dark star of television and newspapers all over the country. Now it was going to happen again. He was sure that it was. After all, it was only fair that he be recognised as the best.

He let the aiming post of the rifle sight gently come to rest on Christine Johnson's forehead. *There, there, isn't that nice.*

(Patterson, 1997: 18–19)

Comments on Task E

We are here placed in Soneji's shoes, watching the family through the killer's telescopic sight, letting the sight 'come to rest' pointed at the head of one of his victims. Here, the aiming post of the rifle sight takes on a life of its own as personified; it is 'allowed' to 'come to rest' on a potential victim's forehead. It is presented as an animate entity, taking responsibility of the crime away from Soneji.

The character's spatio-temporal perspective is communicated through this viewing position, in terms of both time ('Now it was going to happen again.', 'Those were the days') and place ('He saw Alex Cross drop off his two brats ... in front of the Sojourner Truth School', 'right here in Washington').

His ideological perspective is communicated through his description of the scope as 'a rare beauty', the family as an 'oh-so-touching affair of the heart', the children as 'the two brats' and Cross's girlfriend as 'his pretty lady friend', all of which communicate irony and hatred.

His psychological perspective is communicated through his diverting thoughts, distracting him from the task at hand. It is certainly this character's consciousness that is mediated, as only an omniscient narrator would have access to his perceptions ('Gary Soneji squinted through a telescopic sight', 'He watched'. 'He saw'), thoughts ('*Think the unthinkable*, he prodded himself', 'Those were the days, my friend! Those were the days', '*There, there, isn't that nice*'), memories and flashbacks ('Years before he'd almost become famous for kidnapping two school brats right here in Washington', 'For a while he'd been the dark star of television and newspapers all over the country'), feelings ('He was sure that it was') and reactions ('After all, it was only fair that he be recognised as the best').

Task F

What sort of modality is linguistically expressed in the ad slogans below?

1 'A whole lot can happen, Out of the Blue.' (Labatt Blue beer)
2 'Life is harsh. Your tequila shouldn't be.' (Sauza tequila)

3 'Carlsberg – probably the best beer in the world.'
4 'Guinness. Good things come to those who wait.'
5 'Everything you always wanted in a beer. And less.' (Miller Beer Lite)
6 'Clearly it's going to Entice.' (Nestle/Peters Entice ice cream tub)
7 'Any food tastes supreme with Heinz salad cream.'

Comments on Task F

1 The Labatt Blue beer advert expresses epistemic modality, through 'can'. The advertisers communicate that the beer will possibly enable things to 'happen', and could be thought of as a requirement for things to happen. There is a pun on the word 'blue'. The idiomatic expression 'out of the blue' (meaning 'all of a sudden') is here literalised – the meaning of the figurative expression is composed out of the meaning of the individual words it consists of. The expression means both 'all of a sudden' and 'out of drinking our beer brand'. Of course, the reference to 'the blue' also alludes to depression, so the slogan could be interpreted as suggesting that this beer would bring the drinkers out of 'the blue' and so make them cheerful.

2 The Sauza tequila slogan expresses obligation and requirement through the deontic 'shouldn't'. It reinforces the idea that tequila is not (as it should not be) as harsh as life, again literalising 'harsh' which, in the 'life is harsh' sentence, was used metaphorically.

3 The Carlsberg advert employs epistemic modality, as a certain degree of commitment to the proposition is expressed through 'probably'. The advertisers establish a connection between the brand and a quality regardless of the uncertainty communicated here. Though the advertisers are not in a position to communicate absolute certainty that this beer is the best of all beers, they nevertheless succeed in creating a relationship between the brand name and the highest quality.

4 The Guinness advert instead communicates a strong statement and is epistemically non-modal. Note, however, that the certainty in the said conviction is communicated through the reader's extra-textual knowledge. The audience needs to know that it takes longer to pull a draught Guinness than it does to pull any other beer. We are not directly told that Guinness is a 'good thing', but are invited to bring this knowledge in ourselves, solely through our familiarity with the relevant saying.

5 The Miller Lite beer advert expresses boulomaic modality through the use of 'wanted'. The advertisers here presume to know what anyone would want from a beer, and commit themselves to offering it all. At the same time, as Miller Lite is a low-calorie beer, they claim that it does not contain as many calories as other beers do, and in that sense, 'giving you less that what you would get from a beer' is communicated as an equally favourable quality.

6 and 7   The Entice ice-cream advert draws on epistemic and perception modality, as it communicates a strong degree of commitment to the truth of the proposition, which here depends on the reference made to visual human perception ('Clearly'). Also, there is a play on 'entice' which is a word that forms part of the brand name as well as means 'attract'. Similarly, the Heinz salad cream advert communicates certainty through the perception of taste (compare 'any food *tastes* supreme' with 'any food *is* supreme').

Task G

Using Simpson's modal grammar of point of view, how would you classify the passage below?

The fat one, the Radish Torez, he calls me Camel because I am Persian and because I can bear this August sun longer than the Chinese and the Panamanians and even the little Vietnamese, Tran. He works very quickly without rest, but when Torez stops the orange highway truck in front of the crew, Tran hurries for his paper cup of water with the rest of them. This heat is no good for work. All morning we have walked this highway between Sausalito and the Golden Gate Park. We carry our small trash harpoons and we drag our burlap bags and we are dressed in vests the same color as the highway truck. Some of the Panamanians remove their shirts and leave them hanging from their back pockets like oil rags, but Torez says something to them in their mother tongue and he makes them wear the vests over their bare backs. We are on a small hill. Between the tress I can see out over Sausalito to the bay where there are no clouds so thick I cannot see the other side where I live with my family in Berkeley, my wife and son. But here there is no fog, only sun on your head and back, and the smell of everything under the nose: the dry grass and dirt; the cigarette smoke of the Chinese; the hot metal and exhaust of the passing automobiles. I am sweating under my shirt and vest. I have fifty-six years and no hair. I must buy a hat.

(Dubus, 2000: 15)

Comments on Task G

The extract from *House of Sand and Fog* takes the form of first person narration, hence is classifiable as Category A. It features positive shading, as the narrator's opinions ('This heat is no good for work'), reactions ('I am sweating under my shirt and vest') and perceptions ('<u>I can see</u> out over Saulito to the bay', '<u>I cannot</u>

see the other side') are foregrounded. Some deontic modality is evident ('I <u>must</u> buy a hat', 'he <u>makes them</u> wear the vests over their bare backs'), as is some ability ('because <u>I can bear</u> the August sun longer'). Such narratives, Simpson (1993: 56) says, are rich in evaluative adjectives ('this heat is <u>no good</u>', 'the <u>dry</u> grass', 'the <u>hot</u> metal') and 'verba sentiendi', meaning words denoting thoughts, feelings and perceptions ('<u>I am sweating</u>').

Task H

Analyse the prologue below from James Patterson's *Along Came a Spider* (1993). The scene is set in 1932. We share the perspective of the Lindbergh baby kidnapper as he is about to kill for the very first time. How is his criminal mind style linguistically constructed here? In analysing this, also identify indicators of the various types of viewpoint in this same extract.

The Charles Lindbergh farmhouse glowed with bright, orangish lights. It looked like a fiery castle, especially in that gloomy, fir wooded region of Jersey. Shreds of misty fog touched the boy as he moved closer and closer to his first moment of real glory, his first kill ....

Light cast from a hallway lamp illuminated the baby's room. He could see the crib and the snoozing little prince in it. Charles Jr., 'the most famous child on earth.'

On one side, to keep away drafts, was a colorful screen with illustrations of barnyard animals.

He felt sly and cunning. 'Here comes Mr. Fox,' the boy whispered as he quietly slid open the window.

Then he took another step up the ladder and was inside the nursery at last.

Standing over the crib, he stared at the princeling. Curls of golden hair like his father's, but fat. Charles Jr. was gone to fat at only twenty months.

The boy could no longer control himself. Hot tears streamed from his eyes. His whole body began to shake, from frustration and rage—only mixed with the most incredible joy of his life.

'Well, daddy's little man. It's our time now,' he muttered to himself.

He took a tiny rubber ball with an attached elastic band from his pocket. He quickly slipped the odd-looking looped device over Charles Jr.'s head, just as the small blue eyes opened.

As the baby started to cry, the boy plopped the rubber ball right into the little drooly mouth. He reached down into the crib and took Baby Lindbergh into his arms and went swiftly back down the ladder. All according to plan.

The boy ran back across the muddy fields with the precious, struggling bundle in his arms and disappeared into the darkness.

Less than two miles from the farmhouse, he buried the spoiled-rotten Lindbergh baby – buried him alive.

That was only the start of things to come. After all, he was only a boy himself.

He, not Bruno Richard Hauptmann, was the Lindbergh baby kidnapper. He had done it all by himself.

Cool beans.

Comments on Task H

The prologue is given in the form of third person internal narration (Simpson's category B reflector mode), as we get access to the Lindbergh baby kidnapper's consciousness throughout. In terms of psychological perspective, we have access to the boy's often epistemically modalised perceptions ('It <u>looked</u> like a fiery castle', 'he <u>stared</u> at the princeling', 'He <u>could see</u> the crib'), feelings ('He <u>felt</u> sly and cunning', 'His whole body began to shake, from <u>frustration and rage</u> – only mixed with the most incredible <u>joy</u> of his life.'), thoughts ('"the most famous child on earth"') and reactions ('Then he took another step up the ladder and was inside the nursery <u>at last</u>', 'The boy <u>could no longer control</u> himself', 'Cool beans').

His spatio-temporal perspective is indicated through a number of deictic expressions related to place and time, such as demonstratives ('<u>That</u> was only the start', 'It looked like a fiery castle, especially in <u>that</u> gloomy, fir wooded region of Jersey'), adverbials and adverbs ('<u>On one side</u>, to keep away drafts', '<u>Then</u> he took another step up the ladder and was <u>inside</u> the nursery at last', 'Standing <u>over</u> the crib', 'He reached <u>down</u> into the crib and took Baby Lindbergh into his arms and went <u>swiftly back down</u> the ladder.'), and verbs of motion ('he <u>moved</u> closer and closer to his first moment of real glory', '"Here <u>comes</u> Mr. Fox"', 'the start of things to <u>come</u>'). In 'The boy ran back across the muddy fields with the precious, struggling bundle in his arms and <u>disappeared</u> into the darkness', the character moves away from the origo (the viewpoint centre) and is lost from sight, while in 'He, not Bruno Richard Hauptmann, was the Lindbergh baby kidnapper', we are informed by the social deixis who the character actually is, if only that it is someone other than the person we expected it would be.

His ideological viewpoint particularly in reference to his victim often communicates irony: 'he stared at the <u>princeling</u>', 'the boy plopped the rubber ball right into the <u>little drooly mouth</u>', 'The boy ran back across the muddy fields with <u>the precious, struggling bundle in his arms</u> and disappeared into the darkness'. The latter example additionally illustrates a metonymic mapping, as the name of the referent, 'the baby' is replaced by the name of the element that contains it – 'the bundle', therefore bringing out the impression that the baby was as insignificant to its killer as a bundle of clothes to be carried around.

According to Lakoff and Johnson (1980), in metaphor, there are two conceptual domains, and one is understood in terms of the other (for example LOVE is understood as a kind of NUTRIENT in 'I'm drunk with love', 'He's sustained by love', 'I'm starved for your affection' and so on). Creative individuals will often provide unique artistic instantiations of conceptual metaphors that partially structure our experiences. In the Patterson novels, there seem to be a number of such metaphors, which are 'sustained' (see Werth, 1999) or 'extended' (see Nowottny, 1962): that is, they work in even more extended ways across the whole of novels and give rise to related metaphors as well. As previously noted, Werth (1999: 323) refers to such sustained metaphorical undercurrents as megametaphors.

A noticeable one is the KILLERS ARE ANIMALS/INSECTS TO BE FED megametaphor, which is evident in 'Shreds of misty fog touched the boy as he moved closer and closer to his first moment of real glory, his first kill', in '"Here comes Mr. Fox," the boy whispered as he quietly slid open the window', not to mention in the novel's title, *Along Came a Spider*, itself. According to this mapping, the killer is conceived of as the hunter on the loose, while the (potential) victim is the hunted, the (potential) kill under observation. The killing is the feeding, and the anticipation of the crime is the physical reaction the animals get to the killing. To illustrate this 'anticipation', it here correlates with the character's physical and psychological reaction in 'The boy could no longer control himself. Hot tears streamed from his eyes.'

Another pattern that is found when looking into the poetics of the criminal mind is whereby idiomatic expressions are manipulated so as to bring out cruel, inhuman and violent undertones. It is in fact the case that the apparent idioms' meanings are now to be determined through an analysis of the individual meanings of the words they consist of. In a way, the idioms are literalised, or 'unidiomatized'. For instance, in this extract we are told that 'Less that two miles from the farmhouse, he buried the spoiled-rotten Lindbergh baby – *buried him alive*'. As I argue in Gregoriou (2007a), even though the boy is engaged in fantasies at this point in the novel, his choice of idiomatically describing the baby as 'spoilt-rotten' brings out vicious connotations; the baby is in fact soon expected to be literally and physically spoilt rotten.

Task I

Look at the extract below (from Nick Hornby's *A Long Way Down*) and try to determine the extent to which Short's categorisation of speech and thought presentation proves useful in justifying the effects generated.

Can I explain why I wanted to jump off the top of a tower-block? Of course I can explain why I wanted to jump off the top of a tower-block. I'm not a bloody idiot. I can explain it because it wasn't inexplicable: it was a logical decision, the product of proper thought. It wasn't even a very serious thought, either. I don't mean it was whimsical – I just meant that it wasn't terribly complicated, organised. Put it this way: say you were, I don't know, an assistant bank manager, in Guildford. And you'd been thinking of emigrating, and then you were offered the job of managing a bank in Sydney. Well, even though it's a pretty straightforward decision, you'd still have to think about it, wouldn't you? You'd at least have to work out whether you could bear to move, whether you could leave your friends and colleagues behind, whether you could uproot your wife and kids. You might sit down with a bit of paper and draw up a list of pros and cons. You know:

> CONS – aged parents, friends, golf clubs
> PROS – more money, better quality of life (house with pool, barbecue, etc.), sea, sunshine, no left-wing councils banning 'Baa-Baa Black Sheep', no EEC directives banning British sausages etc.

It's no contest, is it? The golf club! Give me a break. Obviously your aging parents give you a pause for thought, but that's all it is – a pause, a brief one, too. You'd be on the phone to the travel agents within five minutes.

(Hornby, 2005: 3)

Comments on Task I

The extract takes the form of first-person narration. It starts with an elliptical address to the reader ('Can I explain [to you, the reader] why I wanted to jump off the top of a tower-block?'). After a series of narrative-like sentences, the character-narrator (Martin) gives us the NRTA ('It was a logical decision, the product of proper thought. It wasn't even a very serious thought, either'). Here, the reader is being told that thought took place, along with some indication of the nature of the thought. We do not, however, have much indication about the actual content of these thoughts at this stage.

From then on, we have the narrator constructing a hypothetical scenario, where the reader (in the form of second-person narration[2]) is instructed to take on the role of an assistant manager who is 'offered a job in Sydney'. The 'you'd been thinking of emigrating' is yet another NRTA instance, whereas the hypothetical job offer would be classifiable as a NRSA, as the speech act verb 'offer' is in use, as is some indication as to the nature of the discussion (about 'a job in Sydney'). The 'you'd still have to think for a bit wouldn't you?' direct reader address again is classifiable as NRTA, as is 'You'd have to work out whether you could bear to move ... uproot your wife and kids'.

What follows is a series of what Short (2004) refers to as writing presentation[3] instances. 'You might sit down with a bit of paper and draw up a list of pros and cons' is classifiable as hypothetical NRWA (narrator's representation of writing act), while the paragraph that follows (containing the actual Cons and Pros list) is actually an instance of hypothetical free direct writing presentation.

From then on, the narrator again addresses the reader directly in a very conversational and ironic tone, anticipating the reader's responses and reacting to them accordingly: 'It's no contest. Is it? The golf club! Give me a break!' Another hypothetical NRTA follows ('your aged parents give you pause for thought'), followed by some hypothetical narration ('you'd be on the phone to the travel agents within ten minutes').

Though a very useful starting point indeed, Short's categorisation proves problematic when it comes to hypothetical constructs in narration, especially those which embed all three presentation types (speech, thought, as well as writing), not to mention second-person narration itself.

Task J

How would you apply possible world theory to Tolkien's [1968] (1991) *The Lord of the Rings?*

Comments on Task J

The Lord of the Rings deals with fantasy, a fantasy perhaps completely unexpected and entirely unpredictable at least by readers unfamiliar with the genre or the author's work. Shippey (2000) even argues that the continuing appeal of this trilogy lies partly in the mere charm of the strangeness of this richly populated and densely textured fictional world of Middle Earth. In other words, alien existence (dwarfs, elves, hobbits and magic) occurs alongside human existence in Tolkien's fictional world in conflict with the readers' knowledge or epistemic worlds where alien existence essentially does not. Possible world conflicts can be found not only in contrast with the textual universe, but also within it.

At the start of the major storyline, we have a conflict between the text actual world that contains the ring in the possession of the hobbits, and Frodo's intention world where the ring is to be forever destroyed. Note that Gollum's intention world is in conflict with Frodo's intention world throughout: Gollum wants to regain possession of the ring that Frodo wants destroyed.

Another conflict arises where Frodo believes that Gandalf the Grey is gone for ever. Here, Frodo's knowledge world contains Gandalf's death whereas the now reborn white wizard is alive and well in the context of the textual actual world. When in battle, the fellowship's lives are in danger and therefore conflicts arise between the text actual world which contains the enemies, and the fellowship's intention and wish worlds that no longer do. A further conflict arises where Frodo's wish world of not wanting to go on with the battle of the ring is in conflict with his moral commitment or obligation world where he knows he simply has to. We also have an additional conflict between Frodo's dream/fantasy world (in entering the world of the ring by wearing it) and the text actual world which contains rather different phenomena and entities.

Note that this analysis is by no means exhaustive; the possible world conflicts within this trilogy are certainly numerous.

Task K

How would you apply possible world theory to the traditional Grimm Brothers' *Little Red Riding Hood* fairy tale (1857)?[4]

Comments on Task K

To start with, we have a conflict between the text actual world which contains talking, cunning and human-eating wolves, and our real world which obviously does not. Our real world also does not allow people to survive having been devoured by beastly animals, or animals to survive having had their stomach filled with large stones. The fictional actual world of this fairy tale, however, allows both of these possibilities.

At the start of the narrative, we have a contrast between the text actual world where the grandmother is sick, and Little Red Riding Hood's intention world to help her recover by taking her food and drink. The mother of the girl advises her not to stray from the required path through the forest to the grandmother's house, not to break the bottle she carries, and to be polite and diligent on arrival, therefore setting an obligation world she is to stick to. On encountering the wolf, the girl is blissfully unaware of the danger he poses, therefore a conflict is formed between the girl's knowledge world and that of the wolf. The wolf wanting to eat the girl forms yet another conflict between his intention and the relevant text actual world where the girl is as yet uneaten. To distract her, the wolf points out the beauty of her surroundings, encouraging Little Red Riding Hood to go against her mother's wishes and stray from her path to collect some flowers for her grandmother. This decision forms another contrast between the girl's obligation world where she ought not to stray from the path, and the text actual world where she does indeed do so. This, of course, gives the wolf the opportunity he needs to reach the grandmother's house before the girl does.

The wolf takes on the identity of the girl for the grandmother to let him in. Another conflict is here formed between the grandmother's knowledge world, where she believes that she is letting in her granddaughter, and the text actual world, where she instead is letting in a dangerous wolf. Little Red Riding Hood eventually makes her way to the grandmother's house only to find what she believes to be her grandmother in bed with the curtains drawn. Another contrast is here formed, since the girl believes she is looking at her grand-mother as opposed to the disguised wolf. We here therefore have a contrast between the girl's knowledge world where the grandmother is alive and well and talking to her, and the text actual world where the grandmother has been eaten by the wolf to whom the girl is talking. The conversation the two have is interrupted by the wolf eating Little Red Riding Hood as well.

In this version of the story, particularly favoured by parents, the contented wolf falls asleep only to have his snoring attract a passing huntsman who enters the house to find the wolf in bed. Realising that the wolf must have eaten the grandmother, he rescues the two females by cutting the wolf's stom-ach open with a pair of scissors. His expectation world contains him saving the old woman, in conflict with the text actual world where he saves both her and her granddaughter. The wolf's stomach is then filled with large stones. When the wolf wakes up and tries to run away, the weight of the stones causes him to fall down at once and die. The wolf's intention world of running away is there-fore in contrast with the text actual world where he does not succeed in doing so. All three humans are satisfied with the result, and Little Red Riding Hood decides never to stray from her path again, and to therefore not ever deviate from the obligation world her mother prescribes.

Task L

Undertake a text world analysis of the opening extract below from Lionel Shriver's *We Need to Talk about Kevin*:

November 8, 2000

Dear Franklin,

I'm unsure why one trifling incident this afternoon has moved me to write to you. But since we've been separated, I may most miss coming home to deliver the narrative curiosities of my day, the way a cat might lay mice at your feet: the small, humble offerings that couples proffer after foraging in separate backyards. Were you still installed in my kitchen, slathering crunchy butter on Branola though it was almost time for dinner, I'd no sooner have put down my bags, one leaking a clear viscous drool, than this little story would come tumbling out, even before I chided that we're having pasta tonight so would you please not eat that whole sandwich.

In the early days, of course, my tales were exotic imports, from Lisbon, from Katmandu. But no one wants to hear stories from abroad, really, and I could detect from your telltale politeness that you privately preferred anecdotal trinkets from close to home: an eccentric encounter with a toll collector on the George Washington Bridge, say. Marvels from the mundane helped to ratify your view that all my foreign travel was a kind of cheating. My souvenirs – a packet of slightly stale Belgian waffles, the British expression of 'piffle' (*codswallop!*) – were artificially imbued with magic by mere dint of distance. Like those baubles the Japanese exchange – in a box in a bag, in a box in a bag – the sheen on my offerings from far afield was all packaging. What a more considerable achievement, to root around in the untransubstantiated rubbish of plain old New York state and scrounge a moment of piquancy from a trip to the Nyack Grand Union.

(Shriver, 2005)

Comments on Task L

The extract takes the form of a letter, and it is therefore written in the first person. The whole of the text thus starts from what appears to be a sub-world. The first-person narrator and Franklin appear to have separated, the two being the primary characters of the storyline, although we later find out that Franklin is dead, having been killed by the couple's own and only son. Although other characters are mentioned (the cat, other couples, the toll collector), as are some objects (the bags, the sandwich, the souvenirs), they do not physically feature in the narrative events, but only within the context of the narrator's imagination.

Another thing to note about this opening is that it is difficult to establish the temporal and spatial boundaries of the text world. We have some indication of time in that the letter is dated 'November 8, 2000' and reads 'this afternoon', although the events described are essentially either hypothetical constructs or memories fused with modalised propositions. It is for this reason that we have difficulty setting a space or location for the extract's primary text world (although the reference to 'home' and 'kitchen' hint that the narrator is at home when writing this).

Instead, we have a number of epistemic sub-worlds generated ('I'm unsure ...', 'I may not miss coming home', 'the way a cat may lay mice', 'Were you still installed in my kitchen' and so on), indicating that the narrator is engaging in memories blended with fantasies rather than actual memories alone. Such epistemic sub-worlds cover any remoteness or hypotheticality expressed within the text world (Gavins, 2000: 22), and there are plenty such hypotheticalities to be found here, ones that remain unrealised and so remote from the originating world.

Sub-worlds are also triggered when we get instances of each of the two characters' speech presentation. Hers is in the FDS form in 'before I chided that we're having pasta tonight so would you please not eat that whole sandwich', and so triggers a deictic sub-world. His is in the FIS form in 'Marvels from the mundane helped to ratify your view that all my foreign travel was a kind of cheating. My souvenirs ... were artificially imbued with magic by mere dint of distance', and so triggers an epistemic sub-world.[5]

A temporal alternation deictic sub-world flashback is triggered in the second paragraph, where the narrator recalls 'the early days' and her partner's reactions to her 'stories from abroad', though modalised propositions feature here also. We get epistemic sub-worlds ('I could detect') alongside attitudinal sub-worlds expressing belief ('you privately preferred ...').

Overall, not much appears to propel the story forward, but the function advancers appear to instead feature primarily arguments and hypotheses as opposed to actions, movement and actual changes of state.

Task M

What are your frame and script expectations of going to (a) a take-away restaurant, (b) an Italian trattoria and (c) the (early 21st-century) chicken specialist Nando's?

Comments on Task M

Although you are likely to activate your 'restaurant' schema in responding to this question, the three sorts of restaurants listed here would more likely warrant different sub-schemata. If you do not share a schema for any of these particular sorts of restaurants, you will not have the sorts of expectations outlined below, and are likely to witness your restaurant schema being violated in some way here.

In entering a traditional restaurant, your script expectations are likely to involve the following sequence: (a) you order on the premises, (b) you eat on the premises, (c) you pay on the premises and (d) you leave the premises. It is possible, however, to make your food order at a take-away restaurant before you arrive, over the phone, something atypical of traditional restaurants. When it comes to a take-away meal, you are expected to pay before you leave, yet not after you eat. In the case of a take-away restaurant, you are likely to hence expect the ordering (a), (c), (d), (b) instead, with (b) not taking place on the premises. When it comes to your frame expectations, you are much more likely to expect plastic cutlery, a menu on the wall rather than on paper, and certainly no waiters.

When it comes to a trattoria in Italy, you are less likely to expect a menu; you simply eat what is available on the day. In addition to your expecting no menu, the service is likely to be more casual than a traditional restaurant, and certainly the prices lower. Though the food is likely to be modest, it is bound to be plentiful, while you might expect it to be served family-style (that is, served at common tables along with the regular clientele).

At Nando's, your script expectations involve being greeted at the entrance, although you order and pay for your meal before you get served or even seated. You help yourself to cutlery, drinks and sauces off a rack. If you have been before, you are likely to be familiar with the restaurant's speciality 'peri peri' sauce. You are more than likely to order chicken to eat, since it is a restaurant specialising in chicken dishes. Your frame expectations are, finally, likely to contain quick service, seeing that it is a fast-food restaurant, along with relatively low prices.

Task N

Read the extract below from Russell Hoban's *Riddley Walker*. Then use schema theory to account for its style, structure and effects.

Walker is my name and I am the same. Riddley Walker. Walking my riddles where ever theyve took me and walking them now on this paper the same.

I dont think it makes no diffrents where you start the telling of a thing. You never know where it begun realy. No moren you know where you begun your oan self. You myt know the place and time and time of day when you ben bearht. You myt even know the place and day and time when you ben got. That dont mean nothing tho. You stil dont know where you begun.

Ive all ready wrote down about my naming day. It wernt no moren 3 days after that my dad got kilt in the digging at Widders Dump and I wer the loan of my name.

Dan and me we jus come off forage rota and back on jobbing that day. The hoal we ben working we ben on it 24 days. Which Ive never liket 12 it's a judgd men number innit and this ben 2 of them. Wed pernear cleart out down to the chalk and hevvy mucking it ben. Nothing lef in the hoal only sortit thru muck and the smel of it and some girt big rottin iron thing some kind of machine it wer you cudnt tel what it wer.

(Hoban, 1980: 8)

Comments on Task N

Hoban's book is futuristic, set in a supposedly post-holocaust south-east of England. Riddley's first person narrative also is not in Standard English, but in what looks like a broken-down version of the language. The extract therefore disrupts our world and language schemata at the same time, in that readers recognise the impossibility of a text supposedly written over 2000 years ahead of our time, along with the consistent and yet non-standard futuristic language portrayed, just one of the numerous results of the supposed catastrophic environmental damage.

Linguistically speaking, words appear to be broken down in their supposed particles (we get 'where ever' for 'wherever', 'all ready' for 'already', 'judgd men' for 'judgement'), perhaps mirroring the splitting of the atom here. We also get phonetic simplification of the voiced dental [d] to a general unvoiced [t] in indicating the past tense (we get 'kilt' for 'killed', 'liket' for 'liked', 'sortit' for 'sorted'), along with various spelling pronunciations (we get 'diffrents' for 'difference', 'realy' for 'really', 'moren' for 'more than', 'oan' for 'own' and so on), southern-imitating rhoticity, and a simplification of terminal consonant clusters ('jus' for 'just', 'lef' for 'left', 'rottin' for 'rotting').

The double negatives ('That dont mean nothing tho'), high use of conjunctions, repetition, tags ('innit') and overall non-standard grammar ('Dad and me' for 'Dad and I', 'hevvy mucking it ben' for 'it was heavy mucking') are more typical of speech than writing, while the simplified spellings are probably also meant to indicate a lack of education on the writer's part. There is also a lack of the possessive apostrophe, evident diachronic semantic change ('walking them' means 'writing them', 'naming day' probably means 'birthday', 'beartht' means 'born', and 'jobbing' means 'working'), and some unusual use of lexis (such as in 'ben got'). Overall, there is such language schema violation here, that one could argue that it could generate a schema for the language of the future. (For a more detailed analysis of the language employed in this book, see Mey, 1995.)

Task O

How would you apply schema theory to the storyline of two of your favourite novels? See below for an analysis of my two favourites: (1) Philip Kerr's *A*

Philosophical Investigation (1992) and (2) Mark Haddon's *The Curious Incident of the Dog in the Night-time* (2003).

Comments on Task O

As I argue in Gregoriou (2007a), Kerr seems to work in the background of the detective genre since the novel is concerned with the pursuit of a serial killer, something which is crime fiction schema preserving or reinforcing. Yet the novel changes our perception of the genre since it questions some of its conventions, and also incorporates a number of aspects that are consistent with the science fiction genre. The book disrupts our detective (or noir crime genre) text schemata along with our world schemata in a number of ways.

Like *Riddley Walker*, Kerr's novel is futuristic, set in 21st-century London where serial killing has reached great proportions. DNA profiling is so advanced that it is possible to identify those men who are genetically predisposed to become serial killers, 'those males whose brains lack a Ventro Medial Nucleus (VMN) which acts as an inhibitor to the Sexually Dimorphic Nucleus (SDN), a preoptic area of the male human brain which is the repository of male aggressive response' (Kerr, 1992: 42). The arguments that men are the only ones capable of serious aggression, and that aggression itself is genetically predetermined, are world schema disrupting. When dead bodies of these individuals are found, the detectives are on a hunt for the potential serial killers' serial killer.

What disrupts our detective fiction schema is the fact that the villain could alternatively be viewed as a hero, seeing that he systematically assassinates those posing a criminal threat to the world. In other words, we could argue that what we have here is a violation of that generic convention whereby in the context of the crime fiction genre, the villain is a threat to the world; Kerr's villain is, in some ways, a saviour to the world instead. Another detective schema disruption is Kerr's view of the potential killers in the novel. These killers are so named before they have committed criminal acts, as well as victimised themselves in the course of the novel.

The generic fuzziness of the novel could also be a result of the fusion of two genres: crime fiction and science fiction; the science-fiction characteristics that this crime novel exhibits do in fact contribute to the difficulty of classifying the novel in a genre category.

Generically, *The Curious Incident* is classifiable as a crime story. Chris's auto-biographical mystery novel details his detective work on a past event of murder, his exploration of the murder clues and his attempts to trace the killer, while we are surprised when we find out who it was that 'did it', all of which reinforce and preserve our crime fiction schema.

Still, the novel certainly disrupts our crime fiction schema in that the detective is a child, the victim a pet, and the book's set-up unconventional (it contains diagrams, lists, maps, pictures, and various oddly prime-numbered chapters). Also, as Walsh (2004) notes, the resolution of the murder mystery halfway through the novel involves a 'disruption of the schema for reading the whodunit, since such a resolution normally marks the point of closure. Instead, in *The Curious Incident*, it affects a shift to an identity quest schema.' In other words, unlike our expectation for the novel to end with the discovery of the killer, *The Curious Incident* does not.

Task P

To what extent is Labov's model applicable to long written narratives such as crime novels?

Comments on Task P

As noted in Gregoriou (2002a), Pratt (1977) was one of those who applied the model with caution to literary written texts, having made a number of adjustments mostly in as far as those narrative aspects dealing with the 'abstract', 'orientation' and 'coda' sections are concerned. More specifically, Pratt (1977: 60) suggested that the abstract of a novel may well be its title, in that it often gives a clue to the nature and genre of the story, and serves as a device for people referring to works and committing themselves to the reading of them. The orientation of books is sometimes set apart at the very start, though it often varies widely in both length and scope. Finally, Pratt (1977: 56) argues that novels do not need codas to signal the end of narratives 'since the end of the text visibly and palpably signals the end of the story'. Nevertheless, novels often have elaborate codas which, much like those of natural narratives, explain, revise and evaluate the story's outcome, informing us of the ultimate consequences of the narrative. (For an application of the refined model to short written stories translated from Greek, see Gregoriou, 2002a.)

In Gregoriou (2007a), I argue that crime novels lend themselves to Labovian analysis. The abstracts of crime novels may well be their titles: for example, those of Patricia Cornwell's *Body of Evidence* (1991) and *Cruel and Unusual* (1993) certainly indicate that they deal with brutal murders and the investigation into the identity of the perpetrators. Titles might also give some indication of perspective: here, that of the medical examiner, as opposed to that of a detective.

The openings of crime novels often function as reader-orientating devices, as these often give an indication of what will follow. Also, as crime novels are often part of a series, the readers are expected to be familiar with the characters and the main circumstances surrounding them. For instance, in the case of

Cornwell's Kay Scarpetta crime series, the readers are likely to know that the protagonist is a single woman and medical examiner in her forties, who has a disastrous love life, yet enjoys close personal relationships with her niece Lucy and colleague Marino. In any case, the writer often summarises this background before the story proper begins, for the benefit of those readers picking up their first Cornwell book half-way through the Scarpetta series.

The complicating action of crime novels is rendered in the form of either narration or dialogue, while summaries often remind readers of the clues and facts to keep in mind and consider. Evaluation takes place in the discussions among the detectives, villains, victims and witnesses, or in the rendering of characters' thought. The resolution takes the form of the discovery of the murderer, who is often either killed or somehow otherwise brought to justice. Evaluations are prevalent in the resolution section, while codas might take the form of detective reflection. At this point, readers are very often told what happened to the main characters after the story's result.

Task Q

In what ways and to what extent do oral narratives of personal experience differ from jokes? Can Labov's model explain the differences?

Comments on Task Q

To begin with, jokes are fictional events narrated most often in the third person, since the narrator is not a character featuring in the storyline, whereas personal narratives are most often factual and related in the first person by a participating character-narrator. Also, while a personal narrative is most usually sequentially ordered, jokes are often not sequentially ordered. In joke-telling, information is often withheld and then released at a later appropriate time, to surprise the reader into a particular reaction.

There are also differences in terms of narrative function. Oral narratives of personal experience are often related to impress, entertain, inform and create various bonds with the addressee, whereas jokes most often primarily aim to entertain in that they are expected to be humorous (though, in turn, this often serves to also create bonds with the addressee, impress and so on).

The role of the addressee also differs accordingly. Besides, McCarthy (1991: 140) argues that joint enterprise with active listeners is very common; stories are not just monologues told to a hushed audience. Listeners are, however, normally allowed to intervene solely to ask for more details (particularly in relation to the orientation), and are certainly not allowed to provide information that was not requested of them. In the case of a personal narrative, the listener is quite likely to interrupt and ask the orientating 'What time did this happen exactly?' or the complicating 'Oh My God! What did you do next?' The listener is, however, unlikely to ask for more information when attending to a joke, assuming that the information related will, in itself, be adequate to generate the relevant effects.

Let's revisit a short narrative first given in Chapter 5 (here named a), and compare and contrast it with a joke of a similar length (here named b):

a) You're never going to believe what happened to me yesterday! I went to this bar to have a quick drink after work. I was on my own, looking for some peace essentially, to wind down after a very stressful day at the office. This woman walks up to me and starts yelling at me for absolutely no reason whatsoever. 'Leave me alone,' I said. She would not go away. Eventually, the barman had to ask her to leave. I tell you, that's the last time I'm going somewhere on my own, ever again!

b. Let me tell you the worst joke ever.
   This duck walks into a bar and asks 'Got any crackers?'
   The bartender says no.
   The duck walks out. The duck walks in the next day and asks, 'Got any crackers?'
   The bartender says no. The duck walks out.
   The duck walks in the next day and asks, 'Got any crackers?'
   The bartender says, 'I told you yesterday and the day before that, no! And if you ask that one more time I'll nail your stupid beak to the bar!' The duck walks out.
   The duck comes back the next day and asks, 'Got any nails?' The bartender says no.
   The duck says, 'Good. Got any crackers?'

It is conventional to establish the activity to be performed and signal the response expected when it comes to story-telling. This prepares the ground, and transfers the participants from the real world to the story world. In the case of a joke, the abstract is most likely to directly make reference to the narrative being a 'joke' ('Let me tell you the worst joke ever') which directly triggers the relevant schema and hence expectations of the reader (in this case, the expectation 'you are supposed to be amused, but won't be'). In comparison, the abstract of the personal narrative could also indicate the sort of reaction required or expected ('You're never going to believe what happened to me yesterday!'), although this is here given in an exaggerated tone; the reader might be surprised but will not necessarily be in disbelief.

In both stories, the orientation is given at the start, setting both events in a bar. As the personal narrative is factual, a lot more orientation is given than for the joke. The listener is told when exactly the events took place ('yesterday', 'after work'), and exactly what circumstances surrounded them ('I was on my own'). Notice, however, the lack of orientation and self-interruptive evaluative elements in the joke pretty much altogether. Effectively, the joke telling does not contain much orientation or evaluation, perhaps with the exception of the bartender's speech (and reaction) at the duck's third entry into the bar.

In terms of the complicating action, both stories are given in the historic present tense, adding vividness and immediacy to the events described. Whereas the personal narrative has a lot of narration and little speech, the fictional narrative introduces a talking (and hence personified) duck walking into a bar and annoying the bartender with irrelevant and unnecessary questions (which is, in itself, I suppose, amusing).

Longacre (1983: 25) defines a narrative peak or climax as essentially 'the zone of turbulence in regard to the flow of the discourse'. According to the same source, by identifying the pre-peak and post-peak episodes (through the story-teller's stylistic choices), we can articulate a considerable amount of the narratives' surface structure, and therefore gain further access to the story-teller's ability insofar as achieving vividness and excitement is concerned.

Whereas the narrative peak of the personal narrative takes the form of narration ('The woman walks up to me and starts yelling at me ...'), we could argue that the narrative peak of the joke takes the form of direct speech ('Good. Got any crackers?'), and hence actually coincides with the joke's resolution. Essentially, the surprise-ending effect of the joke is what constitutes it as such. In contrast, the resolution of the personal narrative is rendered in indirect speech ('the barman had to ask her to leave') and takes place after the narrative peak.

Finally, whereas the coda of the personal narrative is explicitly given here, you could argue that the shock-effect of the joke is what effectively brings it to a close, rendering the need for a joke-coda unnecessary, though this could be marked by the reaction of the listener instead anyway.

Task R

Try to apply Propp's categories (dramatic personae and all 31 functions) to the story of *The Lord of the Rings* trilogy. How well does the analysis work? What does the analysis tell you about the tale?

Comments on Task R

The dramatic personae could be classified as follows.

Hero (also the seeker or victim): this could be the protagonist Frodo, Aragon (the heir of Isildur), or even the whole of the fellowship (Legolas, Sam, Merry and so on).

Villain: this is the Dark Lord Sauron or Saruman the White (the head of Gandalf's order of wizards).

Donor (from whom the hero gets some magical object): this is the elf Galandriel and/or Elrond (the master of Rivendell).

Magical helper (the character who helps the hero in the quest): although everyone is helping the Fellowship, the wizard Gandalf the Grey is the one who fits this category best.

Dispatcher (the character who makes the lack known): this could be Bilbo, Frodo's cousin and mentor, who informs Frodo of his duty to destroy the ring.

False hero (the character who takes credit for hero's actions): this is possibly Gollum, who was once Sméagol, but has since been corrupted by the ring.

Prince/princess (person the hero marries): Arwen, Elrod's beautiful daughter, and/or Sam's Rosie.

Victim (person harmed by the villain if not the hero): this could be the fighter Boromir and Gandalf the Grey, both of whom are wounded/killed by the enemy.

The functions could be classified as follows:

1   ABSENCE: Bilbo leaves the Shire.
2   INTEDICTION: Frodo is told that the ring must be destroyed. He is to take it away from the Shire.
3   VIOLATION: Sauron's power is growing.
4   RECONNAISANCE: Sauron sends his Black Rider servants to find the ring.
5   DELIVERY: Sauron knows where Frodo is when he puts on the ring at the inn.
6   FRAUD: The Riders attempt to kill the hobbits who take refuge at the inn, yet the hobbits are saved by Aragon, who advises them not to sleep in their room.
7   COMPLICITY
8   VILLAINY/ LACK: Frodo is wounded when, at the top of hill Weathertop, the company is forced to defend itself against attacking Riders.
9   MEDIATION: Frodo is wounded. Aragon and the others are worried about him.
10   BEGINNING COUNTER-ACTION: Elrod heals Frodo and then holds a meeting to decide what to do next.
11   DEPARTURE: Frodo and the fellowship head south. Their journey begins.
12   FIRST DONOR FUNCTION: the party is attacked by Balrog, a demon, and Gandalf falls.
13   HERO'S REACTION: Frodo offers Galandriel the ring.

14 PROVISION OR RECEIPT OF MAGICAL AGENT: Lady Galandriel gives the fellowship gifts.

15 SPATIAL TRANSLOCATION: Boromir confronts Frodo who sends him off, and realises the danger that the ring poses to the fellowship's sanity.

16 STRUGGLE: the Fellowship is attacked by Orcs.

17 BRANDING: Frodo leaves alone, hurt by Boromir's treachery.

18 VICTORY: the Orcs mistakenly think that Merry and Pippin are the ring-bearers and capture them.

19 LIQUIDATION: The two escape.

20 RETURN: Gandalf reappears.

21 PURSUIT: Shelob, a giant deadly spider paralyses Frodo.

22 RESCUE: Sam saves Frodo.

23 UNRECOGNISED ARRIVAL: Sam, Frodo and Gollum are captured by Faramir, only to be later released.

24 UNFOUNDED CLAIMS: Gollum, in leading Frodo and Sam up the mountain, deliberately puts them in danger.

25 DIFFICULT TASK: Frodo refuses to give up the ring, overcome by its power.

26 SOLUTION: Gollum falls in the cracks of doom with the evil ring.

27 RECOGNITION: Gandalf saves Frodo and Sam.

28 EXPOSURE: Gollum is revealed to us readers as evil.

29 TRANSFIGURATION: Frodo, wounded by the burden of the ring-quest, decides to leave the Shire and enters beautiful paradise.

30 PUNISHMENT: Darkness disperses from Gondor.

31 WEDDING: Aragon is crowned king of Gondor, while Sam marries Rosie and Aragon marries Arwen.

Although the classification of actions into Proppian functions is not necessarily straightforward and straight-fitting, with function 7 missing, the narrative nevertheless seems pretty much to follow the overall Proppian structure. Could we argue that the trilogy is at least partly successful because of its faithfulness to such a traditional storyline?

Task S

Below are extracts from my translation of Antonis Samarakis's short story 'The river' (in Samarakis, 1954). Can Brémond's narrative cycle, Labov's model and Emmott's frame theory help account for the story's style, structure and effects? I have numbered the (given) paragraphs for ease of reference.

1 The order was clear; swimming in the river was prohibited, and so was coming less than 200 metres from it. There was therefore no room for any

misapprehension. Whoever disobeyed the order would be court-martialled ...

2   It had been about three weeks since they had settled on this side of the river. On the other side of the river rested the enemy, the Others as many had called them.

3   Three weeks of inaction. This state would definitely not last long, yet for the time being stillness prevailed.

4   On both sides of the river, in great depth, lay the forest. Thick forest. It was in that forest that both sides had camped.

5   The intelligence said that the Others had two battalions there. Still, they wouldn't attempt to attack; who knew what they were planning to do. Meanwhile, the guardhouses, of both sides, were hidden in the woods here and there, prepared for all contingencies.

6   Three weeks! How have three weeks passed! They could not remember in this war, which had begun about two and a half years earlier, another break such as this one.

7   When they reached the river, it was still cold. The past few days the weather had settled. It was now spring!

8   The first who crept towards the river was a sergeant. He slipped away one morning and dived. A bit later he was dragged out by his own people, with two bullets in his side. He didn't live long ...

9   It was then that the order of the Division came out ...

10 Having reached the shore, he stood and gazed at it. The river! So that river did actually exist! There had been times when he thought it might not actually exist. That it might be a figure of their imagination, a mass delusion ...

11 In a tree, by the shore, he left his clothes, and upright against the trunk, his rifle. He quickly glimpsed around, and behind him, just in case there were any of his own people, and also peeked at the opposite shore, just in case there were any of the Others. And he entered the water.

12 From the minute his body, all stripped, entered the water – this body that had been tortured for the past two and a half years, and had been so far scarred by two bullets – from that minute on, he felt like a different person. As if a hand with a sponge ran through him and altogether erased the past two and a half years ...

13 In front of him, there was now a branch drifting along with the stream. He put his mind on reaching it with one single dive under water. And he made it. He came out of the water right next to it. He felt such joy! But at the same time, he saw a head before him, about 30 metres ahead.

14 He ceased swimming and tried to take a better look ...

15 For a few minutes, they both stood still in the waters. The silence was broken by a sneeze. It was he who sneezed, and out of habit, he swore

loudly. Then the man before him started swimming fast towards the opposite shore. However, he didn't lose any time either. He swam towards his own shore as fast as he could. He came out first. He ran towards the tree he had left his rifle against and picked it up. The Other was just coming out of the water. He was now also running for his rifle.

16 He raised his rifle and took aim. It was very easy for him to get a bullet in his head. The Other wasn't much of a mark running that way all naked, barely 20 metres ahead.

17 No, he didn't pull the trigger. The Other was there, naked, the way he had come into this world. And he was here, naked, the way he had come into this world. He couldn't pull it. They were both stripped. Two stripped men. Stripped of clothes. Stripped of names. Stripped of ethnicity. Stripped of their khaki selves.

18 He couldn't pull it. The river wasn't pulling them apart any more, it was instead uniting them.

19 He couldn't pull it. The Other had now turned into an other person now, with no capital 'o', nothing more, and nothing less.

20 He lowered his rifle. He lowered his head. And he didn't see anything until the end, but some birds which were fluttering frightened when the shot rang out from the opposite shore, and he kneeled first, and then fell head down against the ground.

Comments on Task S

Samarakis's 'The river' forms part of the short story collection *Hope Wanted*. Each of the stories is, in fact, consistent with Brémond's notion of narrative cycle, in that the opening state of deficiency is followed by a state of equilibrium, only for the story to end on a tragic note. 'The river' agrees with this pattern since it involves a hero trying to find release from war's irrationality by enjoying a cathartic swim in a river, only for him to get tragically shot at the end by an enemy soldier.

The story's title could be thought of as an abstract, in that it indicates the story's subject matter. In this case, the river refers to what separates the soldiers at this time of war, both literally and figuratively. The first few paragraphs give orientating information by making reference to characters ('they', 'the Others'), although no names are given and little overall characterisation is provided. Interestingly, the soldiers are not described; they are merely characterised by virtue of their 'khaki selves' (paragraph 17) and 'scars' (paragraph 12). We also have some references to time ('It had been about three weeks', 'this war which had begun about two and a half years ago'), place ('this side of the river') and accompanying circumstances ('swimming in the river'). In terms of complicating action, the story features a few flashbacks (that is, paragraphs 6,

7 and 8), although most events are given in chronological order. Paragraphs 6, 10, 12 and 17–19 are rather evaluative in nature (in the form of primarily free indirect discourse, where the character's and narrator's voices merge somewhat), while the resolution of paragraph 20 concludes the story with the final event rather ironically, if not metaphorically, especially in its mention of the frightened birds fluttering up above. We share the hero's perspective throughout, particularly his visual viewpoint, something also noticeable at the story's very end.

As I argue in Gregoriou (2002a: 306), since through the story's abstract-title we were allowed to move from the real world into the story world, the readers would, at some point, expect to be brought back into the real world. Nevertheless, at the point where the character dies, we get a 'narrative shot' as well as a 'content shot', since the focaliser is no longer available and so the final resolution denies us readers the possibility of uniting the story world and the real world.

Furthermore, Labov's distinction between 'external' and 'internal' evaluation is not applicable to this extract since the dead character cannot step outside the story and express his current viewpoint; at the end of the story he is dead and no longer available.

The first paragraph primes the third person narrator's river-side frame, while paragraph 2 momentarily switches to the frame of the opposite side of the river. The forest frame is primed in paragraph 4, while we get some frame mixing on paragraphs 5 and 6, with reference to what the intelligence said, and what the soldiers remembered. We have flashbacks to a chronologically earlier frame on paragraph 7, and fleeting frame switches, and hence mixes, in paragraphs 8, 9 and 10. The frame surrounding the tree is primed on paragraph 11. Events are all placed within the hero-swimming frame from then on, with a few switches to the enemy-swimming frame in paragraph 15. We then follow the hero as he returns to the tree to get hold of his rifle, an event that features some frame mixing, where the character realises that he is unable to pull the trigger, only for this hesitation to cause him to be tragically shot dead by the enemy instead.

Task T

Read the following extracts from Liam O'Flaherty's 'The sniper' (1923). Can frame theory account for the plot switch? I have numbered the (given) paragraphs for ease of reference.

1   The long June twilight faded into night. Dublin lay enveloped in darkness but for the dim light of the moon that shone through fleecy clouds, casting

a pale light as of approaching dawn over the streets and the dark waters of the Liffey. Around the beleaguered Four Courts the heavy guns roared. Here and there through the city, machine guns and rifles broke the silence of the night, spasmodically, like dogs barking on lone farms. Republicans and Free Staters were waging civil war.

2 On a rooftop near O'Connell Bridge, a Republican sniper lay watching. Beside him lay his rifle and over his shoulders was slung a pair of field glasses. His face was the face of a student, thin and ascetic, but his eyes had the cold gleam of the fanatic. They were deep and thoughtful, the eyes of a man who is used to looking at death ...

3 Crawling quickly to his feet, he peered up at the corner of the roof. His ruse had succeeded. The other sniper, seeing the cap and rifle fall, thought that he had killed his man. He was now standing before a row of chimney pots, looking across, with his head clearly silhouetted against the western sky.

4 The Republican sniper smiled and lifted his revolver above the edge of the parapet. The distance was about fifty yards – a hard shot in the dim light, and his right arm was paining him like a thousand devils. He took a steady aim. His hand trembled with eagerness. Pressing his lips together, he took a deep breath through his nostrils and fired. He was almost deafened with the report and his arm shook with the recoil.

5 Then when the smoke cleared, he peered across and uttered a cry of joy. His enemy had been hit. He was reeling over the parapet in his death agony. He struggled to keep his feet, but he was slowly falling forward as if in a dream. The rifle fell from his grasp, hit the parapet, fell over, bounded off the pole of a barber's shop beneath and then clattered on the pavement.

6 Then the dying man on the roof crumpled up and fell forward. The body turned over and over in space and hit the ground with a dull thud. Then it lay still ...

7 When the sniper reached the laneway on the street level, he felt a sudden curiosity as to the identity of the enemy sniper whom he had killed. He decided that he was a good shot, whoever he was. He wondered did he know him. Perhaps he had been in his own company before the split in the army. He decided to risk going over to have a look at him. He peered around the corner into O'Connell Street. In the upper part of the street there was heavy firing, but around here all was quiet.

8 The sniper darted across the street. A machine gun tore up the ground around him with a hail of bullets, but he escaped. He threw himself face downward beside the corpse. The machine gun stopped.

9 Then the sniper turned over the dead body and looked into his brother's face.

Comments on Task T

The story, set in the early weeks of Irish Civil War, is told in the third person, from the viewpoint of a Republican sniper. The first paragraph sets the scene on a June night after a day of battle, which here constitutes the primed frame. The machine guns are overt first, and later the snipers are overt and bound into this primed war zone frame. We have some frame modification in the second paragraph, where the Republican sniper is overt: first his face and then his eyes. The information we get in relation to the state of his face and eyes is here classified as episodic, seeing that it is probably not terribly relevant and, for the duration of the story at least, static and unchanging.

I have omitted some text between paragraphs 2 and 3 (for brevity), where the Republican sniper gets hit in the right forearm, making it impossible for him to keep using his rifle. Having treated the wound, he puts his cap on the muzzle of his weapon, tricking the opposite side's sniper into thinking that it is his head underneath the cap. The Free Stater shoots the cap, and hence believes that he has killed the Republican.

When we return to the priming of the Republican's frame in paragraph 3, readers realise that, unlike the Free Stater's belief frame, the Republican is still bound into the frame. Some frame switching and recalling takes place in the course of paragraph 3, as the two frames are modified in both priming and overtness.

In paragraphs 4 to 6, the Republican, despite his pain and the large distance, manages to shoot the Free Stater dead, and he falls into the street below and therefore is bound out of the relevant frame.

Some frame mixing takes place in paragraph 7, where the Republican experiences some remorse, wonders about the identity of the Free Stater, and decides to risk going over to have a look at the corpse. The heavy firing, so far covert, is overt and primed toward the end of paragraph 7.

Some frame modification takes place in paragraph 8, where the Republican moves toward the corpse, in which case the relevant frame becomes primed and the dead body is overted. Some frame repair or even replacement takes place in paragraph 9, where the readers, as well as the Republican sniper himself, realise that the two are brothers. What had appeared to be a pretty straightforward war narrative therefore turns out to be a tragic story of a man killing his own brother.

Structure and Characterisation in Drama

7.1 Analysing drama's discourse levels

What distinguishes drama from other literary genres is the fact that it is mostly made up of dialogue between the characters: '[C]onversation and dramatic speech share areas of commonality in being speech exchange systems, which sets them apart from poetic genres like the ode or the lyric, or narrator language in the novel' (Herman, 1995: 1). It is therefore not surprising that, when it comes to drama, 'the conversational genre' (Short, 1996), stylisticians are mostly interested in actually analysing the conversations that take place between dramatic figures.

It is worth taking the time to differentiate such character–character dialogues from the higher-order interaction that also takes place between a playwright and a reader (where the dramatic text is read), or the playwright and the audience (where the dramatic text is performed on stage). Short (1989, 1996) was one of those who made this distinction:

> Character speaks to character, and this discourse is part of what the play-wright 'tells' the audience. Any play will consist of a series of such embedded discourses, and there can even be more layers, as when one character reports to another the words of a third. But the important thing to notice is the *embedded* nature of drama, because features which, for example, mark social relations between two people at the character level become messages *about* the characters at the level of discourse which pertains between author and reader/audience.
>
> (Short, 1989: 149)

In other words, whatever it is that stylisticians choose to say about dialogues should be analysable at both the *top* playwright–audience/reader level and the *bottom* character–character level. A character lying to another, for instance, communicates one untruth at the bottom communicative level and a character trait (that is, '(s)he is liar') at the top level. Short (1996: 169) further argues that it is this 'doubled' structure that gives rise to the notion of dramatic irony, which typically occurs when the knowledge of some of the characters is less complete than that of the author and the audience at the top level, producing tension for the audience, as they wonder what will happen when that knowledge is revealed to the characters.

Of course, this *doubled* 'discourse level' analysis of drama is relevant to those dramatic texts that are straightforwardly simple, yet things get often more complicated where plays have narrators or voice-overs, where we get multiple conversations, where characters overhear the conversation of other characters, where characters relay the words of another on stage, and so on.

See Chapter 9, Task A

7.2 The form of dramatic conversation

When considering the nature of conversation in drama, it is also worth exploring to what extent real conversation approximates to dramatic dialogue. Short (1996: 174) notes that 'the main way that drama is not like conversation stems from the fact that dramatic dialogue is *written to be spoken*' (author's italics). Various normal non-fluency features are typical of everyday natural speech. Natural speech is relatively grammatically simple and informal. It often lacks clear sentence boundaries, which is why we often talk of speech *utterances* rather than sentences. Words are contracted and grammatical structures blend into each other. Speakers repeat themselves unnecessarily, abandon utterances/sentences, hesitate, and use plenty of verbal and non-verbal fillers. They monitor their speech and often use hedges to avoid committing themselves to their propositions. In natural speech, we often assume a lot of background or contextual knowledge, which is why it is often characterised by inexplicitness. Such features are common and un-interpretable in everyday conversation; due to everyday conversation's impromptu nature and the fast speed with which such speech is produced, non-fluency features inevitably occur and do not mean much. However, how would we interpret such features when encountered in dramatic conversation?

Short argues that such features are indeed *interpretable* in drama:

> Normal non-fluency does not occur in drama dialogue, precisely because that dialogue is written (even though it is written to be spoken). Moreover, if features normally associated with normal non-fluency do occur,

they are perceived by readers and audience as having a *meaningful* function precisely because we know that the dramatist must have included them *on purpose.*

(Short, 1996: 177)

In other words, when such features do occur in drama, they can certainly add a realistic flavour to the conversation, but also often actually give us information about characters and their relationship to each other. For instance, a character could be thought of as anxious if they use many verbal fillers (such as 'erm' and 'hmm', as well words such as 'like' and 'you know'), whereas someone hesitating could give the reader/audience the impression that they have something to hide. Also, changes in a character's use of non-fluency patterns could be indicative not only of their shifting state, but also of their changing relationship with others.

Figure 7.1 (overleaf) is an extract transcribed from the popular British series *The Office* (Series 1, episode 3, 'The quiz', first aired by the BBC on 23 July 2001). The scene takes place during a pub quiz, and there are four male characters (plus a non-speaking woman).

Unlike most scripted conversation, the large amount of normal non-fluency featured in this exchange gives the drama a very realistic effect. Character turns overlap, at times cooperatively (see, for instance, l. 7–9, l. 11–12), yet on other occasions competitively (see l. 30–31). There are various pauses and interruptions, not to mention much inexplicitness, particularly where the characters draw on assumed background or contextual knowledge. See, for instance, Finch's reference to Blockbusters (l. 6), 'your Dostoevsky' (l. 7) and his sexist comment on l. 10, not to mention Brent's reference to the students surrounding them in the pub as 'those lot' (l. 21).

Moreover, the characters use spoken, relaxed utterance grammar. Notice Finch's ellipted first person pronouns in l. 6, Brent's verbal filling 'innit' in l. 11, 15 and 35, and Brent's false starts in l. 17 ('all the (.) everything on the trivia board (.) all those different subjects'). The characters also use various verbal backchannelling signals which, along with laughs (as well as nonverbal nods, smiles, facial expressions and gestures) signal vocally that they are attending to each other's contributions. The verbal backchannels mostly take the form of 'yeah's (l. 5 and l. 16), 'um's (l. 18), 'well's (l. 30) and 'right's (l. 31), although the last two could also be classified as verbal filling, since they allow the contributors to maintain the turn to speak for longer.

The characters also use rather informal and taboo lexis (see respectively Finch's 'a question like that's not <u>gonna catch me out</u>' on l. 7–8, and Brent's 'I <u>bloody</u> 'ate 'im' on l. 34), contractions ('while <u>you're</u> down there', l. 10), casual terms of address ('mate' in l. 2 and 'love' in l. 10), not to mention hedges ('<u>sorry</u> exactly which books do you read every week' on l. 14), monitoring features ('(.)

BRENT:	Yeah er (.) Ricky this is Chris	1
RICKY:	hello [mate	2
FINCH:	I'm] Chris [Finch	3
RICKY:	pleased] to meet [you	4
FINCH:	yeah pleased] to meet you (.)	5
	heard about Blockbusters (.) need more than that tonight (.) heard about	6
	your Dostoevsky (.) I read a book a week (.) so a [question like that's not	7
	gonna catch me out	8
BRENT:	true]	9
	Dawn bends down and picks up her bag	
FINCH:	while you're down there love	10
BRENT:	ha ha (.) close to the bone (.) but harmless [innit	11
FINCH:	Christ give me] 'alf hour with	12
	her I'd be up to my nuts in guts	13
TIM:	sorry exactly which books do you read every week	14
BRENT:	science (.) science and nature [innit	15
FINCH:	yeah]	16
BRENT:	all the (.) everything on the trivia board (.) all those different [subjects	17
FINCH:	um]	18
BRENT:	in [books	19
FINCH:	yeah]	20
BRENT:	those lot sound like they haven't read a book between themselves	21
	[sometimes	22
FINCH:`	yeah]	23
BRENT:	college [boys	24
FINCH:	yeah] (.) bloody [students	25
BRENT:	yeah]	26
FINCH:	waste of space (.) ooh (.) I don't do anything all day but (.) ooh I need	27
	more money to do it	28
BRENT:	political	29
RICKY:	yeah (.) well (.) had a job when I was studying (.) [so	30
FINCH:	yeah (.) right] (.) and	31
	what was your job (.) professor in charge of watching Countdown every	32
	day	33
BRENT:	Ha ha ha ha (.) Clever and funny (.) I bloddy 'ate 'im (.) that's why we get	34
	on (.) I think (.) innit (.) similar	35

Figure 7.1

that's why we get on (.) I think (.) innit (.) similar' in l. 34–35) and repetition ('science (.) *science* and nature' in l. 15).

Overall, the large number of normal non-fluency features certainly gives the text a documentary-like effect, something that has certainly added to this British situational comedy's popularity in Britain as well as in America. Much like reality TV shows, the non-fluency gives the audience the impression of real events being dramatised here, although what is viewed is actually scripted drama. Nevertheless, the non-fluency is further interpretable here, particularly when it comes to the audience being informed about the nature of character relationship and characterisation.

Brent and Finch are trying very hard to impress the others. They exchange sexist comments (l. 10–13), and cooperatively build up a 'bad student' schema (l. 21–28), before directly making fun of Ricky's supposed college job (l. 31–34). In l. 7, Finch claims that he reads 'a book a week', something to which Brent agrees with on l. 9 ('true'), yet Brent's non-fluency in l. 15 and 17 indicates that he is probably lying about having such a habit. Finch's back-channelling in l. 16, 18 and 20 makes him look rather naïve, as he is probably failing to notice that Brent is dishonest. Tim's sole contribution in l. 14 is fluent, which marks him out as someone more assertive, challenging and daring, compared with Brent and Finch, who are here engaging in what appears to be cooperative, yet mindless chatter.

Finch impersonates the 'students' in l. 27–28, complaining about not having enough money and yet doing nothing all day. Ricky then challenges him, by claiming that he was indeed working when studying himself ('yeah (.) well (.) had a job when I was studying (.) so', l. 30), a contribution that is non-fluent and has many non-verbal fillers or pauses, and therefore marks his hesitation about challenging Finch at this stage. Nevertheless, Finch, oblivious to the seriousness of Ricky's comment, proceeds to make a joke of Ricky's supposed college profession. Brent laughs at the joke, but his eagerness to give too much positive feedback ('ha ha ha ha (.) Clever and funny (.) I bloody 'ate 'im (.) that's why we get on (.) I think (.) innit (.) similar' l. 34–35) coupled with the non-fluency presents him, again, in the light of someone awkward, who is simply trying too hard to gain others' acceptance.

See Chapter 9, Task B

As Short (1996: 179) further notes, dramatic conversation is indeed, in many ways, also much *like* real conversation. But what is real conversation like? Research by Sacks, Schegloff and Jefferson (1974) suggests that a complex mechanism regulates smooth turn exchange in natural speech. Consider the 'facts' for the turn-taking nature of ordinary conversation that Sacks et al proposed:

(a) Overwhelmingly, one party talks at a time
(b) Speaker change recurs
(c) Transitions between turns with no gap are common
(d) Turn order is not fixed, but varies
(e) Turn size is not fixed, but varies
(f) Length of conversation not specified in advance
(g) What parties say is not specified in advance
(h) Relative distribution of turns is not specified in advance
(i) Number of parties can vary
(j) Talk can be continuous or discontinuous
(k) Turn allocation techniques are obviously used
(l) Various mechanisms exist for dealing with turn-taking errors/ violations

(Sacks et al, 1974)

On initial inspection, these 'facts' certainly have intuitive appeal. However, it needs to be kept in mind that these generalisations for turn-taking in ordinary conversation are not necessarily universal or relevant for all cultures and all situations. As Graddol, Cheshire and Swann (1994: 173) note, this highly influential turn-taking model developed particularly in relation to conversational data from British and American English, and there are indications that it may work less well in other cultures and contexts.

This, of course, is not to say that all speakers within the same culture follow the same or similar turn-taking rules. Certain speakers may signal their readiness to relinquish their turn by slowing down or repeating themselves, whereas others might instead employ lexical, phonological or paralinguistic signs. It is important to account also for sociolinguistic or socio-cultural variation among speakers of a particular language, not to mention consider to what extent age, sex, rank as well as actual conversation topic influence turn-taking mechanisms. In the course of a board meeting among business colleagues, it is the chairperson who holds the conversational power and determines the distribution, topic and length of turns. In a job interview situation, the interviewer is the one who holds the power, and yet it is the candidate who is ultimately expected to talk the longest, even within the restrictions that the interviewer sets.

Moreover, within any one language and culture, these mechanisms differ across various activity types; some of Sacks et al's (a)–(l) points certainly are realised or favoured, but some might not even come into play. For example, a group of six academics chatting over drinks in a bar are likely to employ different turn-taking mechanisms from those used by the same six academics interacting in the course of a reading group meeting. When in a bar, it is acceptable for the large group to split into smaller groups and engage in separate discussions at the same time. The conversation topic is less likely to be predetermined, as are the conversation length, turn distribution and order. When the same individuals are interacting in the course of a reading group meeting (say, a book club), what they say is, at least to some extent, specified in advance, as are the conversation length and number of participants involved. It would certainly be unusual for the reading group to split into smaller groups and engage in minor, separate conversations, particularly once the meeting gets on its way. Indeed, Graddol et al (1994: 173) note that several critiques of Sacks et al's model have been derived from analyses of multi-party conversations, conversations that do not fit the traditional one-person-at-a-time model of one-to-one talk. (For more on conversation analysis, see Clark, 2007: 66–72.)

See Chapter 9, Task C

According to Coulthard (1985: 182), drama texts, being scripts for the performing of pseudo-conversations, can successfully be approached with techniques originally developed to analyse real conversation. He adds, however, that we need to remember that these are invented sequences, shaped for an artistic purpose, and that some of the rules and conventions are different.

Nevertheless, it is important to use our observations to do with the characters' conversational behaviour to first, infer the things characters assert or suggest when they talk (bottom discourse level), and second, infer things *about* the characters from the way in which that behaviour is constructed (top discourse level).

When dealing with an analysis of dramatic dialogue, we are essentially concerned with establishing who holds conversational control or conversational power. We can start by considering the number of turns and average turn-length (or overall distribution of word count) for each participant. If only two characters are interacting, they are likely to take it in turns to speak. However, if more than two characters interact at the same time, it is important to work out how many turns each character takes. Regardless of the number of characters involved, we can employ simple statistics to work out the average number of words per turn for each of the characters.

Moreover, it is worth exploring whether there is a pattern of a character being interrupted the most or indeed doing the interrupting (mostly, but not exclusively, when self-selecting). Interrupting others can be a powerful conversational strategy which prevents the interrupted from taking the conversational floor. Also, it is useful to explore which character or characters maintain conversational topic control, keeping in mind that topics can be embedded within other topics. Furthermore, we could explore whether there are any characters who keep trying to shift the conversational topic, and if so, whether they succeed or fail in their attempts. A character's failure in shifting the topic is likely to hint at conversational weakness, for instance.

The terms of address that characters use in reference to themselves and each other are also likely to yield important information, as these may be indicative of their personalities, states and relationship with each other. Using a 'title + surname' term to address someone certainly gives the impression of a more formalised and distant relationship between the characters involved than, say, a first-name basis.

Finally, it is useful to consider the 'adjacency pairs' of the dialogue. These are sequences of utterances that are adjacent, produced by different speakers, and ordered as a first and second part. Essentially, the notion of the adjacency pair 'has been posited to account for next turn constancies which underlie the linear structuring of talk' (Herman, 1995: 84). Also, adjacency pairs are of particular types, so that a particular first part requires either a particular second part, or a range of second parts; questions demand to be answered, greetings expect greetings in return, and complaints expect apologies. Essentially, the issuing of the first part of each such adjacency pair (say, an invitation) raises the expectation that the second part will follow (say, the 'preferred' response of an acceptance in this case), yet where this does not take place (say, the invited gives the 'dispreferred' response of a let-down), it is important to interpret why this is so. As Herman (1995: 84) puts it, the absence of the second part of the adjacency pair when the first has been used is 'both noticeable and noticed given the conventional tie'.

Pre-sequences are important to notice, as these indicate that some sort of sequence is likely to occur. Let us look at an example, where A asks B, 'Have you watched the film *Closer*?' This sort of interrogative is likely to indicate that an invitation is coming up next, subject to B responding negatively to the interrogative to start with:

A: Have you watched the film *Closer*? **Pre-sequence Q1 (Question 1)**
B: No, I haven't actually. **Pre-sequence A1 (Answer 1)**
A: Want to watch it tonight? **Actual invitation Q2**
B: Sure. **Actual acceptance A2**

Pre-sequences are useful devices for people to avoid dispreferred second parts. If someone does not actually get to the point where the first part of the adjacency pair is uttered, then they are still in a position to avoid the dispreferred second part altogether. Having said that, pre-sequences often, in themselves, are taken to perform the act they are meant to introduce. In other words, asking whether someone has watched the film often, in itself, functions as an invitation for someone to watch the film with you.

Finally, we refer to adjacency pairs embedded within others as insertion sequences:

A:	Want to come watch a film tonight?	Q1	
B:	What film?	Q2	⎤ Insertion
A:	*Closer*	A2	⎦ sequence
B:	Sure.	**A1**	

B here responds to A's initial question with yet another question. This is a challenge to the first question, and hence a dispreferred response to Q1. It is only when A responds to B's Q2 ('What film?') with A2 ('*Closer*'), that B actually responds to Q1 ('Want to come watch a film tonight?') with A1 ('Sure'). As Herman (1995: 85) puts it, in such cases, 'the adjacency tie does not disappear, since *conditional relevance* is said to hold across the intervening turns, till the second part of the pair is performed' (author's italics).

According to Short, '[a]ll other things being equal, powerful speakers in conversations have the most turns, have the longest turns, initiate conversational exchanges, control what is talked about and who talks when, and interrupt others' (1996: 206). However, much like Sacks et al's conversation management 'facts', Short (1996: 207) notes that not all conversations follow this general pattern exactly and there is at least some room for manoeuvre. He further adds that particular activity types also demand some variation from these general rules.

If we take, for instance, the police interview genre, we would certainly regard the police officer as the one in power, in contrast to the suspect interviewed. Nevertheless, it is the less powerful party that is the one who we would expect to talk the most on this occasion. Also, in a courtroom scenario, we would expect the powerful figure of the judge to take not only the least number of turns (compared with, say, the lawyers, audience and witnesses invited to the stand), but also the shortest turns.

See Chapter 9, Task D

7.3 Text, production and performance

As stylisticians, we are primarily focused on the *language* of the dramatic script: that is, the written text. In fact, most stylistic work on drama from Herman (1995) to Short (1996) tends to treat theatre and film as text, and has traditionally analysed play scripts as if they were mere sociolinguistic transcripts. Nevertheless, when studying such texts, it is important to decide where else we should direct or indeed focus our interpretative attention. Are there not any additional effects that may arise in the *production* and *performance* of the *written text* in question?

Culpeper (2001: 42) notes that producers of plays must be able to read and interpret plays in order to decide how to produce them. He therefore agrees with Short (1989, 1998) that a play text lays down parameters which guide perform- ance. As Short (1998: 8) put it, '[i]n ontological terms, each production of a play would appear to be a play PLUS an interpretation of it, in that the director and actors have to decide which elements to focus on, emphasize in performance, etc'. Therefore, the text is where it is that directors and actors actually start from, but it is not unreasonable to claim that it is only in *performance* that the words of the text can be fully understood.

Stylisticians have recently started to take steps towards treating the 'stylis- tics of production and performance' as separate activities, in addition to the 'stylistics of dramatic text'. In fact, Short and McIntyre are currently working on books that aim to describe this unexplored interaction between these additional communicative levels of drama and the written text. McIntyre (2006: 12, 13) argues that, to some degree, these additional factors or levels can be imagined in an idealised reading of a text, and this is how stylistic analysis can begin to illuminate features of performance. Nevertheless, much as with McIntyre's work, it is the written script's performance indicators, as opposed to particular performances, to which my comments are restricted here.

So what sorts of things are we meant to be looking out for exactly? Inter- preting texts is a verbal, that is, linguistic (and cognitive) process, but inter- preting dramatic texts is a verbal, cognitive, visual as well as aural process. We need to account for what the characters are doing (that is, their actions), wearing (their overall appearance) and saying (their verbal behaviour), but also account for the way in which they say what they say. This includes aspects of their non-verbal behaviour – that is, their gestures, posture, facial expressions, eye contact and so on – and their paralinguistic cues – to do with their use of juncture (timing and pauses), the raising and lowering of their voice, the stress they put on certain words, their intonation, speed and so on – all of which affect their utterance's meaning, and indicate the speaker's state of mind.

Have you ever been misunderstood when text messaging and emailing someone? It is the lack of various non-verbal and paralinguistic features that makes it hard for people to deliver or interpret messages (which are written in a casual, spoken style) as intended. Electronic language users have, therefore, developed other means by which they can communicate non-verbal infor- mation (for example, emoticons such as ':)' for a 'smiley face') and paralin- guistic information (such as the use of capital letters to signal one shouting) to accompany their words on the digitised page. Hence, non-verbal and paralinguistic information supplementary to speech is particularly important to consider. Someone directly looking in your eyes when addressing you could indicate honesty, as opposed to one avoiding your gaze, which could signal dishonesty. When someone talks fast and in a breathy way, people could see stress and anxiety, whereas loud and slow speech often designates anger. Ultimately, the way in which a particular line is delivered by an actor will have an influence on the way in which the line is to be interpreted. Different actors will deliver the same line in different ways. A line such as 'You are good' could be paralinguistically communicated with actual sincerity or with an ironic tone. Therefore, it is only the delivery of the line that eventually allows the viewer to make an appropriate judgement on the line's intended meaning.

See Chapter 9, Task E

7.4 Characterisation

So far, in this chapter, we have discussed a number of ways in which readers and viewers of dramatic texts can develop an impression of the various dramatic personas. We can infer information about characters through their fluency or non-fluency, their verbal and overall turn-taking behaviour, non-verbal and paralinguistic behaviour, not to mention their actions and overall appearance on stage. In the next chapter I focus on the pragmatics of turn-taking behaviour, and show how an analysis of characters' speech acts, linguistic (im)politeness and treatment of various conversational conventions or maxims, can also give us an impression of their – perhaps more implicit this time – characterisation. (For the implicit and explicit characterisation cues distinction, see Culpeper, 2001.) For the remainder of this chapter, I would like to draw on some distinctions that prove useful when engaging in an analysis of characterisation.

One such distinction is Forster's [1927] (1987) analysis of what he refers to as flat and round characters. The former are those characters often thought of as mono-dimensional, that is, those constructed round a single idea or quality. The wolf, in the traditional Brothers Grimm's *Little Red Riding Hood* (1857) fairy tale can be thought of as such a flat character, as his whole personality is structured round his need to capture and eat humans, whatever the cost. Round characters, however, are those that give readers and viewers more than one factor to account for, and are therefore multidimensional. It is when readers and viewers begin to see more of, and to, the characters that we actually see them as round. If, for instance, the wolf was said to want to kill Little Red

Riding Hood and her grandmother so that he could take food to his little ones, we might begin to see that there was more to his need to eat humans; he could be seen to kill out of love, and hence be thought of as a loving and caring persona also.

According to Culpeper (2001: 93), three dimensions are involved in making the flat/round distinction: 1) whether the character is simple or complex, 2) whether the character is static or undergoes change, and 3) whether the character surprises the reader or not. But how straightforward are these dimensions? Would you, for instance, describe the detectives of crime novels as flat or round? We could argue that to some extent, such personas are rather flat; they are merely characterised by their obsessive need to capture criminals. On the other hand, they could be thought of as round as well; they often suffer by associating with, and even aligning themselves with, the criminally minded, enjoy romantic relationships, have families and friendships, and as I argue in Gregoriou (2007a), are pretty much as socially deviant as the criminals they pursue.

In relating this distinction to schema theory (see Chapter 5), Culpeper (2001: 95) argues that flat characters are typically schema reinforcing (that is, schema confirming) and round characters are typically schema refreshing (that is, change the reader's schemata). If we watch a new detective series on television, we are likely to have certain expectations, certain social schemata, about what the featuring detective will be like, expectations derived from, say, the older *Colombo* or *Murder She Wrote* television series. If the new character is pretty much like all the other detectives we have come across before (for example, is highly intelligent despite appearances, and has good memory and deductive skills), and therefore confirms or reinforces our detective schemata, then we are likely to view him or her as rather flat. If, however, the new detective challenges and hence changes/refreshes our existing schemata (by, say, being too young or naive, unintelligent, or having ulterior motives in capturing the perpetrators), then we are likely to perceive him or her as round.

Culpeper argues that schema theory is helpful in analysing characters in drama, since although the scripted text certainly drives our understanding or conception of character (this he refers to as bottom-up processing), our social schemata and hence our background knowledge also drive the impression we get of characters (this he refers to as top-down processing). Culpeper (2001: 75) here draws on a useful distinction between the character social schemata we, readers and viewers, draw on when constructing character impressions. Person schemata include knowledge about particular people's preferences, interests, habits and goals, such as being confident or unconfident, organised or disorganised, interesting or boring. Role schemata include knowledge about people's social or functional roles, such as kinship (father, sister and so on) and relational roles (work colleague, lover). Group (or stereotype) schemata include knowledge about social groups: for example sex, class, race, nationality, religion. (For an analysis of social schemata and the humour in the *Little Britain* television series, see Snell, 2006.)

For instance, when we encounter Brent, the British manager, being sexist when interacting with employees in a pub in the television series *The Office*, we are likely to draw on our 'British' group schema, our 'sexist' group schema, and our 'boss' role schema, in developing a conceptually driven understanding of what this character is bound to be like. We then allow our data-driven text processing to inform our schematic understanding, in order to develop a fully formed characterisation or person schema of 'Brent'.

See Chapter 9, Task F

7.5 Chapter review

In this chapter, we started by examining what it is that distinguishes drama from other literary forms: conversation. We then differentiated between the various discourse levels relevant to the analysis of dramatic discourse, before examining the ways in which dramatic conversation approximates real-life natural speech. Here, we investigated the interpretability of non-fluency features in the context of drama. We also explored 'facts' to do with the turn-taking nature of real-life conversation, conventions that are not only culture, speaker and language dependent, but also conversational topic and activity-variant. We described various turn-taking issues that one needs to consider in analysing drama, including the number and length of turns for each character, the interruptions, terms of address and adjacency pairs of each sequence, not to mention the topic management of the characters involved. Though it is customary to expect powerful dramatic personas to interrupt, maintain topic control, speak the most and the longest, we ought to keep in mind that certain activity types generate an adjustment to these expectations.

We then discussed the extent to which interpreting dramatic texts differs from the interpretation of the written text alone. Analysing drama should include an appreciation of the ways in which the script directions and performance indicators will affect the ways in which we interpret given lines. We finally drew on some distinctions that prove useful when engaging in an analysis of characterisation, including Forster's flat/round distinction and an analysis of the social schemata (inclusive of person, role and group schemata) relevant to the characters we consider.

The next chapter considers more implicit aspects to characterisation, those inherent in the pragmatics of character turn-taking. Here I draw on speech act theory, Grice's cooperative principle and accompanying maxims, and politeness theory, in engaging in further analysis of dramatic discourse.

The Pragmatics of Drama

8.1 What is pragmatics?

Pragmatics is concerned with the study of the meaning as communicated by one human and interpreted by another. In contrast to the study of syntax (how sentences are put together) and semantics (what words and sentences mean and how these relate to the world), pragmatics is the study that actually allows humans into the equation, since it involves an analysis of the relationship between linguistic forms and the users of these forms (Yule, 1996: 4).

As noted in the previous chapter, in order to explore implicit cues to characterisation, stylisticians often engage in analysis of the pragmatics of dramatic discourse. It often proves useful to interrogate the difference between what characters actually say (that is, the *semantics* of their utterances) and what characters mean by what they say (that is, the *pragmatics* of their utterances). Engaging in such pragmatic analyses of drama can enable readers to explain various effects attributed to dramatic scripts, whether these texts are conventional or absurd, whether they generate humour, irony or satire. (For a book on the discourse of satire, see Simpson, 2003.)

In this chapter, I introduce three theories relevant to such pragmatic analyses of drama, namely the theory of speech acts, the theory revolving round Grice's maxims and politeness theory.

8.2 Speech acts

Speech act theory is associated with the philosophy of Austin (1962) and Searle (1969). Utterances, grammatical structures, do not merely describe states of affair in the world, but also actively do things, and have effects on people. 'Speech act' is a term reserved for such speech actions, acts that people perform by saying what they do. Such actions include apologies, promises, threats, commands, warnings, requests and assertions (statements), among many others.

'Performatives' are those speech acts where the relevant action is actually performed by naming, and whose verbs can normally co-occur with 'hereby' (the so-called 'hereby' test). Whereas 'I'm sorry' and 'Sit down!' are respectively speech acts of an apology and a command, 'I (hereby) apologise' and 'I (hereby) command you to sit down' perform the same sort of speech acts, yet *performatively* so.

A useful speech act distinction is that between the act's locution, its illocution and its perlocution. Locution is a term that refers to the actual words uttered, whereas illocution refers to the force or intention behind the words. Perlocution refers to the effect of the illocution on the hearer, and covers the way in which the illocution was actually interpreted by the hearer. To illustrate this distinction, let's have a look at the following example of a customer ordering dinner at a high-class restaurant:

Customer: Can I have fish fingers?
Waiter: This is a high-class restaurant Sir!
Customer: Ok (.) **may** I have fish fingers?

The customer's 'Can I have fish fingers?' is a speech act of a request that requires a response. The actual preferred response here is for the waiter to bring him fish fingers. Seeing that the customer is in a high-class restaurant, the waiter offers the customer a negative, dispreferred ('This is a high-class restaurant Sir!') response that should allow the customer to understand that it does not serve fish fingers. The customer fails to pick up on the implication, and instead thinks that the waiter was merely referring to the high quality of the restaurant, something to which he responds with a slightly more formalised request ('May I have fish fingers?' as opposed to the original 'Can I have fish fingers?'). What we have here is, therefore, a misunderstanding of the waiter's implication on the customer's part.

So what is the locution, illocution and perlocution of the waiter's 'This is a high-class restaurant Sir!' contribution? The locution, the semantic meaning, what the waiter is actually literally saying is 'I'm informing you that this is a high class restaurant'. The illocution, the pragmatic meaning, what the waiter is implying by what he is saying is 'There are no fish fingers in a high-class restaurant such as this so, no, I cannot let you have some'. The perlocution, what the customer understands by what it is that the waiter is saying is 'Speak more formally in a restaurant as formal as this'.

In other words, the locution matches the illocution of utterances where the semantic meaning matches the pragmatic meaning the speaker intends. Where there is a mismatch between the two, the speaker is implying something other than what they are literally saying. The illocution and perlocution of all utterances are ideally matched, but where they are not, the mismatch between the illocution and perlocution leads to misunderstanding between the people involved.

See Chapter 9, Task G

One general speech act classification system is of five main types of speech acts, known as:

- 'declarations', which effectively change the world, such as 'I hereby name you King of Scotland.'
- 'representatives', which state what the speaker believes to be true, such as 'It's a nice day today.'
- 'expressives', which state the speaker's feelings, such as 'I love you.'
- 'directives', which direct the hearer to do something, such as 'Get me my coat.'
- 'commissives', which speakers use to commit themselves to future acts, such as 'I'll come by your house later.'

Another important aspect of speech acts is their 'felicity conditions'. These are conditions that need to be fulfilled in order for the act to count, or be valid.

Let us take the example of a promise, which is a commissive. We cannot promise another person to do something in the past tense ('I promise I was there yesterday'), at least not if the speech act verb is used in accordance to speech act theory. Promises are meant to be made in relation to acts of the speaker set in the future (such as 'I promise I'll meet you there tomorrow'). This is called the promise's 'propositional content'. Similarly, we cannot promise to do something beyond our capabilities ('I promise it will rain next week'), and neither can we promise to do something the hearer does not wish to see done ('I promise I'll hurt you'). Promises are meant to be related to acts the speaker can and the hearer wants to see fulfilled in the future[1] ('I'll buy you a present'). These are called the promise's 'preparatory conditions'. Related to these conditions is a promise's 'sincerity condition': that is, it only counts if you mean it. Finally, the essential condition entails that, having made a promise, we are obliged to see it through. Those speech acts whose felicity conditions are not met are thought of as infelicitous or void. Similar felicity conditions can be given for all sorts of speech acts.

Finally, there is normally a correlation between certain syntactic forms and certain speech acts. Imperatives often correlate with the speech act of a command (such as in 'Be quiet!'), declaratives correlate with assertions or statements ('I am Greek') and interrogatives correlate with questions ('How old are you?') However, we can imagine situations where speech acts are performed indirectly. If I am surrounded by people who are insulting Greeks, my saying 'I am Greek' is likely to be my way of complaining about their behaviour. In that scenario, telling someone I am Greek is more than a mere assertion of my nationality. It could be thought of as a warning sign for them to be more careful with what they are saying, particularly around me. Similarly, if I am surrounded by adults acting like children, my saying 'How old are you?' could be interpreted as a complaint about their immature behaviour, rather than a question about their age. In both these scenarios, the speech act is hence performed indirectly: that is, through the performance of another speech act. As Herman (1995: 170) notes, indirectness means that the form of the utterance need not give any direct indication of the utterance's force. (For more on speech acts, see Chapman, 2006: 118–22 and Clark, 2007: 56–9.)

See Chapter 9, Task H

As Culpeper (2001: 236) argues, analysing a character's speech acts is likely to reveal much about their character. Culpeper adds that, in addition to analysing what speech acts characters use, we also need to consider how they perform their speech acts. What is more, speech act behaviour can allow readers and viewers to infer characters' relationship with others. We shall return to look at this aspect of drama in a moment, but let us first turn to look at yet another closely related theory, that of Grice.

8.3 Grice's maxims

In his 1975 article on 'Logic and conversation', Paul Grice suggested that when conversing with each other, humans say what is necessary for the purpose of the talk; they carry out talk that has mutual communicative ends for all concerned and therefore follows his so-called cooperative principle (also see Jeffries, 2006: 189; Chapman, 2006: 98–102, 136–40; Clark, 2007: 59–63). According to this principle, when conversing, you should 'make your contribution such as is required, at the stage at which it occurs, by the accepted purpose or direction of the talk exchange in which you are engaged' (Grice, 1989: 26). This principle is accompanied by four maxims, four generalised expectations that underlie communication:

The Maxim of Quality

try to make your contribution one that is true, specifically,

(i) do not say what you believe to be false

(ii) do not say that for which you lack evidence

The Maxim of Quantity

(i) make your contribution as informative as is required for the current purposes of the exchange

(ii) do not make your contribution more informative than is required

The Maxim of Relevance

make your contributions relevant

The Maxim of Manner

be perspicuous, and specifically,

(i) avoid obscurity

(ii) avoid ambiguity

(iii) be brief

(iv) be orderly

(Levinson, 1983: 101–2)

According to this theory, it is actually not uncommon for conversants to fail to comply with one or more of these maxims at any one time. Also, it is acceptable to break the maxims in one of two ways.

First, we can 'violate' a maxim, where we intend the hearer *not* to become aware of the maxim being broken. Lying, for instance, is a quality maxim violation. Similarly, suddenly changing the topic of the conversation is a relation maxim violation.

Alternatively, we can 'flout' a maxim, where we intend the hearer to become aware of the maxim being broken and so draw an additional meaning from this. The additional meaning inferred is what Grice calls an implicature; as Coulthard (1985: 35) put it, '[i]n such instances the conversational maxims provide a basis for the listener to *infer* what is being conversationally *implicated*' (author's italics). According to the same source, in a two-stage process, the speaker first recognises the apparent irrelevance, inadequacy or inappropriateness of the utterance, which secondly triggers (Levinson, 1983) the subsequent inferencing.

My saying 'Today, I am 18 years old' violates the quality maxim, if I am trying to mislead whoever is listening about how old I really am. However, this would be a flout if I expect my listener to become aware that this is an untruth (which I expect they will!), and so draw on a relevant implicature (of the 'I am feeling young and carefree today' sort). Here are some examples of flouting the maxims and drawing on implicatures:

A: I'm over the moon today

A's contribution is metaphorical, otherwise known as a quality maxim flout. In fact, all ironies, exaggerations, metaphors, metonymies and idioms are quality maxim flouts. Unless A is literally 'over the moon' and hence in outer space, A's contribution is certainly untruthful. The implicature is, 'I'm feeling great today.'

> B: What did you think of her book?
> C: Let's just say 'The cover was colourful' and leave it at that.

C's contribution is likely to be taken to be a quantity maxim flout. Though probably a truthful and certainly a relevant response, it is certainly not as informative as B expected it to be. The implicature is, 'I didn't think much of the book.'

> D: Do you think we should go away this summer?
> E: I'm still waiting for this promotion at work, you know.

E's contribution is a relation maxim flout. The response is clearly not directly relevant to the question asked. The implicature is, 'No. I can't afford to do so at the moment.' If E is lying, the response is also a violation of the quality maxim.

> F: My student years were not characterised by unbearable happiness.

F's contribution is a manner maxim flout. The contribution is obscure and indirect. The implicature is, 'I was unhappy when I was a student.'

See Chapter 9, Task I

Of course, as Herman (1995: 174) puts it, Grice's theory has been subject to 'intense scrutiny, debate, contention and revision'. It certainly is not a theory without its problems. For example, it is in fact quite common for participants *not* to be on equal terms (say, a mother conversing with a very young child) or cooperative terms (say, people engaging in an actual argument) when conversing, in which case the cooperative principle is not relevant or valid at all. As Coulthard (1985: 32) notes, the theory further fails to explain why speakers choose one form of flouting over another, and it also fails to account for how an utterance with a series of potential implicatures comes to have only one in the context. In other words, how exactly does the hearer get from the actual language to the actual implicature drawn?

Nevertheless, analysing the extent to which dramatic characters flout or violate one or more maxims throughout a text can prove useful not only in explaining the meaning between the lines but also in justifying reader impressions about the characters' power relationship and their individual characterisations.

Let's analyse an extract from Susannah Grant's script for the movie *Erin Brockovich* (2000) (Figure 8.1, overleaf), in terms of both speech acts and Grice's maxims.

In l. 1, Erin, disturbed by all the noise the bikers are making, greets George ('Hey!'), if aggressively so. She does not get the second, preferred part for her 'greeting' adjacency pair, which is why she repeats the first part in l. 2 ('HEY!'). The capital letters in l. 2 indicate loudness and hence change in her pitch, and so signal Erin's aggression at George's failure to respond to her the first time round, again because of all the noise he and his biker friends are making (something made explicit in the directions also). Notice that the use of 'asshole' in the original screen directions adds to the impression of Erin being angry here.

When George eventually does respond to Erin's initial greeting, his response ('Well, hello to you, darling') signals that he likes the looks of her. As the screen directions indicate, he looks rather tough, but appearances might be deceptive ('Everything about GEORGE HALABY is tough – his denim, his leather, his bike, his long hair. Everything but his eyes, which twinkle like Santa's').

Erin's contribution in l. 4 is an indirect directive speech act. Despite its being in the form of an interrogative ('What the hell do you think you're doing, making all that Goddamn noise?'), it is not a genuine question for him to answer. It counts as a command or directive for George to stop making the noise. George, however, responds to this as if it were a genuine question ('Just introducing myself to the neighbours', l. 5). His response is informative and relevant to the question asked, but probably not genuine; he was not trying to actually introduce himself to the neighbours by revving his bike. It therefore violates, or perhaps flouts, the quality maxim.

Erin plays along with the supposed misunderstanding, and repeats her directive ('Stop making the noise') speech act, this time with a couple of declarative representatives instead: 'Well, I'm the neighbours. There, now we're introduced, so you can shut the fuck up' (l. 6–7).

The bikers laugh at the joke, and Erin leaves, only for the impressed George to go after her. He initiates a different topic by paying her an indirect compliment: 'Ooh, now, see, if I'da known there was a beautiful woman next door, I'da done this different.' The compliment-apology is triggered through the flouting of the manner and quantity maxim; his contribution is both ambiguous and over-wordy. 'Let's start over. My name's George. What's yours?' (l. 9) is an attempt to redo the introductions from the two of them. What is asked is merely her name. Erin's response, 'Just think of me as the person next door who likes it quiet, and we'll get along fine' (l. 10–11) is not the required answer to the question posed. She flouts the quantity, relation and manner maxim as she offers an over-wordy, irrelevant and obscure answer. The implicature is 'I

EXT. ERIN'S HOUSE – NIGHT. Erin steps out onto her front stoop and looks over at what used to be Mrs. Morales's house. A few MOTORCYCLES are parked on the lawn; A FEW BIKERS are drinking beer on the stoop; and one asshole is on his bike, REVVING HIS ENGINE.

ERIN Hey!
1

But of course he can't hear her. She walks over to him, stands right in his line of vision

ERIN HEY!
2

He sees her and kills the engine. Everything about GEORGE HALABY is tough – his denim, his leather, his bike, his long hair. Everything but his eyes, which twinkle like Santa's.

GEORGE Well, hello to you, darlin'.
3

ERIN What the hell do you think you're doing, making all that Goddamn noise?
4

GEORGE Just introducing myself to the neighbors.
5

ERIN Well, I'm the neighbors. There, now we're introduced, so you can shut the
6
fuck up.
7

The guys on the porch chuckle. Erin turns and starts back to her house. George hops off his bike and follows her.

GEORGE Ooh, now, see, if I'da known there was a beautiful woman next door, I'da
8
done this different. Let's start over. My name's George. What's yours?
9

ERIN Just think of me as the person next door who likes it quiet, and we'll get
10
along fine.
11

GEORGE Now, don't be like that. Tell you what. How about if I take you out on a
12
date to apologize for my rudeness?
13

Erin shakes her head in disbelief and keeps walking.

GEORGE Come on. Gimme your number, I'll call you up proper and ask you out and
14
everything.
15

She stops at her porch, turns to him.

ERIN You want my number?
16

GEORGE I do.
17

ERIN Which number do you want, George?
18

GEORGE You got more than one?
19

ERIN Shit, yeah. I got numbers coming out of my ears. Like, for instance, ten.
20

GEORGE Ten?
21

ERIN Sure. That's one of my numbers. It's how many months old my little girl is.
22

GEORGE You got a little girl?
23

ERIN Yeah. Sexy, huh? And here's another: five. That's how old my other
24
daughter is. Seven is my son's age. Two is how many times I been married
25
and divorced. You getting all this? 16 is the number of dollars in my bank
26
account. 454-3943 is my phone number. And with all the other numbers I
27
gave you, I'm guessing zero is the number of times you're gonna call it.
28

She turns and heads inside. He calls out after her:

GEORGE How the hell do you know your bank balance right off the top of your head
29
like that? See, that impresses me.
30

Extract from *Erin Brockovich* screenplay, by Susannah Grant. © 2000 Universal City Studios, Inc. and Palisade Investors, LLC. All Rights Reserved. Courtesy of Columbia Pictures.

Figure 8.1

have no interest in becoming acquainted with you. All I want is for you to be quiet.' Therefore, again, she forms an indirect directive ('Stop making the noise') speech act through her declarative response. She appears to not want to miss out on any opportunity to make her wishes known to George.

In response, George tries to calm her down. He indirectly performs the speech act of an apology-invitation for the two of them to go out ('How about I take you out on a date to apologize for my rudeness?'), something to which Erin responds by walking away and shaking her head in disbelief. She hence fails to offer the preferred ('I accept') or indeed dispreferred ('I refuse') second part of the invitation adjacency pair altogether. Her walking away constitutes a non-verbal refusal. George insists by being more direct in lines 14–15. He uses directives ('Come on. Gimme your number') and a commissive ('I'll call you up proper and ask you out and everything'), which at least get Erin to stop walking away and turn to him, something that appears at first to be promising.

Rather than giving George some sort of a response to his invitation or request for her number at this stage, Erin instead initiates a number of insertion sequences with her own questions ('You want my number?' in l. 16 and 'Which number do you want George?' in l. 18). George plays along with her 'game' by responding to her questions at first directly ('I do' in l. 17) and then with an initiation of an insertion sequence of his own ('You got more than one [number]?' in l. 19). At this stage, George appears to be genuinely intrigued by her willing offer of not only one but possibly more than one phone number. It is from l. 20 onwards, that Erin appears to have set him up for a sort of let-down.

In l. 20, she responds to his question with a representative ('Shit yeah [I got more than one number]'), only to then flout the quality maxim by saying 'I got numbers coming out of my ears. Like, for instance, ten.' Erin neither has numbers literally coming of her ears, nor can 'ten' be one of her phone numbers. George picks up on the flout when he repeats 'Ten?' on l. 21, initiating a further insertion sequence. Nevertheless, neither he nor the audience would have picked up on the nature of Erin's implicature at this stage.

In l. 22, Erin yet again responds to his question with, 'Sure. That's one of my numbers. It's how many months old my little girl is.' Her response here is truthful; 'ten' is indeed one of 'her numbers' or 'the numbers relevant to her life', and indeed, that is how many months old her little girl is. Nevertheless, the response is certainly irrelevant and disorderly, therefore flouting the relation and manner maxims respectively, possibly to imply that she has more important things to do than go on dates (that is, bring up a ten-month-old baby). In this way, we begin to realise that she uses 'number' to refer to something other than her phone number alone, which itself explains why she has more than one. Undeterred, George poses another question on l. 23, 'You got a little girl?', initiating yet another insertion sequence. He has in a sense fallen into Erin's trap.

Erin further flouts the relation, manner and quantity maxims again on her longest turn, running from l. 24–28. She offers various representatives (such as 'Seven is my son's age'), one indirect interrogative ('You getting all this?') and one expressive ('I'm guessing') speech act. Here, she lists all of 'her numbers', inclusive of the ages of her other two young children, her marriages and divorces, not to mention her low bank balance, before finally giving George her phone number, declaring that 'with all the other numbers I gave you, I'm guessing zero is the number of times you're gonna call it'. Her implicature, therefore, is that being poor and having that many young children, she does not expect him to call her at all. She makes a value judgement about the sort of man he probably is (someone not genuinely interested in women who are poor or have many young children, which is why he would not call), and the sort of impression that her 'numbers' make of her (someone unsexy and unattractive – 'Yeah. Sexy, huh?' in l. 24).

Having made this major declaration, she turns away and heads inside, only for George to call out after her, 'How the hell do you know your bank balance right off the top of your head like that? See, that impresses me' (l. 29–30). His contribution proves him to remain undeterred. His interrogative is not a genuine question, but more of a representative/expressive speech act. He pretends to be impressed with her good memory, as a way of justifying his own determination. This then is a flout of the quality and manner maxim to imply that not only does he continue to be interested in her, he is even more so now than he was at the conversation's start. In the performance of the script on film, George follows this line by pretend-falling down on the lawn while clutching his chest, as a testament to the extent to which he is taken by her.

Such an analysis can prove very useful in explaining the meaning between the lines, which is where a sort of 'alternative conversation' between the characters is unfolding. At the dramatist–audience discourse level, the characters certainly take shape. Through the analysis, Erin proves herself to be a very determined, aggressive and street-wise woman, while George is impressed, relentless and undeterred by her verbal and non-verbal behaviour. The power relationship between the two characters is an interesting one, and the dialogue proves a good way to explain who has, or indeed wants to maintain, control in this rapport.

See Chapter 9, Task J

In addition to Grice's four conversational maxims, Grice himself (1975: 47) later added a fifth maxim to the mix: 'Be polite.' It is this politeness maxim that is the subject of the next section.

8.4 Politeness theory

Politeness theory is mostly associated with the work of Brown and Levinson (1987). Despite the everyday meaning of the word 'politeness', linguistic politeness is not about humans merely being nice to each other. The linguistic politeness notion is instead about humans efficiently and smoothly achieving whatever goals and satisfying whatever needs they may have. This notion was originally introduced in association with Goffman's (1967) notion of 'face', a concept that involves prestige, people's positive social value and public image. To say that someone is 'losing face', for instance, is to refer to someone's damaged public image. The 'face' notion was said to consist of two associated aspects:

- negative face: the basic claim to territories, personal preserves, rights to non-distraction – i.e. to freedom of action and freedom from imposition
- positive face: the positive consistent self-image or 'personality' (crucially including the desire that this self-image be appreciated and approved of) claimed by interactants.

(Brown and Levinson, 1987: 61)

To put this simply, negative face refers to humans' need to be unimpeded. We want to have neither our space invaded nor our actions dictated by others. Positive face refers to humans' need to be recognised, noticed, liked and approved of. Although face is very much a personal issue, our face can be extended to those close to us. This is why what children do can reflect positively or negatively as much on themselves as it can on their parents' face, their parents' public image.

According to this theory, speech acts that pose a threat to one's positive or negative face are referred to as 'face threatening acts' (FTAs). A request or directive is classified as an FTA toward the hearer's negative face, whereas a criticism is an FTA toward the hearer's positive face. Having said that, we can equally pose FTAs on our own face (see Brown and Levinson, 1987: 65–8). An unwilling promise to do something for someone is self-imposing, and therefore classifiable as an FTA toward the speaker's own negative face. Similarly, a confession constitutes damage to our own public image, and is therefore classifiable as an FTA toward the speaker's own positive face.

Of course, there are a number of variables which affect the extent of the face threat performed, namely the 'absolute ranking', 'distance' and 'relative power' variables (Brown and Levinson, 1987: 74–8). A request to borrow something from someone is a negative FTA, but it is certainly a much smaller imposition to ask to borrow someone's pen during a meeting, than it is to ask to borrow someone's car or, even worse, money in the same sort of context, particularly in certain cultures (ranking). The relationship the people concerned share is also bound to have an effect on the extent of the face threat. Asking for spare change from a friend is less of an imposition than asking for spare change from a stranger (distance), or even worse, asking for money from your boss. In other words, the sort of power that an addressee has in relation to an addresser will also affect the extent of the face threat (relative power).

An FTA can be performed either bald on record or off record. An on-record FTA is performed without redress: that is, efficiently in a direct and concise manner (Brown and Levinson, 1987: 69), so it is in accordance with Grice's maxims (1975). Such acts are often employed in emergency situations, or where the speaker has huge power over the addressee. In the case of a fire roaring through a building, you are likely to burst through a door screaming 'Fire! Get out!' to everyone in the room. Although an act like this is threatening to the addressees' negative face, it is more important for you to perform the act bald on record, without any indirect minimisers (of the 'Would you mind vacating the room, please?' sort), than to worry about inadvertently attacking people's face in doing so. Similarly, where the speaker is overly powerful or the extent of the face threat is small, it is again acceptable to perform the act on record. No negative linguistic politeness is required when, say, a courtroom audience is told to 'Stand' when a judge enters the room, or when you are told to 'Sit down' when entering someone's office, although both these are negative FTAs.

Off-record FTAs are those performed indirectly, meaning in such a way that the speaker can avoid responsibility for performing them. Telling someone that you have a headache might be an indirect way of getting them to give you some painkillers, while telling someone that you are feeling cold might be interpreted as an indirect way of getting them to switch the heating on, make you a cup of tea, close the window or give you their jacket. Hence, both of these are off-record negative FTAs. In other words, the FTA is here triggered through the flouting of a maxim, and the threat lies in the implicature rather than the speech act itself. As Simpson (1995: 174) put it, '[b]y choosing to go off record, speakers adopt a strategy in which the utterance often takes the form of a declarative sentence containing no direct lexical link to the goods and services implicitly demanded of the addressee'. Of course, the speaker can deny the relevant implicature:

A: I'm cold.
B: Do you want me to switch the heating on?
A: I never asked you to do anything.

B might respond to the 'I'm cold' hinting strategy by switching the heating on, but A can claim they never actually performed the FTA, if confronted with it.

Alternatively, people can choose to perform the FTA in such a way that they pay attention to the hearer's positive or negative face wants. Strategies that pay attention to someone's positive face wants are classified as positive politeness, while those that pay attention to negative face wants are classified as negative politeness. Negative politeness occupies a higher position in the hierarchy. Brown and Levinson's study includes a comprehensive list of such strategies.

Positive politeness includes expressing an interest in someone ('What do you do?'), approving of them, ('Excellent lecture!'), complimenting them ('I love your dress'), assuming common ground ('I know exactly what you mean'), seeking agreement ('Don't you think that was a great lecture?'), avoiding disagreement ('It sure was, yeah'), and using in-group or solidarity markers ('Come on, honey'). Negative politeness includes the use of strategies that mollify the force of an utterance, such as hedges ('If possible, I was wondering if maybe ...'), acknowledgements of debt ('I will be forever grateful if ...'), apologising and begging forgiveness ('I'm really sorry for asking, but ...'), indicating deference, say by putting yourself down and treating the hearer as superior ('I'm so silly to be taking up your precious time but ...'), impersonalising by cutting out the pronouns ('The lecture could have been better delivered'), being pessimistic ('I know this is very last minute and you probably don't have the time but ...') and so on.

If you wish for someone to get you some water, you can therefore go bald on record with 'Get me a glass of water', go off record with 'I'm so thirsty', employ negative politeness with 'Sorry for the hassle, but could you give me a glass of water?' or employ both positive and negative politeness with 'It's a hot day today, isn't it, mate? Get me a glass of water, will you?' Finally, if the FTA is too threatening, Brown and Levinson argue that we can of course actively refrain from performing it at all.

See Chapter 9, Task K

Culpeper (2001: 245) notes that the Brown and Levinson politeness ranking has been challenged by a number of researchers. He quotes Blum-Kulka, Danet and Gherson (1985), as researchers who suggested that off-record strategies could be less polite than negative politeness strategies, and Baxter (1984), who suggested that positive politeness may presuppose negative politeness and should therefore occupy a higher position in the hierarchy. Nevertheless, and despite the usefulness of Brown and Levinson's model, we should always take the actual context into account when judging the relevance of these classifications to actual wording. As Culpeper (2001: 245) puts it, an important point to note is that 'politeness is not just determined by a particular strategy: it is determined by a particular strategy in a particular context'. (For more on context, see Clark, 2007: 126–9; for an 'impoliteness' model with particular reference to characterisation, see Culpeper, 2001.)

Let's look at the way in which (im)politeness analysis interacts with the previously introduced pragmatic models in the context of drama. Figure 8.2 is a script extract from the 1997 film *As Good As It Gets*.

Melvin Udall, well past 50, is unliked, unloved, and unsettling. A huge pain in the ass to everyone he's ever met. He lives in an apartment building next to Simon, who is in his 30s and gay. Unbeknown to Simon, Melvin has stuffed Verdell, Simon's tiny dog, in their floor's garbage chute. Melvin is currently in his apartment writing his latest novel, reading aloud as he writes, while Simon is with his friend Frank in the corridor.

MELVIN	Somewhat in the dark, she had confessed and he had forgiven. This is what	1
	you live for, he said. Two heads on a pillow where there is only the safety	2
	of being with each other. How, she wondered, could she find such hope in	3
	the most shameful part of her.'	4

He barely reacts as we hear a LOUD KNOCKING as he reads.

SIMON	Mr. Udall.	5

But Melvin's into it. His fingers flying as he reads.

'MELVIN	At last she was able to define love. Love was ... '	6

More KNOCKING.

SIMON	Mr. Udall, I'd like to talk to you please.	7
MELVIN	'Love was ... '	8

He almost has the rest of the sentence -- the meaning of love -- but the knocking throws him.

MELVIN	... Son-of-a-bitch-pansy-assed-stool-pusher.	9

He bursts from his chair. As Simon hears MELVIN through the door and takes a step back, Melvin throws open the door. He looks demonic.

MELVIN	(*loud and angry*) Yeeeess!!!	10
SIMON	Maybe this can wait.	11

Frank signals encouragement as Melvin opens the door.

SIMON	I found Verdell, Mr. Udall.	12
MELVIN	Well, that's a load off.	13

Melvin walks back into the apartment and is about to close the door when Simon has another burst of bravery.

SIMON	Did you... do something to him?	14
MELVIN	Do you realize that I work at home?	15
SIMON	(*eyes downcast*) No, I didn't.	16
MELVIN	Do you like to be interrupted when you are hanging around in your little garden?	17, 18
SIMON	No... actually, I even shut the phone off and put a little piece of cardboard in the ringer so no one can just buzz me from d...	19, 20

MELVIN Well, I work all the time. So never, never again interrupt me. Okay? I mean, 21
never. Not 30 years from now... not if there's fire. Not even if you hear a 22
thud from inside my home and a week later there's a smell from in there that 23
can only come from a decaying body and you have to hold a hanky against 24
your face because the stench is so thick you think you're going to faint even 25
then don't come knocking or, if it's election night and you're excited and 26
want to celebrate because some fudge-packer you dated has been elected the 27
first queer President of the United States...and he's going to put you up in 28
Camp David and you just want to share the moment with someone... don't 29
knock... not on this door. Not for anything. Got me. Sweetheart? 30

SIMON Yes. It's not a subtle point you're making. 31

MELVIN Okay, then. 32

Melvin enters his apartment and slams the door shut.

Figure 8.2

The initial stage directions present Melvin as a loner, and a grumpy old man. He is older than Simon (Melvin is '*well past 50*', while Simon is '*in his 30s*'), '*unliked, unloved, and unsettling*', and cruel to animals ('*Melvin has stuffed Verdell, Simon's tiny dog, in their floor's garbage chute*'). He later appears to be homophobic also (see l. 9's '... Son-of-a-bitch-pansy-assed-stool-pusher', or l. 27's 'fudge-packer').

Lines 1–4 are in the form of a monologue, where Melvin recites to himself a few lines from his book, '*reading aloud as he writes*'. The book appears to be strongly emotional, revolving round some sort of love affair, a sort of storyline that certainly appears to be very much in contrast to the original description of Melvin himself as a '*huge pain in the ass to everyone he's ever met*'. Melvin's linguistic behaviour nevertheless later reinforces this original description.

The loud knocking in-between l. 4 and l. 5 constitutes an FTA toward Melvin's negative face. Besides, knocking on someone's door is a directive, as it amounts to an imposition for them to get up and open the door for you. Melvin '*barely reacts*' to this FTA. Simon uses a pre-sequence in l. 5 with 'Mr Udall', as the utterance aims to actually get Melvin's attention. This is another negative FTA, another directive, another potential imposition for Melvin. Having said that, the 'Mr + Surname' address format is positive face-giving. Melvin again fails to respond to this directive. Notice that Melvin's behaviour is in itself positive face-threatening to Simon. Failing to notice someone is a major attack to their positive face. Even more so, Melvin continues with his out-loud monologue on l. 6 ('At last she was able to define love. Love was ...'), oblivious or perhaps indifferent to the fact that Simon might be able to hear him reciting and typing away, and hence realise that Melvin is very much in his flat, ignoring him. This strengthens the extent of Melvin's positive FTA toward Simon.

Simon's contribution on l. 7 ('Mr Udall, I'd like to talk to you please') reveals that Simon is certainly aware of Melvin being inside his apartment. In syntactic terms, it's an expressive declarative, although it constitutes an indirect speech act of a request for the two of them to talk. The directive, politeness speaking, is face threatening toward Melvin's negative face again, as it imposes on Melvin. Though rather assertive, the act in fact encodes negative politeness in its use of hedges ('I'd like') and explicit politeness markers ('please'), not to mention the previously mentioned 'title + surname' positive face-giving form of address. Compare, for instance, 'Mr Udall, I'd like to talk to you please' with the bald on-record alternative, 'Talk to me.'

Indifferent to this, Melvin continues to ignore Simon, with yet another dispreferred response to Simon's first part ('Love was ...'). According to the directions, Melvin has almost captured the very important meaning of love, but the knocking *'throws him'*. He responds with '... Son-of-a-bitch-pansy-assed-stool-pusher' (l. 9), a line particularly amusing because it contrasts strongly with the sensitive and emotional theme of the book he is currently writing.

Although this is apparently said 'to himself' rather than to Simon directly, it is certainly referring to Simon, so in speech-act theory terms it constitutes an insult, and a representative speech act. It is also an FTA to Simon's positive face, as it goes against Simon's need to be liked and approved of.

Melvin's performance indicators show him to be very angry and aggressive when opening the door (he *'bursts from his chair'*, *'throws open the door'* and *'looks demonic'*), while Simon picks up on the aggression and is obviously intimidated by it (*'As Simon hears MELVIN through the door and takes a step back ...'*).

Melvin's eventual 'Yeeeess!!!' (l. 10) indicates annoyance. Although this is indeed the second part of the adjacency pair Simon expected, the altered spelling of the word signals that paralinguistically, Melvin draws the word out in agitation. The performance indicators also show that his tone is both *'loud and angry'*. Simon's 'Maybe this can wait' (l. 11) signals that at this point he acknowledges that he is imposing, that he performed an FTA on Melvin's negative face, which is why he employs linguistic politeness in the use of 'maybe' and 'can'. He appears to be weak and certainly intimidated, as he implies that they should talk about his matter later, when it is convenient for Melvin to do so. Nevertheless, according to the directions, Simon's friend Frank non-verbally encourages Simon to go ahead and talk to Melvin anyway.

'I found Verdell, Mr Udall' (l. 12) appears to be an informative assertion.

Though a representative declarative, it actually functions as an indirect speech act of an accusation at this stage. What Simon implies here, through flouting the manner and quantity maxims, is that he knows or suspects that it was Melvin who threw the dog down the garbage chute. The implication is positive face threatening toward Melvin, though performed off record. It is also a first part of an adjacency pair that requires a response on Melvin's behalf.

Melvin's response 'Well, that's a load off' (l. 13), is a dispreferred second part, as it is neither an acceptance nor a refusal in response to Simon's accusation. Melvin flouts the quality maxim as he does not say what he believes to be true. The implicature is, 'I don't care.' Again, this is an FTA toward Simon's positive face, as it goes against Simon's need for his feelings to be considered and accommodated by others. The FTA is performed off record, through the implicature of the utterance rather than the utterance itself.

Melvin's walking back into the apartment, coupled with his attempt at closing the door, is another positive FTA directed toward Simon, yet Simon tries to remain undeterred by this behaviour. He has 'another burst of bravery'.

Simon's 'Did you ... do something to him?' (l. 14) is non-fluent. The pause indicates that, though apparently 'brave', Simon is certainly hesitating still, possibly because he is afraid of Melvin and what he is capable of doing to him. Having Frank there certainly appears to help egg Simon on. Though an interrogative, Simon's utterance is not a genuine question, but functions as an indirect speech act of an accusation. It is doubly threatening to Melvin: it is positive face threatening as the utterance presupposes that Melvin is the kind of man who is capable of hurting a dog, and it is negative face threatening as it imposes on Melvin to engage in further conversation with Simon about Verdell.

Melvin's response, 'Do you realise that I work at home?' (l. 15), is a dispreferred second part to Simon's first part of an accusation, as Melvin again fails to admit or deny having hurt the dog. The utterance constitutes an indirect speech act. Although it is an interrogative in grammatical terms, it implies the directive 'Don't interrupt me' in speech act terms. This implicature is triggered through the flouting of the relation maxim. Besides, whether he works at home or not is not related to whether he hurt the dog. The act therefore constitutes an off-record negative FTA towards Simon.

Simon's contribution on l. 16 ('No, I didn't'), coupled with the 'eyes downcast' performance indicator, reveals him to be sort of ashamed of himself. Although he picked up on Melvin's implicature, he responds to Melvin's l. 15 question as if it were genuine. It also constitutes the second part of the question–answer adjacency pair.

Melvin's 'Do you like to be interrupted when you are hanging around in your little garden?' (l. 17–18) constitutes an off-record FTA toward Simon's positive face; it constructs an unfavourable image of Simon as someone who has nothing important to do with his life, and hence nothing better than hanging around in his 'little [see "unimportant"] garden', and someone who rudely interrupts others when they are working. This FTA is triggered through the flouting of the manner and relation maxims. The implicature is, 'I wouldn't interrupt you, so don't interrupt me.' It's another indirect speech act, as it is not a genuine question. It is also another first part to a question–answer adjacency pair.

Simon is forced to respond with 'No ... actually, I even shut the phone off and put a little piece of cardboard in the ringer so no one can just buzz me from d...' (l. 19–20). Inadvertedly, Simon is trapped into admitting his own supposed rudeness, even though Melvin is obviously the ruder of the two. Again, Simon replies to Melvin as if his (l. 17–18) question was a genuine request for information. Melvin's interruption on l. 21 clearly reveals that this was anything but a genuine question.

Melvin's long turn from l. 21–30 is very explicit and rather direct. He flouts the quantity and manner maxims to emphasize his point. The implicature is that he is very upset and expects such interruption to never ever happen again. The act is both positive and negative face threatening. Melvin attacks Simon's need to be unimpeded with explicit imperative directives ('So never, never again interrupt me', 'don't knock'), and he also attacks Simon's need to be liked and approved of ('some fudge-packer you dated'). Besides, Melvin's use of 'sweetheart' is condescending, and along with the 'queer' references, mocking of Simon's sexuality. The whole of this speech constitutes a threat. The contribution's force, long-windedness and slight non-fluency (notice the pauses and abandoned sentences) add to the impression of Melvin as an angry bully.

Simon's response on l. 31, 'Yes. It's not a subtle point you're making' flouts the manner maxim to imply, 'You weren't subtle.' Therefore, despite the fact that this constitutes a second part to Melvin's first part, it is an off-record FTA on Melvin's positive face ('You are tactless'), triggered through the relevant flout. Finally, Melvin's 'Okay, then' (l. 32) is condescending and therefore possibly a positive FTA directed towards Simon. Equally face threatening is Melvin's rude slamming of the door in Simon's face.

Very cleverly and very nastily, Melvin has managed to completely change the conversation topic away from Verdell, and trap Simon into agreeing with him. Melvin comes across as powerful; he is the one who is asking most questions and performing most FTAs. Simon is intimidated, weak and over-polite; he merely responds to the questions posed, even when these are not genuine. Simon is certainly the one who is powerless conversationally, despite his attempts to be brave here.

One thing this analysis has revealed is that the theories certainly complement each other. It proves useful to consider turn-taking aspects alongside non-fluency, speech acts, the handling of the maxims and linguistic politeness. Also, the performance indicators and actual actions could be classified as various sorts of 'act', much like verbal acts. For instance, knocking on someone's door can be as negative face-threatening as a directive. Nevertheless, and as noted earlier, what is most important is to account for all physical and verbal acts in their situational and verbal context.

See Chapter 9, Task L

8.5 Chapter review

In both Chapters 7 and 8, I have focused on screenplay texts in particular – that is, popular film and television drama rather than stage plays – in the hope that some of my audience will be familiar with the actual dramatic texts as well as the characters. Similar analyses could, of course, be performed on stage plays. It nonetheless proved important to account for the scripts' directions and performance indicators in the course of my analysis, something that an analyst of stage plays should also be concerned with. Such an analyst should consider not only the language the characters use to one another, but also the language the playwright uses to the audience and even to the characters or actors themselves. Moreover, as Toolan (2001: 104) put it, in film there is a blend of modalities: visual representation, non-verbal aural representation, non-verbal human noises, speech and even writing to consider. McIntyre adds that '[i]n film particularly, the notion of point of view can often apply literally, as the camera position can reflect exactly what a particular character would see' (2006: 12). In my various analyses here, I do not pretend to have covered all perspectives necessary to the analysis of film, but I hope to have highlighted some of the aspects that should accompany an interpretation of the written text in plays.

This chapter was concerned in particular with the pragmatic analysis of dramatic texts. In my analysis of speech acts, I distinguished between direct, performative, and indirect speech acts, and highlighted the distinction between an act's locution, illocution and perlocution, with particular reference to jokes and misunderstandings. I then briefly outlined the five-sided speech act classification system, before discussing felicity conditions, using 'promise' as an example. I outlined Grice's cooperative principle and explained its accompanying maxims, then considered the theory's limitations in brief. Following this, I analysed Grice's politeness maxim in some detail, in relation to Brown and Levinson's (1987) politeness theory. I distinguished between positive and negative face, and explained the meaning of FTAs, before outlining the options someone has when performing one of these.

When it comes to the actual analysis of dramatic texts, it proved useful to consider (a) what speech acts characters use and how these are performed, (b) what maxims characters flout and violate, and (c) what linguistic (im)politeness strategies the characters use toward one another. Such analyses can allow someone to infer information about both the characters themselves and their relationship to each other. Finally, the analyses proved to complement each other, while it is also important to account for the classification being done in light of the utterances' verbal and situational context.

Stylistics of Drama Practice

Task A

Figure 9.1 (overleaf) is an extract from the 1999 *Notting Hill* film script. It features William, a shop-keeper, who lives and works in Notting Hill. This scene takes place at the start of the film, where he catches a thief trying to steal a book from his bookshop. Meanwhile a famous actress, Anna, is also browsing through books at the same store. Try to analyse the extract's discourse structure.

Comments on Task A

The extract features three separate conversations.

In the first conversation (lines 1–17), William spots and thereafter confronts the thief trying to steal a book. William gains the thief's attention ('Excuse me', line 1) and thereafter hints that he caught the thief off-guard ('We've got a security camera in this bit of the shop', l. 5). Since this does not appear to have the desired effect of gaining a confession out of the thief, William tries a more direct accusation ('I saw you put that book down your trousers', l. 7), something the thief proceeds to deny ('I haven't got a book down my trousers', l. 10). William then pretends to be giving the thief the benefit of the doubt, pretend-apologises for his direct accusation, and in fact threatens that he will call the police if the thief fails to cooperate ('I tell you what – I'll call the police – and, what can I say? – If I'm wrong about the whole book-down-the-trousers scenario, I really apologize', l.11–13). The thief appears to be frightened into a near-confession ('Okay – what if I did have a book down my trousers?' l. 14). Particularly effective is William's contribution on l.15, ('Well, ideally, when I went back to the desk, you'd remove the Cadogan guide to Bali from your trousers, and either wipe it and put it back, or buy it.', l. 15–17), which gives

Bookstore: William, the shop-keeper, moves toward the back of the shop and approaches a man in slightly ill-fitting clothes.

WILLIAM	Excuse me.	1
THIEF	Yes.	2
WILLIAM	Bad news.	3
THIEF	What?	4
WILLIAM	We've got a security camera in this bit of the shop.	5
THIEF	So?	6
WILLIAM	So, I saw you put that book down your trousers.	7
THIEF	What book?	8
WILLIAM	The one down your trousers.	9
THIEF	I haven't got a book down my trousers.	10
WILLIAM	Right -- well, then we have something of an impasse. I tell you what – I'll call the police – and, what can I say? -- If I'm wrong about the whole book-down-the-trousers scenario, I really apologize.	11 12 13
THIEF	Okay -- what if I did have a book down my trousers?	14
WILLIAM	Well, ideally, when I went back to the desk, you'd remove the Cadogan guide to Bali from your trousers, and either wipe it and put it back, or buy it. See you in a sec.	15 16 17

He returns to his desk. In the monitor we just glimpse, as does William, the book coming out of the trousers and put back on the shelves. The thief drifts out towards the door. Anna, who has observed all this, is looking at a blue book on the counter.

WILLIAM	(*to Anna*) Sorry about that ...	18
ANNA	No, that's fine. I was going to steal one myself but now I've changed my mind. Signed by the author, I see.	19 20
WILLIAM	Yes, we couldn't stop him. If you can find an unsigned copy, it's worth an absolute fortune.	21 22

She smiles. Suddenly the thief is there.

THIEF	Excuse me.	23
ANNA	Yes.	24
THIEF	Can I have your autograph?	25
ANNA	What's your name?	26
THIEF	Rufus.	27

She signs his scruffy piece of paper. He tries to read it.

THIEF	What does it say?	28
ANNA	Well, that's the signature – and above, it says 'Dear Rufus –you belong in jail.'	29 30
THIEF	Nice one. Would you like my phone number?	31
ANNA	Tempting but ... no, thank you.	32

Extract from *Notting Hill* screenplay, by Richard Curtis. © 1999 Universal City Studios, Inc. All Rights Reserved. Courtesy of Universal Studios Licensing LLLP.

Figure 9.1

details about the book stolen, and therefore clearly signals that the allegation was not without basis. The thief is left to choose between one of two options: to either wipe and return the book on the shelf, or instead buy it.

Anna appears to overhear this first conversation, something signalled by her joke on l. 19 ('I was going to steal one [book] myself ...'). This whole first conversation hence is analysable on three discourse levels: William converses with the thief, the conversation is overheard by Anna, and the readers or audience overhear the first two characters' conversation also. This discourse structure enables us to explain what first impressions we get of these two characters. Through this opening conversation, William appears to be cunning, funny and personable, not to mention strong-willed and agreeable, something which perhaps goes a long way to justify Anna's attraction to him in the course of the film. The thief, on the other hand, appears to be rather bad at picking up on William's hints, and hence weak and pathetic where his challenges fail to have the desired effect; he does not get away with his crime, and is eventually humiliated into returning the book to the shelf. The reference to the book being 'wiped' also gives an unpleasant impression of this character's hygiene. Also, the reference to the content of the book makes the thief appear to be a rather obscure character. Why would anyone want a travel company's guide to Bali? If they can't afford the book itself, chances are they are unlikely to afford a trip to Bali.

The second conversation takes place between William and Anna, in lines 18–22. Here, William is back at his desk, and apologises to Anna for having kept her waiting. She accepts his apology, yet her response also hints that she was rather impressed with William's tough treatment of the thief ('I was going to steal one myself but now I changed my mind', l. 19–20). She notices that the book she chose was signed by the author, something that prompts William to joke back, 'Yes, we couldn't stop him. If you can find an unsigned copy, it's worth an absolute fortune', l. 21–22. Here, he ironically pretends that the author damaged the book by signing it, whereas common knowledge suggests that signed copies of books are worth more than unsigned copies, not the other way round.

This second conversation is analysable on two discourse levels. On one, William and Anna jokingly flirt with each other, while on the other, the playwright communicates to the audience information not only about the two characters' good humour, but also about their mutually liking each other at this stage.

The final conversation takes place between the thief and Anna (l. 23–32). The thief, acknowledging Anna's celebrity status, asks for her autograph, to which Anna agrees. What is particularly striking about this scene is that the thief seems entirely unaware how badly everyone thinks of him at this point. He seems to think it quite normal to walk up to a famous actress and talk to her when he has just been caught stealing. Anna asks for his name, something common and so unexceptional for autograph-givers. She then signs his piece of paper, which he struggles to read. She reveals that she wrote 'Dear Rufus – you belong in jail.' (l.29–30), something that certainly is unusual for the autograph-writing genre; she is breaking the conventions with respect to what people write when giving an autograph. At this stage the thief might be expected to pick up on this insult or rejection, but he appears to treat is as some sort of compliment instead, to which he replies by offering Anna his phone number. Anna refuses, but only after she pretends to be flattered by the offer ('Tempting but …no, thank you', l. 32).

This third conversation is also analysable on two discourse levels. On one, the thief interacts with Anna, while on the other, the playwright communicates information about these two characters through their conversation. Anna appears to be good-hearted and agreeable at first, in accepting the request for an autograph. Having signed the thief's paper, however, she appears to be assertive and strong-minded, as she not only remains unthreatened by the request, she also does not hesitate to make it clear what she thinks of him. When she rejects his phone number offer, she also appears to be rather witty, ironic and yet polite. The thief, on the other hand, appears to be entirely oblivious about the consequences of his actions, in both asking the actress for her autograph, then offering her his phone number. He again fails to pick up on Anna's hinting strategies, something that makes him look ignorant and unmindful.

Note that your analysis could differ from mine: normally slightly different analyses are interpreted as variations on the same interpretation.

Task B

Below is another short extract from the 1999 *Notting Hill* screenplay. William has invited famous actress Anna to his sister's (Honey's) birthday dinner party. Anna is wishing Honey goodnight, and Honey is apologising for having followed her to the loo earlier. Consider the meaningfulness of the non-fluency features.

ANNA:	Night, night, Honey!	1
HONEY:	I'm so sorry about the loo thing. I meant to leave but I just … look, ring me if	2
	you need someone to go shopping with. I know lots of nice, cheap places …	3
	not that money necessarily … (*gives up*) nice to meet you.	4

Extract from *Notting Hill* screenplay, by Richard Curtis. © 1999 Universal City Studios, Inc. All Rights Reserved. Courtesy of Universal Studios Licensing LLLP.

Comments on Task B

Anna wishes Honey goodnight, but Honey, anxious to leave Anna with a good impression of her, whole-heartedly apologises for the awkward situation she created earlier ('I'm so sorry').

Despite the extract being short overall, it certainly is easy to spot many non-fluency features here. To start with, whereas Honey is perhaps expected to just say 'goodnight' back, her response proves unnecessarily overlong, in her attempt to impress and befriend Anna. Her reply includes abandoned sentences/utterances or false starts ('I meant to leave but I just ...', 'I know lots of nice, cheap places ...'), something signalled by both the deserted grammatical structures and punctuation ('...') here, the latter further indicating non-verbal fillers or pauses. The grammar is simple and informal ('loo thing'), while it includes contractions ('I'm'), verbal fillers ('look'), hedges which minimise the extent of her imposition ('but I just ...', 'ring me if you need ...'), monitoring features ('not that money necessarily ...'), not to mention inexplicitness and hence assumed background knowledge in the reference to the 'loo thing' to start with.

Overall, although these features are quite typical of everyday conversation, and hence natural and un-interpretable in that context, in this dramatic context they do require interpretation. Honey is very willing for them to have a friendship ('ring me if you need someone to go shopping with') and hence over-eager to appear polite and 'normal' ('I'm so sorry about the loo thing'). She is keen to explain herself ('I meant to leave but I just ...'), and wants to prove useful and therefore worthy a person to have as a friend ('I know lots of nice, cheap places ...'). In this last attempt, she realises that she perhaps inadvertently insulted Anna by implying that she is the sort of person to be interested in 'cheap places'. Besides, Anna is a famous actress and hence very rich. Having realised this, Honey tries to compensate for her potential insult with 'not that money necessarily ...', a contribution that she fails to complete, realising, at this stage that she is trying too hard and therefore potentially sounds intense, over-enthusiastic or even insincere. As the stage directions indicate, it is at this stage that Honey 'gives up' presumably trying to impress and befriend Anna, and instead offers the less fanatical, if perhaps slightly formalised 'nice to meet you', with which she eventually ends the conversation.

Task C

Go through Sacks et al's points (a)–(l) (p. 134), and describe the turn-taking organisation for a television chat show (such as *Jerry Springer* or *Trisha*).

Comments on Task C

A viewer watching a television chat show is told from the very start, normally during the titles, what topic the conversation will follow (such as 'Did you cheat? Lie detection results'). Hence, the conversational topic is strictly controlled. What parties say is to a certain extent also specified in advance (see 'g'), if not actually fully scripted. The conversation length is also specified in advance (see 'f'). A viewer expects a chat show to last a particular amount of time (such as an hour), so all of the chat show conversations are expected to collectively fit into that given time slot. Nevertheless, the individual contributions can vary in length. Such 'chats' normally take place in a television studio, but are filmed prior to the show's actual television screening.

In a chat show, the host holds most, if not all, of the conversational power. Not only are chat show hosts responsible for allocating turns in the course of their show (to either their 'guests' or members of the audience), they also monitor the topic of the conversation throughout. The host is the one meant to ensure that one party talks at a time (see 'a'), and (s)he is also the one who controls the extent to which transition between turns will take place (see 'b'), preferably without over-long gaps (see 'c'). The host is also the one who controls the order and size of turns (see 'd' and 'e'). By the show's start, the host already knows who will talk (see 'i'), when (see 'k'), how long for, and whether continuously or not (see 'j'). In other words, relative distribution of turns is specified in advance (see 'h'), while the number of contributing parties is either predetermined (when they are guests) or controlled (when they are members of the audience who are nominated to speak). Where deviations occur, the host is the one responsible for restoring order. Security officers are often available to control any argument that occurs, while it is not uncommon for the host to ask guests to stop talking, let someone else talk or even leave the room. It is only the host who has this power (see 'l').

The guests have more power than members of the audience. The guests are explicitly introduced, and allowed to speak in some length, and more than once, when on stage. In contrast to this, members of the audience can only contribute if/when nominated, in which case they are asked to stand, talk only once and be brief. Much like a classroom situation, members of the audience are treated like students; they can raise their hands to signal a willingness to contribute, but it is only if and when they are nominated (by the 'teacher-like' host), that they actually contribute.

Task D

Analyse the turn-taking in the excerpt in Figure 9.2 from the script of the 1998 film *There's Something about Mary*. It is set in a Cumberland, Rhode

Island High School. It's the early 1980s, and everyone is arriving at school in the morning.

	We push through the parking lot crowd to a nervous, lanky kid, Ted Peloquin.	
Man's Voice		
	(Voice-Over) When I was sixteen years old I fell in love ...	1
	CLOSE ON – RENISE, a tough girl with stringy brown hair and a shiny forehead, as she turns toward the camera.	
TED	Hey, Renise.	2
	She barely looks at him as he approaches, just drags on her smoke.	
RENISE	Hey.	3
TED	So what's up?	4
RENISE	Eh.	5
TED	Great. Great.	6
	(beat)	
TED	So listen, uh, I was wondering if maybe you wanted to go to the prom you know, with me.	7
		8
	Renise looks unenthused.	
TED	*(cont'd)* It's no big deal, whatever I mean, if you want.	9
RENISE	See, the thing is, I heard a rumour that this guy I like was gonna ask me.	10
TED	Uh-huh.	11
RENISE	Yeah, so ... I'm gonna wait and see what happens there ... But that sounds great, yeah.	12
		13
	Ted nods, confused.	
TED	Okay.	14
	(beat)	
TED	So is that a yes or a no?	15
RENISE	I think I was very clear, Ted. If everything else falls apart, maybe.	16
	Renise throws down her butt and storms off.	
TED	I'm gonna hold you to that.	17

Extract from *There's Something About Mary* screenplay, by Ed Decter and John J. Strauss and Peter Farrelly and Bobby Farrelly. ©1998. Courtesy of Twentieth Century Fox.

Figure 9.2

Comments on Task D

Teenage Ted approaches his 'first love' to ask her out to the prom. He greets her ('Hey, Renise' in l. 2) and then uses an opening type of pre-sequence to smooth the ground for his invitation ('So what's up?' in l. 4). Even though Renise does indeed respond to his initial greeting ('Hey' in l. 3), she somewhat challenges his pre-sequence opening ('Eh' in l. 5), to indicate that she either did not hear him or was simply indifferent to his contribution. This he either fails to pick up on altogether, or simply chooses to ignore ('Great, great' in l. 6).

His non-fluency in l. 7–8 and 9 signals that he is anxious and lacking in confidence when asking her out. He uses fillers, hedges and monitoring features to put the invitation across ('So listen, uh, I was wondering if maybe you wanted to go to the prom you know, with me. It's no big deal, whatever I mean, if you want'), and in doing so presumably wishes to lessen not only the imposition, but also Renise's potential and likely 'let-down' rejection blow.

Rather than giving him a 'yes' (preferred response) or 'no' (dispreferred response), Renise instead mentions a guy she likes, and that there is a rumour he will also ask her to the prom. She then says she will wait and see what happens, after which she says, strangely, 'But that sounds great, yeah.' In other words, her response is neither preferred nor dispreferred. She merely says she would rather leave her options open. Her non-fluency (meaning her pauses) gives an impression of her speaking her mind, oblivious to the effect that her response will have on Ted. She does not appear to appreciate that letting him know she would prefer to go to the prom with someone else will hurt his feelings. Understandably, Ted is (at the very least) confused by her response, and asks for clarification on l. 15 ('So is that a yes or a no?'), something to which Renise snaps, 'I think I was very clear, Ted. If everything else falls apart, maybe' (l. 16). What is amusing about this response is that she neither was clear earlier, nor is clear now. What Ted wanted was a clear 'yes' or 'no' answer, to which he eventually gets a very unsure 'maybe'. Ted's response in l. 17 ('I'm gonna hold you to that') makes him out to be rather pitiable. Not only is he willing to be a runner-up or back-up date for Renise, he also wishes to commit her to keeping him there.

This conversation's turn-taking does not run as smoothly as perhaps we would expect. We expect people taking part in a conversation of two to take it in turns to contribute, but Ted here takes more turns than Renise. Without accounting for the adult Ted's voice-over turn on l. 1 (which functions as a sort of orientating abstract, bringing us into a story-world), the teenage Ted takes a total of nine turns in contrast to Renise's mere five. Also, it is Ted who initiates the conversation with Renise on l. 2, and although she suddenly leaves at the end without saying 'goodbye', it is he again who closes the conversation in l. 17. Notice that she does not bother to respond to him at all here.

Even though Ted speaks on most occasions (that is, turns), it is Renise who appears to speak the longest. Teenage Ted has an average of six words per turn, whereas Renise has an average of nine to ten words per turn. This implies that Renise is the more confident of the two, while Ted appears to be stunned into almost speechlessness by her unwillingness to give him a straight answer to his invitation.

Although Ted initiates the 'prom invitation' conversation topic, Renise tries to shift the topic slightly towards the other guy who might ask her out. Ted attempts to bring the topic back to the pair of them maybe going to the prom (l. 15), but fails to get a desirable response. The characters are on a first-name basis, though Renise's use of his name on l. 16 appears to be more aggressive than caring.

Task E

Revisit the texts for Task A (Figure 9.1) and Task D (Figure 9.2), and consider the extent to which the film directions and performance indicators contribute to your interpretation of them.

Comments on Task E

The *Notting Hill* thief is described as having 'slightly ill-fitting' clothes, something that adds to the impression of him as messy and perhaps chaotic. He gets caught stealing the book, is warned to return it, and drifts 'out toward the door' having returned the stolen book to the shelf. Nevertheless, he is then said to 'suddenly' turn up to ask for Anna's autograph. So he appears at the desk unexpectedly, and perhaps slightly eerily so.

The reference to his 'scruffy piece of paper' in the film directions gives, again, an impression of him as untidy and frenzied. Perhaps the reference to his struggling to read the autograph further alludes to his disarray, though this might also be suggestive of his inability to either read at all, or work out the actress's handwriting. As for Anna, the fact that she 'smiles' at William adds to the impression that she is either flirting with him or responding to his flirting.

The production instructions and performance indicators are also particularly important in the interpretation of the *There's Something About Mary* piece. The initial description of Ted and Renise's appearance constructs a first impression of their character. Ted is described as a 'nervous, lanky kid', in contrast to Renise who is described as a 'tough girl with stringy brown hair and a shiny forehead'. The two make for a rather visually unlikely pair, which adds to their incompatibility when it comes to their linguistic and social behaviour.

As noted earlier, Ted takes a total of nine turns whereas Renise takes a mere five. The '*(beat)*' indicators between l. 6–7 and l. 14–15, and the note that Renise is 'unenthused' between l. 8 and l. 9, indicate that she chooses to be quiet rather than take her turn to speak on these occasions. Overall, Renise's unwillingness to comply with the expected one-person-talks-at-a-time turn-taking rule reveals her to be rather uninterested in conversing with Ted in the first place, something that is certainly *reinforced* by the added performance indicators throughout; she barely looks at him as he approaches, looks unenthused at his invitation, and rather rudely storms off at the end, before or without closing the conversation.

In contrast, Ted is said to be nodding at Renise (between l. 13 and l. 14), and confusingly so. This adds to the impression of him as agreeable and wanting to avoid confrontation (besides, he is 'in love'), despite his bewilderment at her response.

Task F

Outline your schematic expectation of (1) the primary characters from *Friends*, (2) a male protagonist in a romance novel, and (3) a Greek person, having watched a film such as *My Big Fat Greek Wedding* (2002, written by Nia Vardalos) or *300* (2006, written by Zack Snyder and Kurt Johnstad).

Comments on Task F

1 If you are familiar with the popular series *Friends*, you are likely to have developed person schemata for each of the six primary characters.

Rachel enjoyed a very comfortable childhood, and therefore is thought of as rather spoilt. She is kind to others, and often a bit of a push-over. She wants to make a career for herself in the fashion industry, as she loves fashion and shopping. Phoebe is rather eccentric and feeble-minded. She is very generous and friendly, but has the tendency to offer irrelevant and often incoherent contributions when conversing with others. She is the most street-wise of the whole group, as she has spent time literally living in the street, and has hidden depths. She is a vegetarian, and is not afraid to fight for her political beliefs. Monica feels unappreciated and undervalued by her mother, and has a rather obsessive personality, especially when it comes to things like winning in games, cleaning and organising events. She has problems relaxing, and likes to be in control, which is why she can be quite bossy.

Ross is intelligent and accomplished. Although his parents are very proud of him and his academic career, his friends have no interest in it whatsoever. In fact, they think of him as rather boring, particularly when he tries to talk to them about his work and research. He is very loving and giving in relationships, but can also be quite naïve when in love with a woman. Joey is very successful with the ladies, but very unwilling to commit to anyone. He is the least intelligent and informed of the group, which is why he is often ridiculed by the rest. He acts, and wants to succeed in the film industry, but constantly fails in his attempts to do so. He loves food the most, particularly sandwiches, and often stops by Monica's flat just to help himself to some food. Finally, Chandler is probably the most immature of the group. He has had a difficult childhood, with his parents divorcing and his dad becoming a transvestite. He uses humour as a defence mechanism, and also has a fear of commitment. Much like Joey, he enjoys playing games, and is mostly thought of by the others as having a boring job and not much ambition.

Of course, it is important to account for the changing personalities of all of these characters as the series progresses in time, not to mention the ways in which the characters often come to 'surprise' the reader. For instance, though afraid of commitment, Chandler grows very close to Monica and eventually marries her. Similarly, despite Phoebe's strong beliefs when it comes to being a vegetarian, she craves and eats meat when she is pregnant.

2. Your role schema of a male protagonist in a romance novel is likely to depend on the extent to which you are familiar with/have read any novels of this sort. My own role schema for such a persona contains physical characteristics, personality features and certain expectations of his behaviour towards the female persona. I would expect the male protagonist in such fiction to be young (more likely in his thirties than his forties or twenties), tall, handsome, and probably dark-complexioned, with brown hair and a good build. In terms of his personality, I would expect him to be kind, funny, confident, intelligent, and most probably loving to, and protective of, the female persona, at least by the story's very end. The woman would more likely be helping him to 'find' himself, and she would be as much of a saviour to him as he is to her. I would expect him to pursue the female protagonist for some time before she succumbs to his charms. The budding romance between the two is expected to be warm and tender, he would prove himself to be a good and devoted lover, while the love between the two would be lasting. No doubt your romance schema will differ from mine, but I would expect it to at least share some similarities with mine.

3. If you are Greek, or have ever interacted with or somehow familiarised yourselves with Greeks, or have watched such films as *My Big Fat Greek Wedding* or *300*, you are likely to have developed a certain idea or 'group schema' of Greeks. Being Greek myself, I found both of these films interesting and amusing, particularly when it comes to the stereotypical portrayal in both films of my native culture.

In the former film, Greeks (or, at least, migrants to the United States with

Greek ancestry) are presented as very family oriented, yet also rather hard working and business-minded. Women stay at home and do the cleaning, the cooking and the washing up, while the men are out working and supporting the family financially. The parents (and extended family) are often responsible for supporting the children financially and emotionally through life, while it is not atypical for a father to buy his married daughter a house to live in, and for her mother to help bring up any grandchildren. Greek brothers are protective of their sisters, and do not have the same sort of pressure to settle down as young female Greeks do. It is preferable, if not necessary, for Greeks to marry other Greeks, and for potential husbands (and presumably wives) to be approved by the father of the bride (or groom) long before a very long, over-indulgent Greek Orthodox wedding. Any Greek celebration involves dancing, smashing plates, and eating a lot of food, particularly meat.

The latter (and more recent) film *300* presents Greeks in a slightly different light. Although the film again gives a very stereotypical impression of this group, the setting is very different, as the Greeks are in fact Spartans, and the story takes place in ancient history (the 480 BC Battle of Thermopylae, to be more exact). The Greeks are again presented as rather xenophobic, and yet incredibly powerful figures who, despite their small numbers, are capable of fighting and sometimes winning impossible battles against various non-Greeks. Despite the odds, and the inevitable fate that awaits them, King Leonidas's 300 spirited, feisty Spartans secure their honourable place in history by dying in glory in the battle. While the men are fighters, groomed from a very young age to fight against any potential enemies, the women are beautiful, glamorous, and mostly stay-at-home child-bearers. The relationships between the Greeks are very passionate and even homoerotic, while the whole culture is presented as obsessed with physical perfection and beauty.

What we need to keep in mind is that there may or may not be any truth in any of these socially schematic characterisations, but it is important to take into account whatever schematic (or stereotypical) expectations you have of people, roles and groups, especially when interpreting the nature of any dramatic or other fictional characters you encounter. The information you get from the text needs to be coupled with the information that you yourself bring to the text, in order for you to get a clearer conception of how characterisation is created.

Task G

Analyse the locution, illocution and perlocution of the customer's contribution in the following (rather awful) jokes:

1 Customer: Waiter, what's this fly doing in my soup?
  Waiter: Looks like the breast-stroke to me sir!

2 Customer: Waiter, there's a dead fly in my soup.
  Waiter: What do you expect for £1 – a live one?

3 Customer: Waiter, there's a fly in my soup!
  Waiter: Well, keep quiet about it or everyone will want one.

4 Customer: Waiter, your tie is in my soup!
  Waiter: That's all right, sir, it's not shrinkable.

Comments on Task G

1 The customer performs what is syntactically an interrogative. It's meant to be taken as an indirect speech act of a complaint, asking the waiter to do something about this unfortunate occurrence: perhaps get him another soup, give him his money back, get the chef to the table, or get the customer a complimentary bottle of wine. Nevertheless, the waiter takes the customer's contribution to be a genuine question about the fly's activity. Therefore, the customer's 'Waiter, what's this fly doing in my soup?' contribution has both the locution and perlocution of 'Do inform me of the fly's swim-type activity, waiter', although the illocution is, 'Do something about it, waiter!'

2 The customer's contribution is a declarative syntactically. It's meant to be taken as an indirect speech act of a complaint, again asking the waiter to do something about the unfortunate occurrence. Nevertheless, the waiter pretends to have misunderstood what the customer was implying. The customer's 'Waiter, there's a dead fly in my soup' contribution has the locution 'I'm hereby informing you, waiter, that there is a dead fly in my soup', whereas the illocution is 'Do something about it!' The pretend-perlocution is 'I expected a live fly!'

3 The customer's illocution and locution are pretty much the same as in 2. Whereas the customer is actually saying, 'There is a fly in here' (locution), he is implying, 'There shouldn't be one, so do something about it' (illocution). The waiter again pretends to have misunderstood the illocution. He responds as if the illocution actually was more of a speech act of praise: 'I am impressed! There's a complimentary fly in my soup' (perlocution).

4 The customer's 'Waiter, your tie is in my soup' is a declarative, but an indirect speech act of a complaint. The locution is, 'I'm informing you that your tie is in my soup', while the illocution is ,'Take it out of there'. Although the waiter does indeed appear to have picked up on the illocution here, he does not seem to appreciate the reasoning behind it. So, whereas the illocution is much like,

'That's disgusting. Get it out!', the perlocution is, 'I'm worried about your tie. Get it out!'

Task H

How would you describe the following utterances (by a mother to her misbehaving child) in terms of speech act theory?

1 Mind your language!
2 Would you mind your language please?
3 I'm getting a headache here.
4 What sort of a monster are you?

Comments on Task H

1 'Mind your language!' is in syntactic terms an imperative. It is a direct speech act of a command to the child to refrain from misbehaving.
2 'Would you mind your language please?' is in syntactic terms an interrogative. Since it is not a genuine question for the child to answer, it is an indirect speech act, that of a command ('Mind your language!').
3 'I'm getting a headache here' is, in syntactic terms, a declarative. It could be thought of as a genuine assertion that the mother has a headache, but it is probably again meant as an indirect speech act of a command for the child to stop misbehaving (to therefore prevent the mother from getting a full-on headache).
4 'What sort of a monster are you?' is in syntactic terms an interrogative. It is certainly not a genuine question for the child to answer, but is meant as an indirect speech act of an insult ('You are a monster') coupled with a command ('Stop acting like a monster'), again to the child to stop misbehaving.

Even though 'c' appears to be an expressive speech act, and 'd' is perhaps a representative speech act, all of these acts are ultimately classified as directives, since they aim to get the hearer (the misbehaving child) to do something in response to them (that is, behave).

Task I

Look at these brief dialogues. Try to spell out the meanings of them, and to explain your inferences using Grice's maxims.

1 A: What are you doing tonight?
   B: Oh, not much, a bit of this and a bit of that, you know.

2 C: You must be the nicest man in the whole world.

3 D: Will you get me something expensive for Christmas?
   E: I'm not made of money, you know.

4 F: How many times have I asked you to stop annoying me?
   G: Well, it was three times yesterday, and twice this morning.

5 H: War is war.

6 I: I really don't like Judy.
   J: I think we should go get some fresh air.

7 K: Are you watching the horror film with us?
   L: Do pigs fly?

Comments on Task I

B's contribution constitutes a quantity maxim flout as it is not as informative as required. It could also be thought of as a bit of a manner flout, in that it is a bit obscure. The implicature is 'I don't want to get into it' or 'I'd rather not say.' If there is no implicature to be drawn, we are probably looking at a straight violation instead.

C's contribution most probably flouts the quality maxim. Unless C has indeed met all of the men in the world, she (let's assume C is female) is not in a position to make such a claim. The contribution could therefore be thought of as untruthful. The implicature is, 'You are very nice. I am impressed.'

E's contribution is a relation maxim flout. It is indeed truthful (E is not made of money), but irrelevant to what D asked. The implicature is, 'No. I can't afford it.'

G's contribution might indeed be truthful and informative, but G has obviously failed (or pretends to have failed) to pick up on the implication of F's interrogative. F's interrogative indirectly performs the speech act of a complaint, whereas G responds to it as if it were a genuine question. Hence, G's contribution either flouts the manner maxim (the implicature being 'I'm ignoring you') or violates the manner maxim if G has genuinely misunderstood F's implication (in which case there is no implicature to be drawn).

H's apparently pointless and tautological contribution is uninformative, hence it flouts the quantity maxim. The implicature is, 'The results of war are inevitable.'

J's contribution is not relevant to I's utterance, and therefore flouts the relevance maxim, the implicature being 'I don't want to talk about it' or even 'Judy is in the room with us and so might hear us.'

L's contribution flouts both the manner and relation maxims, as it does not directly, unambiguously and relevantly answer the question posed, the implicature being 'The answer to your question is the same as the answer to my question,' meaning 'Very obviously no.'

Task J

Using speech act theory and Grice's maxims, analyse this very short extract from the 1999 *Notting Hill* script. William is in his living room.

	William is looking out the window, lost in thought. His housemate Spike enters.	
SPIKE	Come on – open up – this is me – Spikey – I'm in contact with some	1
	quite important vibrations. What's wrong?	2
	Spike settles on the arm of a chair. William decides to open up a bit.	
WILLIAM	Well, okay. There's this girl...	3
SPIKE	Aha! I'd been getting a female vibe. Good. Speak on, dear friend.	4
WILLIAM	She's someone I just can't – someone who – self-evidently can't be mine	5
	– and it's as if I've taken love heroin – and now I can't even have it	6
	again. I've opened Pandora's box. And there's trouble inside.	7
	Spike nods thoughtfully.	
SPIKE	Yeh. Yeh... tricky... tricky... I knew a girl at school called Pandora ...	8
	never got to see her box though.	9
	He roars with laughter. Williams smiles.	
WILLIAM	Thanks. Yes – very helpful.	10

Comments on Task J

In l. 1–2, Spike encourages his housemate to open up with a series of directives ('Come on – open up'), representatives ('This is me – Spikey', and 'I'm in contact with some quite important vibrations'), and an actual direct speech act of a question as to what is bothering him ('What's wrong?'). Coupled with his non-verbal behaviour – that is, his settling on the arm of a chair – he is trying to initiate a conversational topic surrounding William's thoughtful mood, so as to get him to actually open up and ultimately help ease his friend's pain.

William 'decides to open up' and gives the second part of the adjacency pair;

he responds to 'What's wrong?' with 'Well, okay. There's this girl...', only to be interrupted by Spike. Spike's response is rather enthusiastic and self-indulgent, and displays both representatives ('Aha! I'd been getting a female vibe'), encouraging directives ('Speak on, dear friend') and feedback ('Good'). This adds to an impression of Spike wanting to be helpful, yet perhaps trying too much to be a supportive receiver of William's contributions. Strangely enough, Spike appears to genuinely believe that he is in contact with 'vibrations' and can sense things without actually knowing what's happening. At the playwright–audience discourse level of the drama, the viewers get an impression of Spike being peculiar in believing that he has such powers, perhaps much like Phoebe from *Friends*.

Unlike Spike's opening, William's contribution, particularly in lines 5–7, is less fluent than expected. He abandons utterances, monitors himself, and hedges a lot ('She's someone I just can't – someone who – self-evidently can't be mine – and it's as if I've taken love heroin – and now I can't even have it again'). As indicated by these linguistic features, William is in a rather desperate situation and finds it difficult to explain his feelings to his housemate. The performance indicators throughout (his looking out of the window, being lost in thoughts and hesitating when it comes to opening up) add to this impression. Note that William's response is expressive (stating his feelings), yet flouts the quantity and quality maxims on lines 6–7. He obviously has not taken love heroin, neither has he literally opened Pandora's box, nor is there any trouble inside (the act's locution). The implicature is that 'I am in love and don't know what to do about it' (the act's illocution).

Spike nods thoughtfully between lines 7 and 8, and his later response is non-fluent (notice the use of repetition and pauses), something that signals that he is genuinely thinking it through. Nevertheless, he blatantly violates the relation maxim when he completely changes the topic of the conversation ('I knew a girl at school called Pandora ... never got to see her box though'). Here, he pretends to have not picked up William's earlier implicature. He pretends that the perlocution of l. 7 is the same as the line's locution. At the character–character level, his laughter indicates that this is a pretend-misunderstanding. Nevertheless, at the playwright–audience level, Spike again appears to be decidedly odd; he is rather oblivious to the seriousness of William's situation, and in contrast to his earlier behaviour, perhaps slightly unkind.

According to the performance indicators, William smiles between l. 9–10, something that gives the impression of his taking a light-hearted approach to Spike's earlier contribution. His l. 10 line, though expressive ('Thanks') and representative ('Yes – very helpful'), is obviously ironic, therefore it too constitutes a quality flout. The implicature is that William is not thankful and he does not, in fact, find Spike helpful. The thanking speech act is infelicitous; the sincerity felicity condition is not fulfilled.

Task K

In terms of politeness theory, how would you describe the following utterances, delivered by a lecturer to students during class?

1 'Will you be quiet?'
2 'Be quiet!'
3 'I can't hear myself speak, you guys!'
4 'You make me very proud', uttered with honesty.
5 'You make me very proud', uttered with irony.

Comments on Task K

1 'Will you be quiet?' is an indirect speech act of a request/directive for the students to be quiet. It is a face threatening act damaging the students' negative face, as it is in the interrogative form. It therefore encodes negative politeness also.

2 'Be quiet!' is a direct speech act of a directive as it is in the imperative form. It is again a face threatening act toward the students' negative face, yet performed bald on record this time: that is, directly, and in accordance to Grice's maxims.

3 'I can't hear myself speak, you guys!' is again a directive, yet performed indirectly through the performance of a representative/expressive declarative. It is a negative FTA, but performed off record. The implied 'Be quiet!' FTA is not performed directly (the speaker can avoid responsibility for performing it), and is instead triggered through the flouting of the manner, quality and probably even relation maxims here. In other words, the contribution is neither clear nor true (the speaker most probably can hear herself speak), nor relevant to what the lecturer actually wants the students to do in response to the declaration. Finally, the 'you guys' bit at the end encodes positive politeness to soften the blow of the FTA.

4 'You make me very proud' is a positive face enhancing act directed toward the students. In this case, perhaps more directly even, it is speaker positive face enhancing also. Besides, well-performing students at times reflect well-performing lecturers, their students being an extension of their face perhaps.

5 However, the same contribution could have the effect of being an insult if it is accompanied by an ironic tone. If so, it would be an FTA damaging the students' positive face instead. This sort of accompanying tone would constitute the FTA being performed off record, via the flout of the quality maxim (since the lecturer is not proud) and manner maxim (since she means the opposite of what she is saying).

Task L

Return to (1) the *Erin Brockovich* extract given as Figure 8.1 and (2) the first *Notting Hill* extract for Task A, and analyse them in terms of linguistic politeness.

Comments on Task L

1 Although Erin's greeting is somewhat positive face-enhancing toward George, she then attacks his negative face ('What the hell do you think you're doing, making all that Goddamn noise?' in l. 4) by asking him to keep the noise down. There is some indirectness here, hence some negative politeness. George, on the other hand, compliments and apologises to Erin, both of these being positive face-enhancing acts ('Ooh, now, see, if I'da known there was a beautiful woman next door, I'da done this different', l. 8–9). Further positive face enhancing is his interest in her ('Let's start over. My name's George. What's yours?' in l. 9). Nevertheless, she continues to attack his negative face through her indirect directive ('Just think of me as the person next door who likes it quiet', in l. 10). When asking her out, he imposes on her actions, so he performs an FTA directed toward her negative face. He continues to enhance her positive face by showing an interest in her ('You got more than one [number]?' l. 19, 'You got a little girl?', l. 23) and she continues to attack his positive face by making unfavourable presumptions about his character ('I'm guessing zero is the number of times you're gonna call it', l. 28). We could even argue that she attacks her own positive face when telling him that she is poor and twice-divorced. Nevertheless, he continues to be interested in her, which is positive face enhancing ('How the hell do you know ...? See, that impresses me', l. 29–30).

2 When William tells the thief 'Bad news' (l. 3), he attacks his positive face, by bringing him bad news. When fairly indirectly accusing him of stealing the book ('We've got a security camera in this bit of the shop', l. 5), he attacks the thief's positive face off record; he damages the thief's need to be approved of and liked. When William pretend-apologises to the thief ('If I'm wrong about the whole book-down-the-trousers scenario, I really apologise', l. 12–13), he attacks his own positive face and enhances the thief's face also. Later on, William also apologises to Anna ('Sorry about that ...', l. 18), an act that enhances her positive face. He essentially recognises that she should be apologised to for having had to wait. Her response ('I was going to steal one myself but now I've changed my mind', l. 19–20) is positive face enhancing towards William. It implies that she is impressed by the way he handled the situation. When the thief asks for Anna's autograph ('Can I have your autograph?', l. 25), he attacks her negative face (by imposing on

her actions via a directive) and yet enhances her positive face (she is admired and hence her autograph is worth having). This action gives an impression of a man who is entirely oblivious to the previous damage to his own face. When Anna writes, 'Dear Rufus – you belong in jail' (l. 29–30), she attacks his positive face. Amusingly, he takes this face threatening act to be positive face enhancing instead, which is why he offers her his number in return. Her let-down ('Tempting but ... no, thank you', l. 32) is both positive face enhancing and positive face damaging. It's an enhancement, as she pretends to be 'tempted', but it's a threat, as she eventually refuses the offer.

Concluding Remarks

Afterthought

This book was intended to familiarise readers with recent advances in the stimulating area of stylistics, and to enable them to investigate the effects of literary genres through the structure of their language. In addition to providing a range of stylistic analytical skills for the study of literary texts, the book also enables the reader to develop a critical approach to theory and methodology in the field.

Even though the techniques were introduced in relation to given genres here, this is not to say that the frameworks are exclusively relevant to these genres. For instance, we can explore the figurative language, text worlds and narrative structures of poems and prose as well as drama, not to mention non-literary texts. Consider how useful stylistics is with non-literary text analysis such as that of adverts, newspaper texts, even text messages. For the analysis of verse drama, we might want to particularly employ models relevant to the stylistic analysis of poetry, while there have been attempts to adjust prose's viewpoint technique to drama (see, for instance, McIntyre, 2006). Moreover, the distinction between some prose fiction, poems and dramatic texts is often fuzzy when we considers non-prototypical genre texts, so the techniques that we would use to analyse such texts depend on their very form and nature.

In engaging in such analysis, the reader is encouraged to be systematic, and organise the evidence from the text in tables and/or lists, as well as concentrate on the way in which the features of the language link to meaning. One of the limitations of stylistics, however, is that it forces the reader to concentrate on extracts rather than whole works, a kind of problem particularly likely to arise with fiction or long plays. Computational or corpus stylistics, however, enables you to counter this problem by exploring larger texts in their entirety, although such techniques are not without their own limitations. It is easy, for instance, to identity certain modal verbs (such as 'will') when exploring a large text's modality, but it is hard to spot metaphorical patterns using computational stylistics alone. To check out how writers have used a particular word, phrase or structure, you can use online databases such as Literature Online (aka LION). This database allows you to search a huge range of literary texts, although you might want to focus on a particular period, genre or author, at least to start with.

Moreover, most of the techniques introduced in this book could well be relevant to the stylistics of languages other than English. To a certain extent, we could argue that literary translation constitutes a form of stylistics in itself. A translator tries to maintain the flavour of the original text by sustaining the stylistic choices of the primary author, despite the language employed, and this was certainly my own experience when translating Antonis Samarakis's (1954) *Hope Wanted* collection a few years back.

Stylistics is undoubtedly useful to students of linguistics, literary and cultural critics, but it is also useful to teachers of English language and literature, whether English is taught as a first, second or foreign language. Native as well as non-native students can learn much about the English language through stylistic research, and hence gain linguistic alongside literary competence. The list of ideas for further practice below is not exhaustive, but should prove a good place to start.

Ideas for further stylistic practice

If you are new to stylistic practice, start practising the techniques by engaging in thorough literary stylistic analysis of texts of your own choosing. Having revised the linguistic model or framework you need to use, apply it to your chosen text, and engage in a discussion of the issue of literary interpretation in the context of stylistic analysis. You can analyse prototypical-looking genre texts to start with, but do explore non-prototypical texts also. Explore, for instance, different types of viewpoint shift, or different sorts of humour, and the extent to which genres vary across cultures and/or historical contexts. Why not explore the language typical of one genre in the course of one period or across the work of one author? Here is a possible topic: spend some time browsing through a selection of poetry books and poetry websites. Put together a corpus of (say, 10) poems from different poets, yet from the same period and culture. Analyse the poems stylistically. To what extent does linguistic creativity (sound awareness, word-building, neologism and derivation strategies) contribute to meaning in poems from the same author, era or tradition?

You can also compare and contrast two or more analogous literary or non-literary texts using stylistics to spot patterns, similarities and differences. What are the linguistic and structural differences between the two texts, and what social, historical and/or functional factors account for the differences? Is thought presentation atypical of newspaper articles? What sort of speech presentation is favoured in certain types of fiction and why? Do adverts construct possible worlds or reinforce our schemata in some way?

Alternatively, you may choose to concentrate on one model and find texts which problematise its application. For instance, according to Leech and Short (1981) and Short (1996), all sentences in fiction are either direct address to the reader, narration, or the representation of character speech and/or character thought. As we saw earlier, characters' speech and thought can be slotted into a number of categories, but can you identify any texts where the application of this model is difficult? What does this tell you about the model or the texts themselves?

Similarly, Simpson (1993: 5) argues that the 'feel' of a narrative text is attributable to the type of point of view it exhibits. Starting from this, you could compare and contrast Simpson's model of point of view in narrative fiction: a modal grammar (outlined in detail in *Language, Ideology and Point of View*, chapter 3), and Short's (1996) model of fictional prose and point of view (outlined in detail in *Exploring the Language of Poems, Plays and Prose*, chapter 9).

You could also find texts that portray a deviant conceptualisation of a world through a certain character's perspective. These could be texts that portray the perspective of young children, cognitively impaired characters or psychologically troubled characters. Through systematic analysis, discuss how stylistic linguistic choices affect mind style.

If you feel comfortable with the analytical side of things, you might want to take a thorough critical approach to one of the theoretical models introduced in this book. In compiling a critical review of the chosen model, you would need to undertake a lot of reading on the theory surrounding the model, and engage in the practicalities of applying the model to different texts. Of course, a critical review does not have to 'find fault' with the theory being reviewed. It does have to analyse the theory to identify what major claims the theorists are making, and to unpick the logic and/or the use of evidence that have apparently led the writers to feel able to make such claims. However you might indeed find unsatisfactory aspects of the model in question, which could lead you to make appropriate suggestions for the model's adjustment.

You might want to analyse unusual or made-up languages in fiction. What makes these literary texts linguistically deviant? Such languages can be found in Orwell's *Nineteen Eighty-Four* (1948), Suzette Haden Elgin's *Native Tongue* (1984), Ursula Le Guin's *The Dispossessed* (1974), Russell Hoban's *Riddley Walker* (1980) and Jonathan Swift's *Gulliver's Travels* (1726), among many others. These 'invented' languages (respectively Newspeak, Láadan, Pravic, Riddlespeak, the

Chapter 1 Naming poetic parts

1 *Content* or lexical words, such as nouns, adjectives and most verbs, are those that indicate concepts in English. *Function* or grammatical words, on the other hand, such as articles, prepositions and conjunctions, indicate relationships between concepts.

2 Wales (2001: 346) describes end-rhyme as the end-of-the-line matching of identical sound sequences. The rhyming words are usually monosyllabic, while the rhyme stretches from the (most usually stressed) vowel to the end of the word, with the initial sound of the relevant word being the one that varies.

3 Note that the decisions you make on metre are a lot more personal when there is no overriding metre for the whole. There are at least two possible ways of saying lines 15 and 16, so disagreements are indeed possible, even likely.

4 Linguists make use of phonetic symbols to transcribe human sounds from any language down on paper. Such representations are commonly written in slash lines. Henceforth I follow the set of symbols adopted in Jeffries (2006). See that book for the full chart.

5 In accordance to Jeffries (2006: 127), I use 'predicator' in reference to the verbal 'slot' of clause *functions*. The term 'predicator' is used to differentiate it from the verb phrase *form*.

6 Interestingly, following the success of *Through the Looking Glass*, many of Carroll's neologisms, such as the word 'chortle', have actually made their way into the English language and the *OED*. For instance, the *OED* currently lists 'chortle' as an intransitive verb, 'a factitious word introduced by the author of *Through the Looking-Glass*, and jocularly used by others after him, app. with some suggestion of *chuckle*, and of *snort*.' Nevertheless, for the purposes of the above analysis, such words are still treated as neologisms here.

Chapter 2 Poetic figures, foregrounding and metaphor

1 To exemplify the intertextual reference to this 'verse', 'This little piggy' is essentially a language 'game' used with young children. The adult recites each line of the verse while picking on the child's toes and fingers one at a time, with the first piggy 'going to the market', the second 'going home', the third 'having roast beef', the fourth 'having none', and the fifth going 'wee wee wee all the way home' (for a multimedia illustration of this game, see Short, 2005, and click on 'Topic 1–6 Roundup').

2 For a detailed analysis of the whole of this poem, see Short's (2005) Language and Style Homepage online, and click on 'Topic 1–6 Round-up and Self Assessment'.

3 As noted in Jeffries (2006: 89), transitive verbs are those verbs that take objects, whereas intransitive verbs are those verbs that do not.

4 The non-standard linguistic choices to portray the child could here be seen as dialectal, although it is perhaps odd that the mother accords to Standard English when the child does not.

5 In case this sounds familiar, it is the same version as was used in the 1994 movie *Four Weddings and a Funeral*, directed by Mike Newell.

Chapter 3 Stylistics of poetry practice

1 Note, however, that the repetition of phonemes does not always coincide with a repetition of the graphemes within the words themselves; remember that it is the sound, and not the spelling, that creates such effects as alliteration, assonance and rhyme.
2 Conversion is the linguistic process whereby new words are created by changing the grammatical category of an existing word, for instance the noun 'bottle' is verbed in 'I'll bottle the wine from the cask.'

Chapter 4 Narrators, viewpoint, speech and thought

1 Quite the contrary is in fact the case when it comes to newspaper reports, where a reader can assume that the views of the writer/real author actually correlate to those of the implied author; here, the author and implied author levels collapse.
2 Short later on came to use NV (Narrator's representation of Voice) as an alternative term for NS (narrator's representation of speech).
3 FID, in some of the stylistic literature, such as Toolan (2001), is used to refer to instances of both free indirect speech and free indirect thought, but I use it as synonymous to the latter term.
4 DT is perceived as more artificial than more indirect forms.

Chapter 5 Narrative worlds, schemata and frames

1 The main bulk of text world theory publications became available in the mid to late 1990s (see Werth, 1994, 1995a, 1995b, 1997a, 1997b). The comprehensive exposition of text world theory was completed shortly before Werth's sudden death in 1995.
2 For detailed transitivity models, see the models by Simpson (1993, chapter 4) or Stockwell (2002: 71), adapted from Berry (1977) and Halliday (1994).
3 Labov works on the broad assumption that what is said (by yourself or others) will not be the core of the story; rather, what is done (by you and others) will be.

Chapter 6 Stylistics of prose practice

1 Moretti here seems to presuppose that there is such a thing as a universal aim of narration, which is to do with a change from some initial situation, presentation of plot as conflict, character development and so on. I would tend to disagree with this point, as all sorts of narration cannot be said to share identical aims at a general level.
2 Simpson (1993: 84) notes that the use of a second-person narrative might warrant an extra category to his framework, say a 'category C', though he adds that such a category might be too peripheral to justify such an extension.
3 Writing presentation, Short proposes, would warrant the addition of a third parallel scale to his speech and thought presentation diagram. Short adds that writing and speech presentation scales would arguably be identical, though speech presentation would supposedly lack the sort of faithfulness claims that writing would warrant, particularly where non-fiction writing is concerned.

4   There are various versions of this fairy tale. See the relevant online reference in the bibliography (under Grimm and Grimm, 1857), for the version I analyse here.

5   Gavins (2001a) argues that whereas direct speech and thought presentations generate deictic sub-worlds, indirect versions move one tense backwards, suggesting a shift in epistemic distance rather than temporal setting.

Chapter 8 The pragmatics of drama

1   Note that if the hearer does not wish to see the act fulfilled, we are more likely to be looking at a threat instead.

Bibliography

Andrus, M. (1997) *As Good As It Gets,* screenplay (TriStar Pictures, Inc.).

Auden, W. H. and Isherwood, C. (1936) *The Ascent of F6: A Tragedy in Two Acts* (London: Faber & Faber).

Auster, P. (2002) *The Book of Illusions* (New York: Faber & Faber).

Austin, J. L. (1962) *How to do Things with Words* (Oxford: Oxford University Press).

Bagwell, J. T. (1983) 'Who's afraid of Stanley Fish?', *Poetics Today,* vol. 4, pp. 127–33.

Bal, M. (1985) *Narratology: Introduction to the Theory of Narrative* (Toronto: Toronto University Press).

Barry, P. (1988) 'The limitations of stylistics', *Essays in Criticism,* vol. 38, no. 3, pp. 175–89.

Bartlett, F. C. (1932) *Remembering: A Study in Experimental and Social Psychology* (Cambridge: Cambridge University Press).

Baxter, L. A. (1984) 'An investigation of compliance-gaining as politeness', *Human Communication Research,* vol. 9, pp. 135–61.

Berry, M. (1977) *Introduction to Systemic Linguistics* (2 vols) (London: Batsford).

Berry-Dee, C. (2003) *Talking with Serial Killers: The Most Evil People in the World Tell their Own Stories* (London: John Blake).

Blake, W. (1925) *Songs of Innocence and of Experience, Showing the Two Contrary States of the Human Soul* (ed. G. Cowling) (London: Methuen).

Blum-Kulka, S., Danet B. and Gherson, R. (1985) 'The language of requesting in Israeli society', pp. 113–39 in J. Forgas (ed.), *Language and Social Situations* (New York: Springer-Verlag).

Bockting, I. (1994), 'Mind style as an interdisciplinary approach to characterisation in Faulkner', *Language and Literature,* vol. 3, no. 3, pp.157–74.

Booth, W. (1961) *The Rhetoric of Fiction* (Chicago: University of Chicago Press).

Brémond, C. (1966) 'La logique des possibles narratifs', *Communications,* vol. 8, pp. 60–76.

Brown, P. and Levinson, S. (1987) *Politeness: Some Universals in Language Usage* (Cambridge: Cambridge University Press).

Carroll, L. and Gardner, M. (2001) *The Annotated Alice* (Harmondsworth: Penguin).

Carter, R. (ed.) (1991) *Language and Literature: An Introductory Reader in Stylistics* (London: Routledge).

Carter, R. and Nash, W. (1990) *Seeing Through Language: A Guide to Style of English Writing* (Oxford: Basil Blackwell).

Carter, R. and Simpson, P. (eds) (1989) *Language, Discourse and Literature: An Introductory Reader in Discourse Stylistics* (London: Unwin Hyman).

Chapman, S. (2006) *Thinking About Language: Theories of English* (Basingstoke: Macmillan).

Clark, U. (2007) *Studying Language: English in Action* (Basingstoke: Macmillan).

Connelly, M. (1995) *The Concrete Blonde* (London: Orion).

Connelly, M. (1996) *The Poet* (London: Orion).

Connelly, M. (1997) First Person. Available at: <http://www.michaelconnelly.com/Other_Words/First_Person/first_person.html> (last accessed 14 April 2007).

Connelly, M. (1999) *Angels Flight* (London: Orion).

Cook, G. (1994) *Discourse and Literature* (Oxford: Oxford University Press).

Cornwell, P. (1991) *Body of Evidence* (London: Warner Books).

Cornwell, P. (1993) *Cruel and Unusual* (London: Warner Books).

Coulthard, M. (1985) *An Introduction to Discourse Analysis,* 2nd edn (London: Longman).

Culler, J. (1975) *Structuralist Poetics: Structuralism, Linguistics and the Study of Literature* (London: Routledge & Kegan Paul).

Culpeper, J. (2001) *Language and Characterisation: People in Plays and Other Texts* (London: Longman).

Curtis, R. (1999) *Notting Hill,* screenplay (Universal City Studios, Inc.).

Decter, E., Strauss, J. J., Farrelly, P. and Farrelly, B. (1998) *There's Something About Mary,* screenplay (Twentieth Century Fox).

Dubus, A. III (2000) *House of Sand and Fog* (New York: Vintage).

Elgin, S. [1984] (2001) *Native Tongue* (New York: Spinifex Press).

Eliot, C. W. (1909) *English Poetry II: From Collins to Fitzgerald,* vol. 41 (New York: Collier/Harvard Classics).

Elton, B. (1999a) *Blast from the Past* (London: Black Swan).

Elton, B. (1999b) *Inconceivable* (London: Bantam).

Emmott, C. (1997) *Narrative Comprehension: A Discourse Perspective* (Oxford: Oxford University Press).

Fish, S. (1980) *Is There a Text in This Class? The Authority of Interpretive Communities* (Cambridge, Mass.: Harvard University Press).

Forster, E. M. [1927] (1987) *Aspects of the Novel* (Harmondsworth: Penguin).

Fowler, R. (1971) *The Language of Literature* (London: Routledge & Kegan Paul).

Fowler, R. (1977) *Linguistics and the Novel* (London: Methuen).

Fowler, R. (1986) *Linguistic Criticism* (Oxford: Oxford University Press).

Fowler, R. (1991) *Language in the News* (London: Routledge).

Frost, R. (1920) *Mountain Interval* (New York: Henry Holt).

Fuller, J. (ed.) (2002) *The Oxford Book of Sonnets* (Oxford: Oxford University Press).

Gavins, J. (2000) 'Absurd tricks with bicycle frames in the text world of The Third Policeman', *Nottingham Linguistic Circular,* vol. 15, pp. 17–33 (also available at <http://www.nottingham.ac.uk/english/nlc/nlc15.htm>)

Gavins, J. (2001a) *An Exposition of Text World Theory in Relation to Absurd Prose Fiction*, unpublished PhD thesis, Sheffield Hallam University.

Gavins, J. (2001b) 'The absurd worlds of Billy Pilgrim', pp. 402–16 in I. Biermann and A. Combrink (eds), *Poetics, Linguistics and History: Discourses of War and Conflict* (Potchefstroom: University of Potchefstroom Press).

Gavins, J. (2003) 'Too much blague? An exploration of the text worlds of Donald Barthelme's Snow White', pp. 129–44 in J. Gavins and G. Steen (eds), *Cognitive Poetics in Practice* (London: Routledge).

Genette, G. (1980) *Narrative Discourse* (Oxford: Basil Blackwell). (Originally published in French as *Figues III*, by Seuil: Paris, 1972.)

Gibbs, R. W. (1994) *The Poetics of Mind: Figurative Thought, Language, and Understanding* (Cambridge: Cambridge University Press).

Goffman, E. (1967) *Interaction Ritual: Essays on Face-to-Face Behaviour* (New York: Doubleday Anchor).

Graddol, D., Cheshire, J. and Swann, J. (1994) *Describing Language*, 2nd edn (Milton Keynes: Open University Press).

Grant, S. (2000) *Erin Brockovich*, screenplay (Universal City Studios, Inc. and Palisade Investors, LLC).

Gregoriou, C. (2002a) 'Samarakis in search of hope: a Labovian analysis of Antonis Samarakis's 'Hope Wanted' with a focus on 'evaluation'', pp. 302–7 in S. Csábi and J. Zerkowitz (eds), *Textual Secrets: The Message of the Medium* (Proceedings of the 21st PALA Conference) (Budapest: Akadémiai Nyonda, Martonvásár).

Gregoriou, C. (2002b) 'Behaving badly: a cognitive stylistics of the criminal mind', *Nottingham Linguistic Circular*, vol. 17, pp. 61–73. (also available at <http://www.nottingham.ac.uk/english/nlc/gregoriou.pdf>)

Gregoriou, C. (2003a) 'Demystifying the criminal mind: linguistic, social and generic deviance in contemporary American crime fiction', *Working With English* 1, pp. 61–73 (available at <http://www.nottingham.ac.uk/english/working_with_english>)

Gregoriou, C. (2003b) 'Criminally minded; the stylistics of justification in contemporary American crime fiction', *Style*. vol. 37, no. 2, pp. 144–59.

Gregoriou, C. (2007a) *Deviance in Contemporary Crime Fiction* (Basingstoke: Palgrave Crime Files).

Gregoriou, C. (2007b) 'The stylistics of true crime: mapping the minds of serial killers', in M. Lambrou and P. Stockwell (eds), *Contemporary Stylistics* (London: Continuum).

Grice, H. P. (1975) 'Logic and conversation', pp. 41–58 in P. Cole and J. Morgan (eds), *Syntax and Semantics III: Speech Acts* (New York: Academic Press).

Grice, H. P. (1989) *Studies in the Way of Words* (Cambridge, Mass.: Harvard University Press).

Grimm, J. and Grimm, W. (1857) *Little Red Riding Hood*. Available at: <http://www.fln.vcu.edu/grimm/redridinghood.html > (last accessed 15 June 2008).

Haddon, M. (2003) *The Curious Incident of the Dog in the Night-Time* (London: Vintage).

Halliday, M. A. K. (1971) 'Linguistic function and literary style: an enquiry into the language of William Golding's *The Inheritors*', pp. 325–60 in D. Freeman (ed.), *Essays in Modern Stylistics* (London: Methuen).

Halliday, M. A. K. (1994) *An Introduction to Functional Grammar,* 2nd edn (London: Edward Arnold).

Harrison, T. [1984] (1995) *Selected Poems* (Harmondsworth: Penguin).

Heaney, S. (trans.) (1999) *Beowulf* (London: Faber & Faber).

Herman, V. (1995) *Dramatic Discourse: Dialogue and Interaction in Plays* (London: Routledge).

Hidalgo Downing, L. (2000a) *Negation, Text Worlds and Discourse: The Pragmatics of Fiction* (Stanford, Calif.: Ablex).

Hidalgo Downing, L. (2000b) 'Alice in pragmaticland: reference, deixis and the delimitation of text worlds in Lewis Carroll's *Alice* books', *Círculo de Lingüística Aplicada a la Comunicación* (CLAC), vol. 2 (available at: <http://www.ucm.es/info/circulo/no2/hidalgo.htm>).

Hidalgo Downing, L. (2003) 'Text world creation in advertising discourse', *CLAC*, vol. 13 (available at: <http://www.ucm.es/info/circulo/no13/hidalgo.htm>).

Hoban, R. (1980) *Riddley Walker* (Bloomington: Indiana University Press).

Hornby, N. (2005) *A Long Way Down* (London: Penguin).

Jakobson, R. (1956) 'Two aspects of language and two types of aphasic disturbances', pp. 55–82 in R. Jakobson and M. Halle (eds), *Fundamentals of Language* (The Hague: Mouton).

Jeffries, L. (1993) *The Language of Twentieth-Century Poetry* (Basingstoke: Macmillan).

Jeffries, L. (2000) 'Don't throw the baby out with the bath water: in defence of theoretical eclecticism in stylistics', Poetics and Linguistics Association (PALA) occasional papers 12 (available online from PALA website).

Jeffries, L. (2001) 'Schema affirmation and white asparagus: cultural multilingualism among readers of texts', *Language and Literature*, vol. 10, no. 4, pp. 325–43.

Jeffries, L. (2006) *Discovering Language: The Structure of Modern English* (Basingstoke: Macmillan).

Kant, E. (1963) *Critique of Pure Reason* (London: Macmillan).

Kay, J. (1991) *The Adoption Papers* (Newcastle upon Tyne: Bloodaxe).

Keats, J. (1850) *The Poetical Works of John Keats* (London: Edward Moxon).

Kerr, P. (1992) *A Philosophical Investigation* (London: Chatto & Windus).

Labov, W. (1972) *Language in the Inner City: Studies in the Black English Vernacular* (London: Basil Blackwell).

Labov, W. and Waletsky, J. (1967) 'Narrative analysis: oral versions of personal experience', pp. 12–44 in J. Helms (ed.), *Essays on the Verbal and Visual Arts* (London: University of Washington Press).

Lakoff, G. and Johnson, M. (1980) *Metaphors We Live By* (Chicago: University of Chicago Press).

Lambrou, M. (2003) 'Collaborative oral narratives of general experience: when an interview becomes a conversation', *Language and Literature*, vol. 12, no. 2, pp. 153–74.

Lambrou, M. (2007) 'Oral accounts of personal experiences: when is a narrative a recount?', in M. Lambrou and P. Stockwell (eds), *Contemporary Stylistics* (London: Continuum).

Le Guin, U. [1974] (1999) *The Dispossessed* (London: Millennium).

Leech, G. N. (1969) *A Linguistic Guide to English Poetry* (London: Longman).

Leech, G. N. and Short, M. (1981) *Style in Fiction* (London: Longman).

Levinson, S. C. (1983) *Pragmatics* (Cambridge: Cambridge University Press).

Longacre, R. E. (1983) *The Grammar of Discourse* (London: Plenum Press).

MacCabe, C. (1985) 'Language, linguistics, and the study of literature', in *Theoretical Essays: Film, Linguistics, Literature* (Manchester: Manchester University Press).

McCarthy, M. (1991) *Discourse Analysis for Language Teachers* (Cambridge: Cambridge University Press).

McIntyre, D. (2006) *Point of View in Plays* (Amsterdam: John Benjamins).

McRae, J. (1991) *Literature with a small 'l'* (London: Macmillan).

Mey, J. (1995) 'The last of the Canterbury Tales: artificial intelligence in the fifth millennium', pp. 261–94 in E. Hajicová, M. Cervenka, O. Leška and P. Sgall (eds), *Prague Linguistic Circle Papers*, vol 1 (Amsterdam: John Benjamins).

Milic, L. (1996) 'Unconscious ordering in the prose of Swift', pp.79–106 in J. Leed (ed.), *The Computer and Literary Style* (Kent, Ohio: Kent State University Press).

Moretti, F. (1983) *Signs Taken for Wonders: Essays in the Sociology of Literary Forms* (London: Thetford Press).

Mukarovský, J. (1970) 'Standard language and poetic language', pp. 40–56 in D. C. Freeman, *Linguistics and Literary Style* (New York: Holt, Rinehart & Winston).

Nowottny, W. (1962) *The Language Poets Use* (London: Athlone Press).

O'Flaherty, L. (1923) 'The sniper', *The New Leader*, 12 January.

Orwell, G. [1948] (2000) *Nineteen Eighty-Four* (Harmondsworth: Penguin).

Oxford English Dictionary (1989) 2nd edn, ed. J. A. Simpson and E. S. C. Weiner; Additions 1993–7, ed. J. A. Simpson, E. S. C. Weiner and M. Proffitt; 3rd ed. (in progress) Mar. 2000–, ed. J. A. Simpson. OED Online (Oxford University Press) <http://oed.com> (last accessed 14 April 2007).

Patterson, J. (1993) *Along Came a Spider* (London: Harper Collins).

Patterson, J. (1997) *Cat and Mouse* (London: Headline).

Picasso, P. et al (2004) *Pablo Picasso: The Burial of the Count of Orgaz and other Poems* (New York: Exact Change).

Plath, S. (1981) *The Collected Poems of Sylvia Plath* (ed. T. Hughes) (London: Faber).

Pratt, M. L. (1977) *Toward a Speech-Act Theory of Literary Discourse* (London: Indiana University Press).

Propp, V. (1975) *Morphology of the Folktale* (Austin and London: University of Texas Press).

Propp, V. (1984) *Theory and History of Folklore* (Manchester: Manchester University Press).

Richards, I. A. (1936) *The Philosophy of Rhetoric* (London: Oxford University Press).

Rose, A. (1995) 'Lewis Carroll's 'Jabberwocky': non-sense not nonsense', *Language and Literature*, vol. 4, no. 1, pp. 1–15.

Ryan, M. L. (1991a) *Possible Worlds, Artificial Intelligence and Narrative Theory* (Bloomington and Indianapolis: Indiana University Press).

Ryan, M. L. (1991b) 'Possible worlds and accessibility relations: a semantics typology of fiction', *Poetics Today*, vol. 12, no. 3, pp. 553–76.

Ryan, M. L. (1998) 'The text as world versus the text as game: possible worlds semantics and postmodern theory', *Journal of Literary Semantics*, vol. 27, no. 3, pp. 137–63.

Sacks, H., Schegloff, E. A. and Jefferson, G. (1974) 'A simplest systematic for the organisation of turn-taking for conversation', *Language*, vol. 50, no. 4, pp. 696–735.

Saeed, J. I. (1998) *Semantics* (Oxford: Blackwell).

Samarakis, A. (1954) *Hope Wanted* (Athens, Greece: Eleftheroudakis Publishing) [in Greek].

Schank, R. C. (1982a) 'Dynamic memory: a theory of reminding and learning', in *Computers and People* (Cambridge: Cambridge University Press).

Schank, R. C. (1982b) *Reading and Understanding: Teaching from the Perspective of Artificial Intelligence* (Hillsdale, N.J.: Lawrence Erlbaum Associates).

Schank, R. C. (1984) *The Cognitive Computer* (Reading, Mass.: Addison-Wesley).

Schank, R. C. (1986) *Explanation Patterns* (Hillsdale, N.J.: Lawrence Erlbaum Associates).

Schank, R. C. and Abelson, R. (1977) *Scripts, Plans, Goals and Understanding* (Hillsdale, N.J.: Lawrence Erlbaum Associates).

Searle, J. R. (1969) *Speech Acts* (Cambridge: Cambridge University Press).

Semino, E. (1997) *Language and World Creation in Poems and Other Texts* (London: Longman).

Shakespeare, W. (1911) *The Complete Works of William Shakespeare* (ed. W. J. Craig) (London: Oxford University Press).

Shen, D. (1988) 'Stylistics, objectivity convention', *Poetics,* vol. 17, no. 3, pp. 221–38.

Shippey, T. A. (2000) *J. R. R. Tolkien: Author of the Century* (London: Harper Collins).

Shklovsky, V. (1925) *O Teorii Prozy* (Moscow: Federatsiya).

Short, M. (1982) ''Prelude I' to a literary linguistic stylistics', pp. 55–61 in R. Carter (ed.), *Language and Literature: An Introductory Reader in Stylistics* (London: Allen and Unwin).

Short, M. (1989) 'Discourse analysis and the analysis of drama', pp. 138–68 in R. Carter and P. Simpson (eds), *Language, Discourse and Literature: An Introductory Reader in Discourse Stylistics* (London: Routledge).

Short, M. (1994) 'Understanding texts: point of view', pp. 170–90 in G. Brown, K. Malmkjaer, A. Pollitt and J. Williams (eds), *Language and Understanding* (Oxford: Oxford University Press).

Short, M. (1996) *Exploring the Language of Poems, Plays and Prose* (London: Longman).

Short, M. (1998) 'From dramatic text to dramatic performance', pp. 6–18 in J. Culpeper, M. Short and P. Verdonk (eds), *Studying Drama: From Text to Context* (London: Routledge).

Short, M. (2004) *Corpus Stylistics: A Corpus-based Study of Speech, Thought and Writing in a Corpus of English Writing* (London: Routledge).

Short, M. (2005) The Language and Style Homepage <http://www.lancs.ac.uk/fass/projects/stylistics/index.htm> (last accessed 14 April 2007).

Shriver, L. (2005) *We Need to Talk about Kevin* (London: Serpent's Tail).

Simpson, P. (1993) *Language, Ideology and Point of View* (London: Routledge).

Simpson, P. (1995) 'Politeness phenomena in Ionesco's *The Lesson*', pp. 171–93 in R. Carter and P. Simpson (eds), *Language, Discourse, and Literature: An Introductory Reader in Discourse Stylistics* (London: Hyman).

Simpson, P. (2003) *On the Discourse of Satire: Towards a Stylistic Model of Satirical Humour* (Amsterdam: John Benjamins).

Simpson, P. (2004) *Stylistics: A Resource Book for Students* (London: Routledge).

Simpson, P. and Montgomery, M. (1995) 'Language, literature and film', pp. 138–64 in P. Verdonk and J. J. Weber (eds), *Twentieth Century Fiction: From Text to Context* (London: Routledge).

Snell, J. (2006) 'Schema theory and the humour of *Little Britain*', *English Today,* vol. 22, pp. 59–64.

Stockwell, P. (2002) *Cognitive Poetics: An Introduction* (London: Routledge).

Stockwell, P. (2003a) 'Schema poetics and speculative cosmology', *Language and Literature*, vol. 12, no. 3, pp. 252–71.

Stockwell, P. (2003b) 'Surreal figures', in J. Gavins and G. Steen (eds), *Cognitive Poetics in Practice* (London: Routledge).

Swift, J. [1726] (1997) *Gulliver's Travels* (Harmondsworth: Penguin).

Thompson, J. [1952] (2002) *The Killer Inside Me* (London: Orion).

Toolan, M. (1990) 'Stylistics and its discontents, or, getting off the Fish 'hook'', in *The Stylistics of Fiction* (London: Routledge); reprinted in Weber (1996), pp. 117–37.

Toolan, M. (2001) *Narrative: A Critical Linguistic Introduction*, 2nd edn (London: Routledge).

Tolkien, J. R. R. [1968] (1991) *The Lord of the Rings* (London: Harper Collins).

Tolkien, J. R. R. (1974) *The Hobbit*, 4th edn (London: Unwin).

Tolkien, J. R. R. (1977) *The Silmarillion* (London: Allen & Unwin).

Turner, G. W. (1973) *Stylistics* (Harmondsworth: Penguin).

Ungerer, F. and Schmid, H-J. (1996) *An Introduction to Cognitive Linguistics* (London: Longman).

Wales, K. (2001) *A Dictionary of Stylistics*, 2nd edn (London: Longman).

Wales, K. (2006) 'Stylistics', in *Encyclopedia of Language and Linguistics,* 2nd edn, vol. 12, pp 213–17.

Walsh, C. (2004) 'The poetics of children's and young adult fiction: problems and prospects', unpublished paper presented at PALA Conference.

Weber, J. J. (ed.) (1996) *The Stylistics Reader: From Roman Jakobson to the Present* (London: Edward Arnold).

Werth, P. (1994) 'Extended metaphor: a text world account', *Language and Literature*, vol. 3, no. 2, pp. 79–103.

Werth, P. (1995a) ''World enough and time': deictic space and the interpretation of prose', in P. Verdonk and J. J. Weber (eds), *Twentieth Century Fiction: From Text to Context* (London: Routledge).

Werth, P. (1995b) 'How to build a world (in a lot less than six days and using only what's in your head', in K. Green (ed.), *New Essays in Deixis* (Amsterdam: Rodopi).

Werth, P. (1997a) 'Conditionality as cognitive distance', pp. 243–71 in A. Athanasiadou and R. Dirven (eds), *On Conditionals Again* (Amsterdam: Benjamins).

Werth, P. (1997b) 'Remote worlds: the conceptual representation of linguistic would', pp. 84–115 in J. Nuyts and E. Pederson (eds), *Language and Conceptualization* (Cambridge: Cambridge University Press).

Werth, P. (1999) *Text Worlds: Representing Conceptual Space in Discourse* (Harlow: Longman).

Williams, W. C. (1988) *The Collected Poems of William Carlos Williams 1939–1962, vol. 2* (ed. C. MacGowan) (Manchester: Carcanet).

Wordsworth, W. (1888) *The Complete Poetical Works* (London: Macmillan).

Woudhuysen, H. R. (ed.) (1993) *The Penguin Book of Renaissance Verse* (London: Penguin).

Yule, G. (1996) *Pragmatics* (Oxford: Oxford University Press).

Zephaniah, B. (1996) *Propa Propaganda* (Newcastle upon Tyne: Bloodaxe).

Index

This index includes references only to those pages where there is substantial treatment of the subject entries. Bold font indicates where the entry terms are defined.

abstract, 89, **90**, 118, 120, 125, 126, 170
accent, 32, 47–8, 58–9
act, *see* speech act
adjacency pairs, **136**, 149, 151, 158, 159, 160, 178
    embedding of, **137**
alliteration, **17**, 21, 32, 48, 49, 51–3, 56, 58, 59, 60, 189
assonance, **17**, 21, 32, 48–9, 51–4, 56, 59, 189

Brémond's cycle, **64**, 98, 99, 125
Brown and Levinson, *see* politeness theory

character, 2, 3, 24, 29, 36, 64, 66, 67, 72–3, 93, 95, 122
    characterisation, 172–4
    in drama, 139–41
    flat, **139**–41
    round, **139**–40
    see also schema

coda, 89, **91**, 118, 119, 121
commissives, **145**, 151
complicating action, 89, **90**, 119, 120, 121, 125

declarations, **145**, 152
deviation/deviance, 2, **27**, 28–36, 38, 55–9, 72–3, 87, 187
    discoursal, **29**, 34, 35, 36, 56, 58
    external, **28**, 58
    grammatical, 29, **31**, 34, 36, 55–6, 58, 59
    graphological, 29, **32**, 33, 35, 36, 56, 58
    internal, **29**, 34, 36, 58, 59, 61
    lexical, 29, **30**, 31, 34, 55, 56, 58
    linguistic, 29, 55, 57
    phonological, 29, **31**, 32, 36, 55–7, 58, 59
    semantic, 29, **30**, 32, 34, 36, 38, 55–7, 58
    see also foregrounding, parallelism
directives, **145**, 149, 151, 153, 157, 158, 160, 176, 178, 179, 180, 181, 182
discourse, 29, 63, 65, 72, 82, 98–100
    free indirect, **75**, 126
    levels in drama, 129–30, 135, 163–6, 179

see also plot, speech, thought
drama, 129–30, 135
    embedded nature of, 130
    non-fluency in, 130–1, 133
    see also discourse levels in drama

enactors, *see* frame theory
enjambment, **17**, 18, 19, 22, 49–53
evaluation, 89, **90**, 119, 121, 126
expressives, **145**, 152, 158, 176, 179,
    180

face, **153**
    enhancing act, 180–2
    negative, **153**
    positive, **153**
    threatening act (FTA), **153**:
        negative, **153**, 154, 157–61,
        180–2; positive, **153**, 157–61,
        180–2; self, **153**; *see also*
        impoliteness, politeness
felicity conditions, **145**, 161, 179
    see also speech act
fiction, 2, 63, 79, 119
    crime or detective, 2, 3, 65, 73,
        93, 94, 96, 98, 99, 117, 118–19,
        140, 187
    romance, 64, 172–3
    science, 80, 117, 186
    see also jokes
figurative language, **38**, 39, 61, 104,
    125, 183
    see also irony, metaphor
figure, **24**–6, 54
    see also ground
foregrounding, **26**–41, 57–9
    see also deviation, parallelism
frame, **87**, **94**–6, 114–15, 123–8
    contextual, **94**
    primed, **94**, 95, 126, 128
    repair, **96**, 128
    replacement, **96**, 128

theory, **94**–6, 114–5, 123–8
    unprimed, **95**
    see also schema, script
function
    advancers, **82**–5, 114
    narrative, 119
    Proppian, **91**, 121–3
    words, 12, 16, 22, **188**

Grice, **146**–52
    see also implicature, maxim
ground, **24**–6, 54
    see also figure

illocution, **144**, 145, 174–5, 179
implicature, **147**–54, 159–60, 177–9
    see also Grice, maxim
implied author, 61, **65**–6, 72, 101, 189
implied reader, **65**–6, 100–2
impoliteness, 155
    see also face, politeness
irony, 75, 103, 107, 130, 143, 180

jokes, 29, 119–21, 174–6, 187
    see also fiction

Labov's narrative structure, **89**–91,
    118–21, 123, 126, 189
    see also abstract, coda,
       complicating action,
       evaluation, orientation,
       resolution
lexical words, 16, **188**
locution, **144**, 145, 174–5, 179

maxim, 146–52, 176–80
    flout, **147**–52, 176–80
    manner, **147**, 148, 149, 151, 152,
       159, 160, 177–8, 180
    politeness, **152**
    quality, **147**, 148, 149, 151, 152,
       159, 177–80

quantity, **147**, 148, 149, 152, 159, 160, 177, 179

relation/relevance, **147**, 148, 149, 151, 152, 159, 160, 177–80

violation, **147**, 148, 149, 177, 179

see also implicature

meronymy, **40**, 41

metaphor, 2, 26, **30**, 32, 36, **38**–41, 62, 73, 79, 104, 108, 126, 148, 184, 187

cognitive/conceptual, **41**

literary, **41**

mega- or sustained, 2, **39**, 108

ontological, **41**

orientational, 41

structural, **41**

see also figurative language; maxim, quality; mind style

metonymy **40**, 41, 56, 107, 148

metre, **8**–17, 18, 19, 22, 43–7, 48, 188

anapaest, **9**, 11, 14, 16, 22, 46, 48

dactyl, **9**

iambic, **9**, 10, 14, 16, 22, 45, 51, 53, 61

trochaic, **9**

see also rhythm

mind style, **72**–3, 106

see also metaphors; viewpoint, ideological

modality, **69**–71, 103–6

ability, **70**, 106

boulomaic, **70**, 71, 104

deontic, **69**, 70, 71, 104, 106

epistemic, **70**, 71, 79, 85, 104, 105, 107

negative, **71**

neutral, **71**

perception, **70**, 71, 105

positive, **71**, 105

narration, 64–6

external, **67**, 71

heterodiegetic or third person, 29, **64**, 67, 71, 76, 107, 119, 126, 128

homodiegetic or first person, **64**, 66, 69, 71, 72, 90, 101, 105, 109, 113, 116, 119

internal, **67**, 71, 75, 76, 107

omniscient, *67*, 72, 103

neologism, **21**, 30, 31, 188

onomatopoeia, **17**, 22, 32, 36, 48, 49–52, 60

orientation, 89, **90**, 118–21, 125, 170

parallelism, **27**, 36–8, 42, 57–61

see also deviation/deviance, foregrounding

performance, 15, 46, 137–9, 152

indicators, 141, 158, 159, 161, 171–2, 179

see also production, text

perlocution, **144**, 145, 174–6, 179

phonemes, 58, 189

plot, **63**–4, 80–1, 85, 91, 98–100, 126

see also discourse

poetry, 8–9, 11, 15, 17, 26, 27

point of view, *see* viewpoint

politeness, **153**

negative, **155**, 158, 180, 181

positive, **155**, 180

theory, 153–61, 180–2

see also face, impoliteness

possible worlds, 79–85

production, 137–9

see also performance, text

Propp's morphology, 91–4, 121–3

representatives, **145**, 149, 151, 152, 158, 159, 176, 178, 179, 180

resolution, 64, 89, **90**, 99, 118, 119, 121, 126

rhyme, 11, 17, 18, 19, 32, 38, 45, 46, 48, 50, 53, 55–61
  end-, 13, **22**, **188**
  internal, 19, **22**, 60
rhythm, 8–**9**, 12, 14, 16, 19, 22
  see also metre

schema, **86**
  accretion, **88**
  disruption, **87**, 88, 116, 117, 118
  group or stereotype, **141**, 173
  language, **88**, 116
  person, **140**, 141, 172
  preservation, **88**, 117
  refreshment, **96**
  reinforcement, **88**, 117, 140
  role, **140**–1, 173
  text, **88**, 117
  theory, 86–8, 114–18, 172–4
  world, **88**, 117
script, **87**, 88, 114–5
  see also frame
speech
  act, *see entry below*
  direct (DS), 29, **74**, 83, 85, 90, 121, 176, 178, 180, 190
  free direct (FDS), **74**, 77, 114
  free indirect (FIS), **74**, 75, 90, 114, 189
  indirect (IS), 67, **74**, 121
  narrator's representation of (NRS), **74**, 189
  non-fluency in, 130–1, 133, 139, 159, 160, 166, 170
  non-standard, 36, 48, 116, 118
  Short's model of presentation of, 73–8
speech act, **144**
  direct, **146**
  indirect, **146**, 149, 151, 158–61, 175, 176, 177, 180
  narrator's representation of (NRSA), **74**, 109
  performative, **144**
  theory, 143–6, 149–52, 174–9
  see also commissives, declarations, directives, expressives, felicity conditions, representatives
stress, 9, 10, 13, 14–16

text, 137–9
  worlds, 79–85
  see also performance, production
theory, *see* frame, possible worlds, schema, speech act, text world
thought
  act, **74**: narrator's representation of (NRTA), **74**, 75, 109, 110
  direct (DT), **74**, 75, 77, 78, 189
  free direct (FDT), **74**, 77, 78
  free indirect (FIT), **74**, 75, 76, 77, 189
  indirect (IT), **74**, 75, 189
  narrator's representation of (NRT), **74**
  Short's model of presentation of, 73–8
transitivity, 35, 82, 188, 189
turn-taking, 133–4
  in drama, 168–71
  in real conversation, 133–5

world, **63**
  actual or real, 79, **82**, 111
  builders, **82**–4
  expectation or speculative extension, **79**, 80, 112
  fantasy, **79**, 80, 111
  fictional, 64, 68, 79, 82, 100, 110
  intention, **79**, 80, 81, 85, 110–12
  knowledge or epistemic, **79**, 80, 81, 110–12